# AN EXEGETICAL SUMMARY OF
# 1 PETER

# AN EXEGETICAL SUMMARY OF
# 1 PETER

**Second Edition**

**David Abernathy**

**SIL International**

Second Edition
© 2008 by SIL International

Library of Congress Catalog Card Number: 2008923519
ISBN: 978-155671-193-0

Printed in the United States of America

All Rights Reserved
No part of this publication may be reproduced, stored in a retrieval system, or transmitted in any form or by any means without the express permission of SIL International. However, brief excerpts, generally understood to be within the limits of fair use, may be quoted without written permission.

Copies of this and other publications
of SIL International may be obtained from

International Academic Bookstore
SIL International
7500 West Camp Wisdom Road
Dallas, TX 75236-5699, USA

Voice: 972-708-7404
Fax: 972-708-7363
academic_books@sil.org
www.ethnologue.com

# PREFACE

Exegesis is concerned with the interpretation of a text. Exegesis of the New Testament involves determining the meaning of the Greek text. Translators must be especially careful and thorough in their exegesis of the New Testament in order to accurately communicate its message in the vocabulary, grammar, and literary devices of another language. Questions occurring to translators as they study the Greek text are answered by summarizing how scholars have interpreted the text. This is information that should be considered by translators as they make their own exegetical decisions regarding the message they will communicate in their translations.

**The Semi-Literal Translation**

As a basis for discussion, a semi-literal translation of the Greek text is given so that the reasons for different interpretations can best be seen. When one Greek word is translated into English by several words, these words are joined by hyphens. There are a few times when clarity requires that a string of words joined by hyphens have a separate word, such as "not" (μή), inserted in their midst. In this case, the separate word is surrounded by spaces between the hyphens. When alternate translations of a Greek word are given, these are separated by slashes.

**The Text**

Variations in the Greek text are noted under the heading TEXT. The base text for the summary is the text of the fourth revised edition of *The Greek New Testament,* published by the United Bible Societies, which has the same text as the twenty-sixth edition of the *Novum Testamentum Graece* (Nestle-Aland). The versions that follow different variations are listed without evaluating their choices.

**The Lexicon**

The meaning of a key word in context is the first question to be answered. Words marked with a raised letter in the semi-literal translation are treated separately under the heading LEXICON. First, the lexicon form of the Greek word is given. Within the parentheses following the Greek word is the location number where, in the author's judgment, this word is defined in the *Greek-English Lexicon of the New Testament Based on Semantic Domains* (Louw and Nida 1988). When a semantic domain includes a translation of the particular verse being treated, **LN** in bold type indicates that specific translation. If the specific reference for the verse is listed in *A Greek-English Lexicon of the New Testament and Other Early Christian Literature* (Bauer, Arndt, Gingrich, and Danker 1979), the outline location and page number is given. Then English equivalents of the Greek word are given to show how it is translated by commentators who offer their own translations of the whole text and, after a semicolon, all the versions in the list of abbreviations for translations. When reference is made to "all versions," it refers to only the versions in the list of translations. Sometimes further comments are made about the meaning of the word or the significance of a verb's tense, voice, or mood.

**The Questions**

Under the heading QUESTION, a question is asked that comes from examining the Greek text under consideration. Typical questions concern the identity of an implied actor or object of an event word, the antecedent of a pronominal reference, the connection indicated by a relational word, the meaning of a genitive construction, the meaning of figurative language, the function of a rhetorical question, the identification of an ambiguity, and the presence of implied information that is needed to understand the passage correctly. Background information is also considered for a proper understanding of a passage. Although not all implied information and background information is made explicit in a translation, it is important to consider it so that the translation will not be stated in such a way that prevents a reader from arriving at the proper interpretation. The question is answered with a summary of what commentators have said. If there are contrasting differences of opinion, the different interpretations are numbered and the commentaries that support each are listed. Differences that are not treated by many of the commentaries often are not numbered, but are introduced with a contrastive 'Or' at the beginning of the sentence. No attempt has been made to select which interpretation is best.

In listing support for various statements of interpretation, the author is often faced with the difficult task of matching the different terminologies used in commentaries with the terminology he has adopted. Sometimes he can only infer the position of a commentary from incidental remarks. This book, then, includes the author's interpretation of the views taken in the various commentaries. General statements are followed by specific statements, which indicate the author's understanding of the pertinent relationships, actors, events, and objects implied by that interpretation.

**The Use of This Book**

This book does not replace the commentaries that it summarizes. Commentaries contain much more information about the meaning of words and passages. They often contain arguments for the interpretations that are taken and they may have important discussions about the discourse features of the text. In addition, they have information about the historical, geographical, and cultural setting. Translators will want to refer to at least four commentaries as they exegete a passage. However, since no one commentary contains all the answers translators need, this book will be a valuable supplement. It makes more sources of exegetical help available than most translators have access to. Even if they had all the books available, few would have the time to search through all of them for the answers.

When many commentaries are studied, it soon becomes apparent that they frequently disagree in their interpretations. That is the reason why so many answers in this book are divided into two or more interpretations. The reader's initial reaction may be that all of these different interpretations complicate exegesis rather than help it. However, before translating a passage, a translator needs to know exactly where there is a problem of interpretation and what the exegetical options are.

# ABBREVIATIONS AND BIBLIOGRAPHY

## COMMENTARIES AND REFERENCE BOOKS

Alf     Alford, Henry. *The Greek New Testament.* Vol. 4. 1857. Reprint with revisions by E. F. Harrison. Chicago: Moody Press, 1968.

BAGD     Bauer, Walter. *A Greek-English Lexicon of the New Testament and Other Early Christian Literature.* Translated and adapted from the 5th German edition, 1958, by William F. Arndt and F. Wilbur Gingrich. 2d English ed. revised and augmented by F. Wilbur Gingrich and Frederick W. Danker. Chicago: University of Chicago Press, 1979.

BNTC     Kelly, J. N. D. *The Epistles of Peter and Jude.* Black's New Testament Commentary. Peabody, Mass.: Hendrickson, 1969.

EGT     Hart, J. H. A. "The First Epistle General of Peter." In *The Expositor's Greek Testament,* n.d. Reprint. Grand Rapids: Eerdmans, 1980.

ICC     Bigg, Charles. *A Critical and Exegetical Commentary on the Epistles of St. Peter and Jude.* The International Critical Commentary. Edinburgh: Clark, 1901.

IVP     Marshall, I. Howard. *1 Peter.* The IVP New Testament Commentary Series. Downers Grove, Ill.: InterVarsity Press, 1991.

LN     Louw, Johannes P., and Eugene A. Nida. *Greek-English Lexicon of the New Testament Based on Semantic Domains.* 2 vols. New York: United Bible Societies, 1988.

NCBC     Best, Ernest. *1 Peter.* The New Century Bible Commentary. Grand Rapids: Eerdmans, 1971.

NIBC     Hillyer, Norman. *1 and 2 Peter, Jude.* New International Biblical Commentary. Peabody, Mass.: Hendrickson, 1992.

NIC     Davids, Peter H. *The First Epistle of Peter.* The New International Commentary on the New Testament. Grand Rapids: Eerdmans, 1990.

NTC     Kistemaker, Simon J. *Exposition of the Epistles of Peter and of the Epistle of Jude.* Grand Rapids: Baker, 1987.

Sel     Selwyn, E. G. *The First Epistle of Peter.* New York: Macmillan, 1946.

TG     Bratcher, Robert G. *A Translator's Guide to the Letters from James, Peter, and Jude.* New York: United Bible Societies, 1984.

TH     Arichea, Daniel C., and Eugene A. Nida. *A Translator's Handbook on the First Letter From Peter.* New York: United Bible Societies, 1980.

TNTC     Grudem, Wayne. *1 Peter.* Tyndale New Testament Commentaries. Grand Rapids: Eerdmans, 1988.

WBC     Michaels, J. Ramsey. *1 Peter.* Word Biblical Commentary, vol. 49. Waco. Texas: Word, 1988.

## GREEK TEXT AND TRANSLATIONS

GNT    The Greek New Testament. Edited by B. Aland, K. Aland, J. Karavidopoulos, C. Martini, and B. Metzger. 4th ed. London, New York: United Bible Societies, 1993.
CEV    The Holy Bible, Contemporary English Version. New York: American Bible Society, 1995.
KJV    The Holy Bible, Authorized (or King James) Version, 1611.
NAB    The New American Bible. Camden, New Jersey: Thomas Nelson, 1971.
NIV    The Holy Bible, New International Version. Grand Rapids: Zondervan, 1984.
NJB    The New Jerusalem Bible. Garden City, New York: Doubleday, 1985.
NLT    The Holy Bible, New Living Translation. Wheaton, Ill.: Tyndale House, 1996.
NRSV    The Holy Bible, New Revised Standard Version. New York: Oxford University Press, 1989.
REB    The Revised English Bible. Oxford: Oxford University Press and Cambridge University Press, 1989.
TEV    Good News Bible, Today's English Version. 2d ed. New York: American Bible Society, 1992.
TNT    The Translator's New Testament. London: British and Foreign Bible Society, 1973.

## GRAMMATICAL TERMS

| act. | active | opt. | optative |
| fut. | future | pass. | passive |
| impera. | imperative | perf. | perfect |
| indic. | indicative | pres. | present |
| infin. | infinitive | subj. | subjunctive |
| mid. | middle | | |

# EXEGETICAL SUMMARY OF 1 PETER

**DISCOURSE UNIT: 1:1–2** [IVP, NIC, NTC, Sel, TG, TH, WBC; CEV, NAB, NIV, NJB, NLT, NRSV, REB, TEV]. The customary address of a letter in the ancient world was usually A to B: greetings [BNTC, IVP, NCBC, NIBC, WBC] or A (title) to B: greetings [ICC, TH]. The customary Greek χαίρειν 'greeting' was transformed to the Christian χάρις 'grace' and to it was added the typically Jewish 'peace' [BNTC, EGT, ICC, NCBC, NIBC, NIC].

### 1:1 Peter, apostle[a] of-Jesus Christ

LEXICON—a. ἀπόστολος (LN 53.74) (BAGD 3. p. 99): 'apostle' [BAGD, BNTC, LN, NIC, WBC; all versions], 'special messenger' [LN].

QUESTION—What is meant by the title 'apostle'?
An apostle is an authorized representative or messenger [BNTC, TG, TH], an accredited messenger [NIBC], an agent or ambassador [NCBC]. The office is equal to that of the prophets of old, designating one who spoke or wrote God's words [TNTC].

QUESTION—How are the nouns related in the genitive construction ἀπόστολος Ἰησοῦ Χριστοῦ 'apostle of Jesus Christ'?
It means an apostle who is sent by Jesus Christ [TH], who speaks or acts on behalf of Jesus Christ [NIBC, TH], who represents Jesus Christ [TG, TH]. In the NT 'of Jesus Christ' is not used to describe any ministry office other than that of apostle and therefore the office has paramount importance [NIBC, Sel, TNTC].

**to-(the)-chosen[a] aliens[b] of-(the)-dispersion[c] of-Pontus, Galatia, Cappadocia, Asia and Bythinia,**

LEXICON—a. ἐκλεκτός (LN 30.93) (BAGD 3. p. 99): 'chosen' [BAGD, LN], 'God's chosen people' [NLT, TEV], 'God's elect' [NIV], 'God's people' [CEV], 'the people of God' [REB], 'those whom God the Father has deliberately chosen' [TNT]. Some move this word so as to connect it directly with κατά 'according to' in 1:2: 'chosen and destined by' [NRSV], 'elect according to' [KJV], 'men chosen according to' [NAB], 'who have been chosen in the foresight of God' [NJB]. Some repeat the idea of 'chosen', connecting it with κατά 'according to' in 1:2: 'the people of God ... chosen in (the foresight)' [REB], 'elect ... who have been chosen according to' [NIV], 'God the Father chose you' [NLT], 'God's chosen people ... you were chosen according to' [TEV], 'God's people ... God the Father decided to choose you' [CEV].
   b. παρεπίδημος (LN **11.77**) (BAGD p. 625): 'alien' [**LN**; NJB, REB], 'stranger' [LN; KJV, NAB, NIV], 'foreigner' [CEV, NLT], 'temporary resident' [LN], 'exile' [BAGD; NRSV, TNT], 'refugee' [TEV], 'pilgrim' [NIC].
   c. διασπορά (LN 15.137) (BAGD p. 625): 'dispersion' [BAGD; NJB, NRSV], 'region in which people are scattered' [LN]. The phrase

παρεπιδήμοις διασπορᾶς 'aliens of the dispersion' is translated 'who are scattered like foreigners' [CEV], 'strangers scattered throughout . . .' [KJV], 'scattered' [BNTC], 'strangers in the world scattered throughout . . .' [NIV], 'who live as strangers scattered throughout . . .' [NAB], 'who are living as foreigners in the lands of . . .' [NLT], 'who live as refugees throughout . . .' [TEV], 'who are living as exiles scattered through . . .' [TNT], 'the scattered people of God now living as aliens' [REB], 'all those living as aliens in the Dispersion' [NJB].

QUESTION—Who chose them?

God is the implied actor or agent [BAGD, ICC, NTC, TH; CEV, NIV, NLT, TEV, TNT]. God has chosen them to become his own people [TH; CEV]. His chosen ones now become heirs of the privileged status and responsibility of Israel of old [BNTC, EGT, NIBC, Sel, TH, TNTC]. They are joined to other believers and separated from the world by the fact of his choosing [ICC, NTC].

QUESTION—What is meant by the term παρεπίδημος 'alien'?

The real citizenship of such a person is not in this world but in heaven [NIC, Sel, TG, TH, WBC]. 'Sojourner' fits best with the idea since 'stranger' implies being unknown to neighbors and 'exile' implies being forced to flee [NIBC, TNTC]. The word refers to temporary residents, such as foreigners who settle in a place without intending to reside there permanently [TH].

QUESTION—What is meant by διασπορά 'dispersion'?

Isolated groups or individual believers were to be found in various places similar to the way Jewish communities were dispersed after the exile [IVP, NTC]. This term is meant to include all Christians, whether Gentile or Jewish [Alf, BNTC, ICC, IVP, NIBC, NIC, NTC, TG, TH, TNTC, WBC].

QUESTION—What are the places named, and is there any significance in the order in which they are named?

These were regions in northern Asia Minor (modern Turkey), from which presumably copies of the letter could be made and distributed [NIBC, Sel]. The order probably indicates the route of the messenger [BNTC, EGT, NIBC, NIC, NTC, TNTC, WBC].

**1:2** **according-to[a] (the) foreknowledge/predestination[b] of-God (the) Father**

LEXICON—a. κατά with accusative object (LN 89.8): 'according to' [KJV, NAB, NIV, TEV], 'in accordance with' [LN], 'in' [NJB, REB], not explicit [CEV, NLT, NRSV, TNT].

b. πρόγνωσις (LN **28.20**) (BAGD p. 704): 'foreknowledge' [BAGD, LN; KJV, NAB, NIV, REB], 'what (God) had known beforehand' [**LN**], 'foresight' [NJB], 'predestination' [BAGD], 'purpose' [TEV]. This noun is also translated as a verb: 'to be destined' [NRSV], 'to be deliberately chosen' [TNT], 'to decide' [CEV], 'to choose long ago' [NLT].

1 PETER 1:2

QUESTION—What relationship is indicated by κατά 'according to'?
It indicates congruence with being chosen [TH; CEV, KJV, NAB, NIV, NJB, NRSV, REB, TEV]: you were chosen in accordance with God's foreknowledge/predestination.

QUESTION—What is meant by πρόγνωσιν 'foreknowledge/predestination'?
1. It refers to what is known beforehand [LN; KJV, NAB, NIV, REB]: he chose you in accordance with what he knew beforehand. It is the personal intimacy of a loving father, not just a knowledge of facts [TNTC]. It speaks of a relationship that has its origin in God himself [NIC].
2. It refers to what is predestined by God [BAGD, NIBC, NTC, Sel, TH, WBC; CEV, NLT, NRSV, TEV, TNT]: he chose you in accordance with what he had foreordained to do. God makes sure that what he knows beforehand will happen [TH].

**by/in[a] sanctification[b] of-(the)-Spirit**
LEXICON—a. ἐν with dative object (LN 89.76, 90.6) (BAGD III.1.a. p. 260): 'by' [BAGD, LN; REB], 'through' [KJV, NIV], not explicit [CEV, NAB, NJB, NLT, NRSV, TEV, TNT].
  b. ἁγιασμός (LN 53.44) (BAGD p. 9): 'sanctification' [BAGD; KJV], 'consecration' [BAGD, LN], 'sanctifying work' [NIV], 'consecrating work' [REB], 'holiness' [BAGD]. This noun is also translated as a verb: 'to be made holy' [NJB], 'to be made a holy people' [TEV], 'to make holy' [CEV, NLT], 'to be consecrated' [NAB], 'to be sanctified' [NRSV], 'to be purified' [TNT].

QUESTION—What relationship is indicated by ἐν 'by/in'?
1. It indicates the means by which God chose them [BAGD, BNTC, NIBC, NTC; NIV, REB, TEV]: chosen by being sanctified by the Spirit.
2. It indicates the purpose of being chosen [NJB, TNT]: chosen to be sanctified.
3. It indicates a second comment about the chosen ones [CEV, NAB, NLT, NRSV]: and you were sanctified by the Spirit.

QUESTION—How are the nouns related in the genitive construction ἁγιασμῷ πνεύματος 'sanctification of the Spirit'?
Sanctification is accomplished by the agency of God's Spirit [EGT, ICC; CEV, NAB, NJB, NLT, NRSV, TEV, TNT].

QUESTION—What is meant by ἁγιασμός 'sanctification'?
1. It refers to their relationship with God, as being set apart to be a member of God's people [NAB, REB].
2. It refers to their character, as being made holy in a moral sense [TEV, TNT].

**for[a] obedience[b] and sprinkling[c] of-(the)-blood of-Jesus Christ,**
LEXICON—a. εἰς with accusative object (LN 89.48, 89.57): 'for' [NIV, REB], 'to' [NAB, NRSV, TEV, TNT], 'unto' [KJV], 'for the purpose of, in order to' [LN (89.57)], 'as a result' [NLT], 'with the result that, to cause' [LN (89.48)].

b. ὑπακοή (LN 36.15) (BAGD 1.b. p. 837): 'obedience' [BAGD, LN; KJV, NAB, NIV, REB]. This noun is also translated as a verb: 'to be obedient' [NJB, NRSV], 'to obey' [CEV, NLT, TEV, TNT].
　　c. ῥαντισμός (LN 47.16) (BAGD p. 734): 'sprinkling' [BAGD, LN; KJV, NIV, REB], 'purification' [NAB]. This noun is also translated as a verb: 'to be sprinkled' [BAGD; CEV, NJB, NRSV, TNT], 'to be cleansed' [NLT], 'to be purified' [TEV].

QUESTION—What relationship is indicated by εἰς 'for'?
1. It indicates the purpose for their being chosen [NIV, REB, TNT]: you were chosen for obedience.
2. It indicates the purpose for their being sanctified [NAB]: sanctified to a life of obedience.
3. It indicates the purpose of their being both chosen and sanctified [NRSV, TEV]: you were chosen and sanctified for obedience.
4. It indicates the result of their being chosen and sanctified [NLT]: you were chosen and sanctified, with the result that you obeyed.
5. It introduces a third comment about them [CEV]: God chose you, the Spirit sanctified you, and you have obeyed.

QUESTION—What is the obedience spoken of here?
1. It is obedience to Jesus Christ [NIBC, NTC, TNTC; CEV, NAB, NIV]. It is initial acceptance of Jesus as Lord of one's life [NIBC].
2. It is obedience to the gospel [BNTC, Sel, WBC]. It refers to the initial acceptance of and submission to the gospel [BNTC, WBC]. It refers to the entire life of faith, and not to initial conversion [TNTC].

QUESTION—What is meant by 'sprinkling of the blood of Jesus Christ'?
Paired with 'obedience', this is a metaphor comparing the believer's entering into the new covenant with Israel's entering the covenant in Exodus 24 [BNTC, EGT, IVP, NIBC, NIC, NTC, Sel, TG, TH, WBC]. It can also refer to consecration to priestly service as in Leviticus 8:30 [NIBC]. It refers to Leviticus 14:6–7 and Psalm 51:7, where the same verb is used in the LXX to describe cleansing of sin for on-going fellowship with God [TNTC]. It is the means whereby we are transformed to be like Christ [ICC]. The sprinkling brings about an on-going cleansing process [NTC]. 'Blood' is a metonymy referring to the sacrificial death of Jesus, so this means that believers share in the benefits arising out of Jesus' death, such as forgiveness, purification, or simply a new relationship with God, realized primarily in the church [TH].

QUESTION—To what does the genitive Ἰησοῦ Χριστοῦ 'of Jesus Christ' refer?
1. It refers only to 'sprinkling of the blood' [BNTC, LN, Sel, WBC]: for obedience and for the sprinkling of Jesus Christ's blood. Obedience means the initial acceptance of and submission to the gospel [BNTC, WBC].
2. It refers to both obedience and sprinkling [NIBC, NTC, TNTC; CEV, NAB, NJB, NLT, NRSV, REB, TEV, TNT]: for obedience to Jesus Christ and the sprinkling of his blood.

**grace<sup>a</sup> to-you and peace<sup>b</sup> be-multiplied.<sup>c</sup>**
LEXICON—a. χάρις (LN 25.89, 88.66) (BAGD 2.c. p. 877): 'grace' [BAGD, LN (88.66); all versions except CEV, NAB, NLT], 'favor' [BAGD, LN (25.89); NAB], 'special favor' [NLT], 'goodwill' [LN (25.89)]. This noun is also translated as a verb: 'to be kind' [CEV].
  b. εἰρήνη (LN 22.42) (BAGD 2. p. 227): 'peace' [LN; all versions]. This word corresponds to the Hebrew greeting *shalom*, a wish for welfare and health [BAGD].
  c. aorist pass. opt. of πληθύνω (LN 59.68) (BAGD 1.b. p. 669): 'to be multiplied' [BAGD, LN; KJV], 'to be in abundance' [NAB, NIV, NJB, NRSV], 'to be increased' [BAGD], 'to be increased greatly' [LN], 'to have more and more' [NLT], '(to be given) in full measure' [TEV], '(to be given) in fullest measure' [REB], '(to be given) abundantly' [TNT], 'to keep on giving' [CEV].
QUESTION—What was meant by this greeting?
  'Peace', the typical Jewish greeting [WBC], is a prayer and wish for all blessings spiritual and material [BNTC, NIC], and is the result of grace [NTC, WBC]. Grace epitomizes all that believers receive from God, including mercy, love, and forgiveness of sin [NIBC, NTC, WBC]. Grace and peace are to be multiplied to match the increasing hate and persecution of the world toward the believers [EGT].

**DISCOURSE UNIT: 1:3–2:10** [TNTC, WBC]. The topic is general doctrine about the greatness of your salvation [TNTC], the identity of the people of God [WBC].

**DISCOURSE UNIT: 1:3–12** [IVP, NIC, NTC, Sel, TG, TH, TNTC, WBC; CEV, NAB, NIV, NLT, TEV]. The topic is a real reason to hope [CEV], thanksgiving [IVP, NIC; NAB], a prayer of thanksgiving [TH], a living hope [NLT, NRSV, TEV], a great salvation [WBC], growing as Christians through a joyful faith [TNTC], the Christian joy [TG], the first doctrinal section [Sel].

**DISCOURSE UNIT: 1:3–9** [REB]. The topic is the giving of thanks.

**DISCOURSE UNIT: 1:3–5** [Sel, TH, WBC; NJB]. The topic is the introduction and the inheritance of Christians [NJB], salvation as hope [WBC], thanksgiving for the new life [TH], praise to God for the resurrection of Christ and for new life [Sel].

**1:3 Blessed<sup>a</sup> (be) the God and Father of our Lord Jesus Christ,**
LEXICON—a. εὐλογητός (LN 33.362) (BAGD 322): 'blessed be' [BAGD, BNTC, NIC, WBC; KJV, NJB, NRSV], 'praised be' [BAGD, LN; NAB, REB], 'praise be to' [NIV], 'all honor to' [NLT], 'praise God' [CEV], 'let us give thanks to' [TEV], 'may he be praised' [TNT].

QUESTION—What is the significance of the title 'the God and Father of our Lord Jesus Christ'?

It expresses the core of the Christian gospel and its theology about God and Christ [BNTC, NIC]. Jesus was equal with God, but by becoming a human being, he could acknowledge God as his God and address God as his Father [TH]. The application of the term 'Lord' to Jesus Christ is a clear ascription of deity [BNTC, IVP, NCBC, NIBC, NTC, TH]. The use of the name 'Jesus' with the title 'Christ' refers to both his earthly ministry and his messianic status [NIBC, NTC].

**the (one who) because-of[a] his great[b] mercy[c] us having-caused-to-be-born-again[d] into[e] (a) living[f] hope[g]**

LEXICON—a. κατά with accusative object (BAGD II.5.a.δ. p. 407): 'because of' [BAGD; TEV], 'as a result of' [BAGD], 'in' [NAB, NIV, NJB, REB, TNT], 'by' [NLT, NRSV], 'according to' [KJV], not explicit [CEV].

b. πολύς (LN **78.3**) (BAGD I.1.b.β. p. 688): 'great' [BAGD, LN; all versions except CEV, KJV, NLT], 'abundant' [KJV], 'boundless' [NLT]. The phrase τὸ πολὺ αὐτοῦ ἔλεος 'his great mercy' is translated 'God is so good' [CEV].

c. ἔλεος (LN 88.76) (BAGD 2.b. 250): 'mercy' [BNTC, NIC, WBC; all versions except CEV]. This noun is also translated as a verbal clause: 'God is good' [CEV].

d. aorist act. participle of ἀναγεννάω (LN **13.55**) (BAGD p. 51): 'to cause to be born again' [BAGD, LN], 'to beget again' [BAGD; KJV], 'to give new birth' [NAB, NIV, NJB, NRSV, REB], 'to give new life' [CEV, TEV, TNT], 'to give the privilege of being born again' [NLT].

e. εἰς with accusative object (LN 89.48, 89.57): 'into' [NIV, NJB, NRSV, REB], 'unto' [KJV, NAB], 'with the result that, so that as a result' [LN (89.48)], 'for the purpose of, in order to' [LN (89.57)], not explicit [CEV, NLT, TEV].

f. pres. act. participle of ζάω (LN 23.88) (BAGD 4.b. p. 337): 'to live' [LN; CEV, NLT], 'to draw life (from)' [NAB]. The participle is also used adjectivally to describe the hope: 'living' [BAGD, LN; NIV, NJB, NRSV, REB, TEV, TNT], 'lively' [KJV].

g. ἐλπίς (LN 25.61) (BAGD 2.b. p. 253): 'hope' [all versions except NLT], 'wonderful expectation' [NLT].

QUESTION—What relationship is indicated by κατά 'because of'?

It indicates the reason that God caused us to be born again to a living hope [TH; NLT, NRSV, TEV]: because God is merciful, he caused us to be born again.

QUESTION—What relationship is indicated by εἰς 'into'?

1. It indicates the goal or purpose for being born again [NIC; NLT, TEV]: born again to have a hope.

2. It indicates a result of being born again [IVP, NIBC, TH, TNTC].

QUESTION—In what way can hope be described as 'living'?
This hope is characterized by firmness and certainty [TH]. It grows and increases in strength, as living things do [TNTC]. It possesses or brings life from God [BAGD]. It brings life to God's elect [NTC]. It is certain as well as fruitful and effective [BNTC]. It is founded on a substantial reality, which is the resurrection of Christ [NIC]. It is valid and will not disappoint, in sharp contrast with the hopelessness of pagan religion [WBC].

**through[a] the resurrection[b] of Jesus Christ from[c] the dead,[d]**
LEXICON—a. διά with genitive object (LN 89.26, 89.76): 'through' [BNTC, LN (89.76), NIC, WBC; NIV, NJB, NRSV], 'by' [LN (89.76), WBC; KJV, REB, TEV, TNT], 'from' [NAB], 'by means of' [LN (89.76)], 'because' [NLT], 'because of, on account of' [LN (89.26)].
b. ἀνάστασις (LN 23.93) (BAGD 2.a. p. 60): 'resurrection' [BNTC, NIC; KJV, NAB, NIV, NJB, NRSV, REB]. This noun is also translated as a participle 'raising' [WBC; CEV, TEV, TNT] and as a verb 'rose again' [NLT].
c. ἐκ with genitive object (LN 84.4) (BAGD 1.b. p. 234): 'from' [BAGD, BNTC, LN, NIC, WBC; all versions].
d. νεκρός (LN 23.121): 'dead' [BNTC, NIC, WBC; KJV, NAB, NIV, NJB, NLT, NRSV, REB], 'death' [CEV, TEV, TNT].

QUESTION—What relationship is indicated by διά 'through'?
1. It indicates the reason we have a living hope [IVP, TH; NLT]: we hope because God resurrected Jesus Christ.
2. It indicates the means by which we received the new birth [BNTC, EGT, TG, TH, TNTC, WBC; NAB]: he caused us to be born again by resurrecting Christ.
3. It is the means for both the new birth and the living hope [NTC, TNTC; CEV, TEV, TNT].

**1:4 into[a] an-inheritance[b] (that is) imperishable[c] and undefiled[d] and unfading[e]**
LEXICON—a. εἰς with accusative object (LN 89.48, 89.57, 90.23): 'into' [NIV, NJB, NRSV], 'to' [KJV, NAB], 'so' [TEV], 'with the result that, so that as a result' [LN (89.48)], 'for the purpose of, in order to' [LN (89.57)], 'concerning, with reference to, about' [LN (90.23)], not explicit [CEV, REB, TNT].
b. κληρονομία (LN 57.132) (BAGD 3. p. 435): 'inheritance' [BAGD, BNTC, NIC, WBC; KJV, NAB, NIV, NLT, NRSV, REB], 'priceless inheritance' [NLT], 'possession' [LN; TNT], 'heritage' [NJB]. This noun is also translated as a verb phrase: 'to possess rich blessings' [TEV], 'God has something for you' [CEV].
c. ἄφθαρτος (LN 23.128) (BAGD p. 125): 'imperishable' [LN; NAB, NRSV], 'indestructible' [WBC], 'incorruptible' [NIC; KJV], 'immortal' [LN]. This adjective is also translated as a verb phrase: 'which cannot be destroyed' [BNTC], 'that can never perish' [NIV], 'which nothing can

destroy' [REB], 'which will last forever' [TNT], 'beyond the reach of decay' [NLT], 'it will never decay' [CEV], 'they cannot decay' [TEV], 'that can never be spoilt' [NJB].

d. ἀμίαντος (LN 53.36) (BAGD 1. p. 46): 'undefiled' [LN; KJV, NRSV], 'pure and undefiled' [NLT], 'untainted' [LN], 'incorruptible' [WBC]. This adjective is also translated as a verb phrase: 'it will never be ruined' [CEV], 'incapable of defilement' [NAB], 'that can never spoil' [NIV], 'that can never be soiled' [NJB], 'which nothing can spoil' [REB], 'they cannot spoil' [TEV], 'it cannot be spoiled' [TNT].

e. ἀμάραντος (LN **79.23**) (BAGD 2. p. 42): 'unfading' [LN, WBC; NRSV], 'incapable of fading' [NAB], 'beyond the reach of change' [NLT], 'not losing brightness' [LN]. This adjective is also translated as a verb phrase: 'it will never disappear' [CEV], 'that fadeth not away' [KJV], 'that can never fade' [NIV], 'that can never fade away' [NJB], 'which nothing can wither' [REB], 'they cannot fade away' [TEV], 'it cannot fade' [TNT].

QUESTION—What relationship is indicated by εἰς 'into'?

1. This is a second purpose for being born again [NIC; NAB, NIV, NJB, NRSV]: you are born again into a living hope, and also born again for an inheritance.
2. This explains the hope [REB, TNT]: the living hope is the hope for an inheritance.
3. This is the result of having a living hope [TEV]: because we have a living hope, we look forward to the inheritance.

QUESTION—What is meant by κληρονομίαν 'inheritance'?

It refers to salvation after this life [NTC], future blessings or eternal life [TG], a heavenly reward for the chosen [NIC], a portion in the new creation and all its blessing [TNTC], salvation, grace, glory, and a crown [Alf].

**having-been-kept[a] in (the) heavens[b] for you**

LEXICON—a. perf. pass. participle of τηρέω (LN 13.32, 37.122) (BAGD 2.a. p. 814): 'to be kept' [NAB, NIV, NRSV], 'to be preserved' [BNTC], 'to be reserved' [WBC; KJV, NJB, NLT, REB], 'to be guarded' [NIC], 'to be stored' [CEV]. The perfect passive is also translated as present active: '(God) keeps' [TEV, TNT].

b. οὐρανός (LN 1.11) (BAGD 2.d. p. 595): 'heaven' [BNTC, NIC, WBC; all versions]. There is no significance in the use of the plural; it is a normal Hebrew way of speaking of heaven [ICC, LN, NTC, TH].

QUESTION—What is meant by the use of the perfect passive participle τετηρημένην 'having-been-kept'?

Use of the perfect tense indicates the inheritance already exists and is currently being kept safe [NCBC, NIBC, Sel]. It is a completed past activity with a continuing present result [NTC, TNTC]. God is the implied actor of the passive construction [NTC].

QUESTION—What is the significance of εἰς ὑμᾶς 'for you' in this passage?

It not only refers to the fact that the inheritance reserved in heaven is for the readers, it also marks a shift from the 'we' of 1:3–4 to a more homiletic 'you' style of address in the rest of the epistle [WBC]. The shift to the second person plural serves to make much more personal the promise that the inheritance will not be denied them [TNTC].

**1:5** the ones by[a] (the) power[b] of-God being-protected[c] through[d] faith[e]

LEXICON—a. ἐν with dative object (LN 89.76): 'by' [LN; KJV, NIV, NJB, NRSV, TEV], 'with' [NAB], 'in' [NLT], not explicit [CEV, REB, TNT].

b. δύναμις (LN 76.1): 'power' [BNTC, LN, NIC, WBC; all versions].

c. pres. pass. participle of φρουρέω (LN 37.119) (BAGD 2. p. 867): 'to be protected' [WBC; NRSV], 'to be under someone's protection' [REB], 'to be kept' [NIC; KJV, NAB], 'to be kept safe' [BNTC; NJB, TEV], 'to be shielded' [NIV]. This passive verb is also translated actively: 'to protect' [CEV, NLT, TNT].

d. διά with genitive object (LN 89.76, 89.26): 'through' [LN (89.76); KJV, NAB, NIV, NJB, NRSV, TEV] 'by means of, by' [LN (89.76)], 'because' [NLT, REB, TNT], 'because of, on account of' [LN (89.26)], not explicit [CEV].

e. πίστις (LN 31.85) (BAGD 2.d. α. p. 663): 'faith' [BAGD, BNTC, LN, NIC, WBC; KJV, NAB, NJB, NRSV, REB, TEV]. This noun is also translated as a verb: 'to have faith' [CEV], 'to trust' [NLT], 'to believe' [TNT].

QUESTION—What relationship is indicated by ἐν 'by'?

It indicates the means by which they are protected [LN; KJV, NIV, NJB, NRSV, TEV]: you are protected by means of God's power.

QUESTION—What is the relation between τηρέω 'kept' in 1:4 and φρουρέω 'protected' in 1:5?

The latter is a military term referring to being guarded by a garrison [BNTC, ICC, NIBC, NTC, Sel, TNTC]. It is used in this context almost as a synonym for the former word for rhetorical balance [WBC]. Φρουρέω can mean to protect someone from danger or to prevent him from escaping [NTC, TNTC] and by implication can mean that God preserves us from losing faith [TNTC]. The present participle indicates the ongoing nature of that protecting and preserving [TNTC]. The inheritance is kept for the believers who, in turn, are preserved in order to come into their inheritance [NCBC, WBC]. God is acting in heaven to preserve the saints' future, and on earth to preserve them for the present [NIC].

QUESTION—What relationship is indicated by διά 'through'?

1. It indicates the means by which they are protected [Alf, TG, TH; KJV, NAB, NIV, NJB, NRSV, TEV]: you are protected by your faith. God's power is the source of a believer's protection and faith is the means whereby that power works [Alf, TG, TH].

2. It indicates the reason they are protected [NLT, REB, TNT]: you are protected by God because you believe.

**for/until<sup>a</sup> a-salvation<sup>b</sup> ready to-be-revealed<sup>c</sup> in (the) time last.**

LEXICON—a. εἰς (LN 67.119, 89.57): 'for' [NRSV], 'unto' [KJV], 'until' [NIV, NJB, NLT, REB], 'then' [CEV], 'when' [TNT], 'for the purpose of, in order to' [LN (89.57)], not explicit [NAB, TEV].
  b. σωτηρία (LN 21.18) (BAGD 2. p 801): 'salvation' [BNTC, NIC, WBC; all versions except CEV, TNT], 'his saving purpose' [TNT]. This is also translated as a verbal clause in the future tense, 'he will save you' [CEV].
  c. aorist. pass. inf. of ἀποκαλύπτω (LN 28.38) (BAGD 4. p. 92): 'to be revealed' [KJV, NAB, NIV, NRSV, TEV], not explicit [CEV]. This future infinitive verb is also translated as present indicative: 'is revealed' [NJB, REB]: as future indicative: 'will be revealed' [NLT]; as present active infinitive '(ready) to reveal' [TNT].

QUESTION—What relationship is indicated by εἰς 'for/until'?
  1. It indicates the purpose for which they are protected [TH; NRSV]: God protects you in order to save you in the last time.
  2. It indicates the time during which they are protected [NIV, NJB, NLT, REB]: God protects you until you are saved in the last time.

QUESTION—What is the salvation that is referred to?
It is future vindication [WBC]. It is eschatological fulfillment of all God's plans for creation [NCBC, NIBC], the future full possession of all the blessings of our redemption [TNTC]. It is all God's blessings, protection, and well-being [IVP]. It is the full enjoyment of eternal glory, the object of 'living hope', and the content of the 'inheritance' [BNTC]. It is synonymous with 'inheritance' in 1:4 [NTC]. Salvation is the actual possession of the inheritance with its fullness of life and open vision of God [Sel]. It is the final deliverance from Satan, persecution, and sorrow [ICC].

QUESTION—What is meant by 'the last time'?
It is not generalized 'times' or 'ages' but one decisive moment [WBC]. It is the time of final judgment [TNTC], the final scene of judgment and reward [NIC], the end of the world when Christ appears [IVP], the final days of darkness and suffering [ICC], God's appointed time [NTC, TH].

**DISCOURSE UNIT: 1:6–9** [Sel, TH, WBC; NJB]. The topic is rejoicing in trial through faith and love for Christ [Sel], exhortation to rejoice even in difficult circumstances [TH], salvation as joy [WBC], faithfulness to Christ and love of Christ [NJB].

**1:6 In this you-greatly-rejoice<sup>a</sup>**

LEXICON—a. pres. mid. indic. of ἀγαλλιάω (LN 25.133) (BAGD p. 4): 'to rejoice greatly' [LN; KJV, NIV], 'to be extremely joyful' [LN], 'to exult' [BNTC], 'to rejoice' [NIC, WBC; NRSV], 'to be truly glad' [NLT], 'to be glad' [CEV, TEV]. This verb is also translated as a verbal clause: 'there is cause for rejoicing here' [NAB], 'this is a great joy to you' [NJB], 'this is a cause for great joy' [REB], 'here is cause for rejoicing' [TNT]. This verb is translated as a present imperative [NLT, TEV] or as future indicative [WBC; CEV].

QUESTION—What is the antecedent to which ᾧ 'this' refers?

It is a masculine or neuter relative pronoun in the dative case, and cannot refer individually to 'hope', 'inheritance', or 'salvation', which are all feminine and would require a feminine relative pronoun. While ᾧ could refer to God or Jesus Christ, none of the commentators take that view, choosing to link ἐν ᾧ 'in this' either with one or more of the blessings of the previous verses (which collectively could take a neuter relative pronoun) or with 'in the last time' which immediately precedes it.

1. 'In this' refers to the preceding context. It refers to the experience of rebirth and anticipation of salvation [BNTC, NTC], to all the blessings enumerated in 1:3–5 [EGT, IVP, NCBC, Sel, TG, TH, TNTC].
2. 'In this' refers to 'the last time', and ἀγαλλιᾶσθε 'you rejoice' refers to rejoicing at a future time even though it is a present tense verb [Alf, ICC, WBC; CEV]. It refers to the coming salvation which will be revealed in the last time [NIBC].
3. 'In this' refers to hope, not to 'inheritance' or 'salvation', since all of 1:4–5 explains the content of the hope [NIC].

**(though) now[a] for-a-little-while[b] if necessary[c]**

LEXICON—a. ἄρτι (LN 67.38) (BAGD 3. p. 110): 'now' [BNTC, WBC; KJV, NIV, NRSV, TEV], 'yet' [NJB], not explicit [NIC; CEV, NAB, NLT, REB, TNT].

b. ὀλίγος (LN 67.106) (BAGD 3.a. p. 563): 'for a little while' [NIC, WBC; NIV, NRSV, REB, TNT], 'for a short time' [LN; NJB], 'for a short while' [BNTC], 'for a while' [CEV, NLT, TEV], 'for a season' [KJV], 'for a time' [NAB].

c. δεῖ (LN 71.34) (BAGD 6. p. 172): 'to be necessary' [LN; TEV], 'must' [LN; NJB], 'since it has to be' [BNTC], 'it is necessary' [NIC; NLT], 'if need be' [KJV]. It is also translated with implied subject 'you': 'you must' [WBC], 'you have to' [CEV, NAB, NIV, NRSV, REB, TNT].

QUESTION—What is the meaning of 'if necessary'?

1. It is stated as an actual fact [BNTC, WBC; NJB, NLT, NRSV, TNT]: even though you actually are grieved now by various trials. The suffering is a divine necessity or serves God's sovereign purposes in some way [BNTC, IVP, NCBC, NIBC, NIC, WBC].
2. It is stated as a hypothetical case [CEV, KJV, NAB, NIV, REB, TEV]: even though you may have to be grieved by various trials now.

**having-been-made-sad[a] by various[b] trials[c]**

LEXICON—a. aorist pass. participle. of λυπέω (LN 25.275) (BAGD 2.a. p. 481): 'to be made sad' [BAGD, LN], 'to be made distressed' [BAGD], 'to be in heaviness' [KJV], 'to suffer distress' [NAB, TNT], 'to suffer grief' [NIV], 'to suffer' [NRSV, REB, TEV]. This participle is also

translated as a verb phrase: 'to go through many trials' [CEV], 'to bear all sorts of trials' [NJB], 'to endure many trials' [NLT].
  b. ποικίλος (LN 58.45) (BAGD 1. p. 683): 'various' [NRSV], 'of various kinds, diversified' [BAGD, LN], 'manifold' [KJV], 'many' [CEV, NAB, NLT], 'all kinds' [NIV], 'all sorts of' [NJB], 'many kinds' [REB, TEV, TNT].
  c. πειρασμός (LN 27.46) (BAGD 1., 2.b. p. 640): 'trial' [BAGD (1.); NAB, NIV, NJB, NLT, NRSV, REB, TEV, TNT], 'testing' [LN], 'test' [BAGD (1.)], 'hard trial' [CEV], 'temptation' [BAGD (2.b.); KJV].

QUESTION—What is the significance of the use of the aorist participle λυπηθέντες 'having been made sad'?

The use of ἄρτι 'now' with the aorist participle refers to an action or event just begun or concluded [Sel]; it gives the participle a perfect meaning, that is, it extends to the present time [WBC]. The aorist participle is simultaneous in time with the 'rejoicing' earlier in the verse [TNTC].

**1:7 so-that<sup>a</sup> the genuineness<sup>b</sup> of-your faith<sup>c</sup>**

LEXICON—a. ἵνα (LN 89.59): 'so that' [BNTC, LN, WBC; NIV, NJB, NRSV, REB], 'that' [KJV], 'in order that' [NIC], 'their purpose is' [TEV], 'there is a purpose in this' [TNT], 'this is so that' [NAB], 'these trials are only to' [NLT], not explicit [CEV].
  b. δοκίμιον (LN **73.3**) (BAGD 2. p. 203): 'genuineness' [BAGD, LN, NIC, WBC; NAB, NRSV], 'sterling quality' [BNTC], 'trial' [KJV]. This noun is also translated as an adjective: 'genuine' [**LN**], 'to prove to be genuine' [TEV], 'to show to be genuine' [TNT], 'to show to be strong and pure' [NLT]; as a verb phrase: 'to stand the test' [REB], 'to prove the worth' [NJB], 'to prove to be worth much more' [CEV].
  c. πίστις (LN 31.85) (BAGD 2.d.α. p. 663): 'faith' [BAGD, BNTC, LN, NIC, WBC; all versions], 'piety, genuine religion' [BAGD].

QUESTION—What relationship is indicated by ἵνα 'so that'?

This indicates the purpose of the sufferings mentioned in 1:6. That is, you suffer so that your faith may be found worthy of praise, glory, and honor [BNTC, ICC, IVP, NIC, TH, WBC; all versions].

QUESTION—What is the 'faith' spoken of here?
  1. It refers to steadfast loyalty [BNTC], faithfulness to God [IVP, NCBC, WBC], loyalty to Christ, especially under trial [NIBC], or commitment [NIC].
  2. It refers to trust in Christ [TH], or saving faith in Jesus Christ [TG].

**more-valuable<sup>a</sup> (than) perishing<sup>b</sup> gold**

LEXICON—a. πολυτιμότερος comparative of πολύτιμος (LN **65.3**) (BAGD p. 690): 'more valuable' [NJB], 'of much greater value' [TNT], '(to have) much more value' [LN], 'more precious' [BNTC, WBC; NAB, NRSV], 'far more precious' [NLT], 'much more precious' [NIC; REB, TEV], 'very precious' [BAGD], 'of greater worth' [NIV], 'worth more' [CEV].

b. pres. mid. participle of ἀπόλλυμι (LN **13.96**) (BAGD 2.a.β. p. 95): 'to perish' [NIC; KJV, NIV, TNT], 'to cease to exist, to come to an end' [LN], 'to be lost, to be ruined' [BAGD], 'can be destroyed' [CEV, TEV]. This participle is also translated as an adjective: 'perishable' [BNTC, WBC; NJB, NRSV, REB], 'mere' [NLT].

QUESTION—What is referred to as being 'more valuable than gold'?
1. It is faith that is more valuable than gold [Alf, ICC, NTC, TG, TH; CEV, NAB, NIV, NJB, NLT, NRSV, TEV, TNT].
2. It is the quality of genuineness of faith that is more valuable than gold [BNTC, EGT, IVP, NCBC, NIBC, NIC, TNTC, WBC; REB].

**even-though**[a] **tested**[b] **by fire,**
LEXICON—a. δέ (LN 89.124): 'even though' [BNTC; NIV, TNT], 'though' [WBC; KJV, NRSV], 'even if' [NJB], not explicit [NIC; CEV, NAB, NLT, REB, TEV].
  b. pres. pass. participle of δοκιμάζω (LN 27.45) (BAGD 2.a. p. 202): 'proved by testing' [BAGD], 'examined' [LN], 'tried' [KJV, NAB], 'refined' [NIV]. This participle is translated as a verb or verb phrase in various translations; 'tests' [NLT], 'is tested' [BNTC, LN, WBC; NRSV, TEV], 'having been tested' [NIC], 'has been tested' [CEV, NJB], 'passes through the fire' [REB], 'has been through the refiner's fire' [TNT]. This passive is also translated actively: 'fire tests and purifies' [NLT], 'gold passes through the fire' [REB].

QUESTION—What relationship is indicated by δέ 'though'?
1. It is concessive with reference to the testing of gold [TH; KJV, NIV, NJB, TNT]: even though gold is tested by fire, it is perishable (unlike your faith). Or, it is concessive with reference to gold's quality of perishability; that is, although gold is perishable, it is tested by fire (as your faith is) [WBC; NRSV, REB, TEV].
2. It is concessive with reference to the testing of faith [NIC]: the genuineness of your faith, even though it is tested by fire is more precious than gold.

**may be-found**[a] **to-result-in**[b] **praise**[c] **and glory**[d] **and honor**[e]
LEXICON—a. aorist pass. subj. of εὑρίσκω (LN 27.1) (BAGD 2. p. 325): 'to be found' [BNTC, NIC, WBC; KJV, NRSV], 'to lead to' [NAB], 'to result in' [NIV], 'to bring' [NLT], 'to be proved' [NJB], 'to prove itself' [REB] 'to show that' [CEV], not explicit [TEV].
  b. εἰς with accusative case (LN 89.48) (BAGD 4.e. p. 229): 'to result in' [WBC; NIV, NRSV], 'so that' [BAGD], 'with the result that, to cause' [LN], 'to' [NIC; NJB], 'redound to' [BNTC], 'worthy of' [REB], 'unto' [KJV], 'to lead to' [NAB], 'you will be given' [CEV], 'it will bring you' [NLT, TNT], 'then you will receive' [TEV].
  c. ἔπαινος (LN 33.354) (BAGD 1. a.β. p. 281): 'praise' [BNTC, LN, NIC, WBC; all versions].

d. δόξα (LN 33.357): 'glory' [BNTC, NIC, WBC; all versions except NJB], 'praise' [LN], not explicit [NJB].

e. τιμή (LN 87.4) (BAGD 2.b. p. 817): 'honor' [BNTC, LN, NIC, WBC; all versions].

QUESTION—What is meant by the use of the passive verb 'to be found'?

1. It is a stronger equivalent of the verb εἶναι 'to be' [WBC], that is, your faith will result in praise, glory, and honor.
2. It is used in the sense of 'enduring', that is, when the perishable is gone, real faith that endures the test is all that is found [ICC, TG, TH; TEV].
3. It is used in the sense of being 'reckoned as' the same as something else [Sel].
4. It means 'to find', God being the implied actor or finder [EGT, ICC, IVP, NTC].

QUESTION—What relationship is indicated by εἰς?

1. It indicates the result of the believers' tested faith which will cause them to be given praise, glory, and honor [BNTC, NIC, WBC; all versions except CEV].
2. It indicates the purpose of the trials; that is, the trials will show that you will be given praise, glory, and honor [CEV].

QUESTION—To whom or what is 'praise, glory, and honor' directed?

1. It is the believer whose faith is genuine who will receive praise, glory, and honor [Alf, EGT, ICC, IVP, NIBC, Sel, TH, TNTC; CEV, NJB, NLT, TEV, TNT]. God will praise them and give them honor and glory [TH]. God shares his own praise, glory, and honor with the believer [BNTC, NIC].
2. It is the faith of the believer that will receive praise, glory, and honor from God [NCBC, TG, WBC; NJB].
3. God will receive praise, glory, and honor, although the believer will also share in it [NTC].

**at[a] (the) revelation[b] of Jesus Christ;**

LEXICON—a. ἐν with dative object (LN 67.33) (BAGD II.2. p. 260): 'at' [BNTC, LN, NIC; KJV], 'when' [BAGD, WBC; all versions except KJV].

b. ἀποκάλυψις (LN 28.38) (BAGD 3. p. 92): 'revelation' [LN], 'revealing' [BAGD], 'appearing' [KJV]. This noun is also translated as a verb: 'to return' [CEV], 'to appear' [NAB], 'to be revealed' [NIV, NJB, NLT, NRSV, REB, TEV, TNT].

QUESTION—What is meant by 'the revelation of Jesus Christ'?

It refers to the return of Christ, that is, the parousia [Alf, ICC, IVP, NCBC, NIBC, NIC, NTC, TG, TH], the day of the Lord [BNTC, Sel], the day of judgment [TNTC], the last day [WBC]. 'Revelation' is reflexive rather than passive, that is, he will reveal himself. All that Christ is will be made known [TH]. The focus is not so much on his presence but his being revealed, since he is already invisibly present with the believer [NCBC, WBC].

## 1:8 whom not having-seen[a] you-love,[b]

LEXICON—a. aorist act. participle of ὁράω (LN 24.1) (BAGD 1.a.α p. 577): 'to see' [BAGD, LN, NIC, WBC; all versions], 'to set eyes on' [BNTC].
- b. pres. act. indic. of ἀγαπάω (LN 25.43) (BAGD 1.a.β. p. 4): 'to love' [BAGD, BNTC, LN, NIC, WBC; all versions].

QUESTION—What relationship is indicated by the use of the aorist participle ἰδόντες 'having seen'?

It indicates concession [NIC; CEV, NAB, NIV, NJB, NLT, NRSV, REB, TEV, TNT]: although you have not seen him, yet you love him.

### in whom now[a] not seeing[b] but[c] believing[d]

LEXICON—a. ἄρτι (LN 67.38) (BAGD 3. p. 110): 'now' [LN, WBC; all versions except NJB, NLT], 'yet' [NIC], 'at present' [BNTC], 'at the present time' [BAGD], 'still' [NJB], not explicit [NLT].
- b. pres. act. participle of ὁράω (LN 24.1) (BAGD 1.a.α. p. 577) 'to see' [BAGD, BNTC, LN, WBC; all versions], 'to observe' [NIC].
- c. δέ (LN 89.124): 'but' [LN; CEV], 'yet' [KJV], not explicit [BNTC, NIC, WBC; all versions except CEV, KJV].
- d. pres. act. participle of πιστεύω (LN 31.85) (BAGD 2.a.β. p. 661): 'to believe' [BAGD, BNTC, LN, NIC, WBC; all versions except CEV, NLT, REB], 'to have faith' [CEV], 'to trust' [NLT, REB].

QUESTION—What relationship is indicated by the use of the present participle ὁρῶντες 'seeing'?

It indicates concession [BNTC, NIC, TH; CEV, KJV, NIV, NLT, NRSV, TEV, TNT]: although you do not now see him, yet you believe in him.

### you rejoice[a] (with) joy[b] inexpressible[c] and having-been-glorified[d]

LEXICON—a. pres. mid. indic. of ἀγαλλιάω (LN 25.133) (BAGD p. 4): 'to rejoice' [NIC, WBC; KJV, NAB, NRSV, TEV], 'to rejoice greatly' [LN], 'to be filled with joy' [NIV, NJB, REB], 'to be happy' [NLT], 'to exult' [BNTC], 'to be extremely joyful, to be overjoyed' [LN]. The phrase ἀγαλλιᾶσθε χαρᾷ 'you rejoice with joy' is translated 'how glad and happy you are' [CEV]. This verb is also translated as a future tense 'you will rejoice' because it is viewed as being contingent on the perfect participle κομιζόμενοι 'obtaining' in the following verse. That is, when you have received the outcome of your faith, you will rejoice [WBC]. See this word at 1:6.
- b. χαρά (LN 25.123) (BAGD 1. p. 875): 'joy' [BAGD, BNTC, LN, NIC; all versions except CEV], 'delight' [WBC], 'gladness, great happiness' [LN].
- c. ἀνεκλάλητος (LN 33.96) (BAGD p. 64): 'inexpressible' [BAGD, BNTC, WBC; NAB, NIV, NLT], 'unspeakable' [NIC; KJV], 'what cannot be expressed in words' [LN], 'indescribable' [NRSV], 'no words can tell' [CEV], 'cannot be described' [NJB], 'too great for words' [REB], 'which words cannot express' [**LN**; TEV], 'which no words can express' [TNT].
- d. perf. pass. participle of δοξάζω (LN **65.5**) (BAGD 2. p. 204): 'glorious' [LN, WBC; NIV, NJB, NLT, NRSV, REB, TEV, TNT], 'full of glory'

[BNTC; KJV], 'filled with glory' [NIC], 'touched with glory' [NAB], not explicit [CEV].

QUESTION—What is the basis of the joy of the believer?

It is the assurance or experience of the salvation of the soul as the goal or reward of faith [BNTC, ICC, NCBC, NIBC, NTC, Sel, TH, WBC; NIV]. It is love for Christ [TNTC]; it is their relationship to Christ [IVP, NIC].

**1:9** obtaining<sup>a</sup> the outcome/goal<sup>b</sup> of-your faith, (the) salvation<sup>c</sup> of-(your)-souls.<sup>d</sup>

TEXT—The word ὑμῶν 'your' in the phrase 'of your faith' does not occur in some manuscripts. It is included by GNT with a C rating, indicating difficulty in deciding whether or not to place it in the text.

LEXICON—a. pres. mid. participle of κομίζω (LN 57.126) (BAGD 2.a. p. 442): 'to obtain' [LN], 'to receive' [BAGD, BNTC, LN, NIC, WBC; KJV, NIV, NRSV, TEV, TNT], 'to get' [BAGD], 'to achieve' [NAB], 'to be sure of' [NJB], not explicit [CEV]. The present participle is also translated as future indicative: 'you will receive' [WBC]. The phrase 'obtaining the outcome/goal' is translated 'your reward will be' [NLT], 'to reap the harvest' [REB].

b. τέλος (LN 89.40, 89.55) (BAGD 1.c. p. 811): 'outcome' [BAGD, LN (89.40), WBC; NRSV], 'result' [LN (89.40)], 'end' [BAGD, LN (89.40); KJV], 'end result' [NIC], 'consummation' [BNTC], 'harvest' [REB], 'reward' [NLT], 'final reward' [TNT], 'goal' [BAGD, LN (89.55); NAB, NIV, NJB], 'purpose' [LN (89.55); TEV]. This is also translated as a purpose clause: 'that's why you have faith' [CEV].

c. σωτηρία (LN **21.25**) (BAGD 2. p 801): 'salvation' [BAGD, BNTC, LN, NIC, WBC; all versions except CEV]. This noun is also translated as a verb: 'to be saved' [CEV]. See this word at 1:5.

d. ψυχή (LN 9.20) (BAGD 1.c. p. 893): 'soul' [BAGD, BNTC, NIC; all versions except CEV, NAB], 'inner self' [LN], not explicit [WBC; CEV, NAB]. The genitive form ψυχῶν is translated 'of your souls' by all who translated 'souls' explicitly except REB, which renders it 'for your souls'.

QUESTION—What relationship is indicated by the participle κομιζόμενοι 'obtaining'?

1. It indicates the reason they are rejoicing [TH; CEV, NAB, NIV, NRSV, TEV]: you rejoice because you obtain the salvation of your souls.
2. It indicates an additional comment [NJB, NLT, REB, TNT].

QUESTION—What is meant by τέλος 'outcome/goal'?

1. It means the result or outcome of their faith [BNTC, NIC, WBC; NLT, NRSV, REB, TNT]: you have faith, and as a result, you are saved.
2. It means the purpose or goal of their faith [BAGD; CEV, NAB, NIV, NJB, TEV]: you have faith in order to be saved.

QUESTION—Does 'the salvation of your souls' refer to the believer's present experience or a future experience?

1. It refers to the present experience [IVP, TNTC; all versions except NLT].

2. It refers to a future experience [Alf, WBC; NLT].
3. It refers to both a present as well as a future experience [BNTC, ICC, NCBC, NIC, NTC, TH].

QUESTION—What is meant by ψυχή 'soul'?

It is not used in the Pauline sense of man's lower nature [BNTC, ICC, NCBC, NIC]. It represents the central self or personality [Alf, EGT], the total person [NCBC, NIC], a person's whole life and self-identity [WBC], the whole inner nature of man [ICC]. It is used as an equivalent to a personal pronoun meaning 'yourselves' [BNTC, IVP, TG].

**DISCOURSE UNIT: 1:10–2:10** [REB]. The topic is the calling of a Christian.

**DISCOURSE UNIT: 1:10–12** [Sel, WBC; NJB]. The topic is the witness of prophecy to the universality of the gospel [Sel], the witnesses of salvation [WBC], the hope of the prophets [NJB].

**1:10** Concerning<sup>a</sup> which salvation (the) prophets searched<sup>b</sup> and inquired<sup>c</sup>

LEXICON—a. περί with genitive object (LN 90.24): 'concerning' [LN, NIC, WBC; NIV, NRSV, TEV], 'about' [LN], 'of' [LN; KJV], not explicit [BNTC; CEV, NAB, NJB, NLT, REB, TNT].

b. aorist. act. indic. of ἐκζητέω (LN **27.35**) (BAGD 1. p. 240): 'to search for' [BAGD, BNTC], 'to search out' [NAB], 'to seek out' [BAGD], 'to make a careful search' [**LN**; NRSV, TEV], 'to search intently' [NTC; NIV], 'to search earnestly' [Alf], 'to search hard' [CEV], 'to seek diligently to learn, to make an examination' [LN], 'to explore' [TNT], 'to make diligent inquiry' [WBC], 'to investigate' [NIC], 'to inquire' [KJV]. This verb is also translated as a noun: 'the search' [NJB, REB].

c. aorist act. indic. of ἐξεραυνάω (LN **27.35**) (BAGD p. 247): 'to inquire carefully' [BAGD], 'to inquire earnestly' [TNT], 'to search with great care' [NIV], 'to make careful inquiry' [NRSV], 'to make careful investigation' [TEV], 'to search diligently' [KJV], 'to examine' [NAB], 'to make a careful examination' [LN]. This verb is also translated as a noun: 'investigation' [NJB]. The phrase ἐξεζήτησαν καὶ ἐξηραύνησαν 'searched and inquired' is translated 'was the subject of intense search' [REB], 'they searched hard to find out' [CEV], 'wanted to know more about' [NLT].

QUESTION—What is meant by προφῆται 'prophets'?

1. These were the OT prophets who had prophesied about the coming of Christ [BNTC, EGT, IVP, NCBC, NIBC, NIC, NTC, TG, TH, TNTC, WBC].
2. These were the NT prophets [Sel].

QUESTION—What is the distinction between ἐκζητέω 'searched' and ἐξεραυνάω 'inquired'?

1. The first word, ἐκζητέω, is often used of seeking God, and the second, ἐξεραυνάω, while not used elsewhere in the NT, is used in the LXX to

refer to searching the Scriptures and in extra-biblical literature to refer to searching through a place to find a person or thing [Sel, TNTC].
2. The two words have nearly the same meaning [TG, TH, WBC] and are used together for rhetorical effect [WBC] to intensify the thought [TH]. Both are recapitulated by the participle ἐραυνῶντες 'searching' in 1:11 [WBC]. LN uses the same entry for both words.

**the (ones) having-prophesied[a] concerning[b] the grace[c] for[d] you,**
LEXICON—a. aorist act. participle of προφητεύω (LN 33.459) (BAGD 3. p. 723): 'to prophesy' [BAGD, BNTC, LN, NIC, WBC; KJV, NAB, NLT, NRSV, REB, TEV, TNT], 'to tell' [CEV], 'to speak' [NIV, NJB].
b. περί with genitive object (LN 90.24): 'concerning' [LN], 'about' [BNTC, LN; NLT, REB, TEV, TNT], 'of' [LN, NIC, WBC; KJV, NIV, NJB, NRSV], not explicit [CEV, NAB].
c. χάρις (LN 57.103, 25.89) (BAGD 3.b. p. 878): 'grace' [BAGD, BNTC, NIC, WBC; KJV, NRSV, REB, TNT], 'gift' [LN (57.103); TEV], 'gracious gift' [LN (57.103)], 'favor, good will' [LN (25.89)], 'divine favor' [NAB]. This noun is also translated as an adjective modifying 'salvation': 'gracious' [NLT].
d. εἰς with accusative object (LN 90.41, 90.59) (BAGD 4.d. p. 229): 'for' [BAGD, LN], 'on behalf of' [LN (90.41)], not explicit [CEV]. The phrase εἰς ὑμᾶς 'for you' is translated 'that should come unto you' [KJV], 'destined to be yours' [NAB], 'that was to be yours' [NRSV], 'that was to come to you' [NIV], 'you were to receive' [NJB], 'prepared for you' [NLT], 'awaiting you' [REB].

**1:11 searching[a] for who/what[b] or what/what-kind-of[c] time[d]**
LEXICON—a. pres. act. participle of ἐραυνάω (LN 27.34) (BAGD p. 306): 'to search' [BAGD, LN, NIC; CEV, KJV, NJB], 'to investigate' [BAGD; NAB], 'to inquire' [BNTC, WBC; NRSV], 'to wonder' [NLT], 'to try to learn' [LN], 'to try to find out' [LN; NIV, REB, TEV, TNT].
b. τίς (LN 92.14) (BAGD 2. p. 819): 'what' [LN; KJV], 'what sort of' [BAGD], 'who' [LN; CEV], 'to whom' [NLT], 'the person' [NRSV]. This is also combined with καιρός 'time' to mean 'the times' [NAB], 'the time' [NJB, REB], 'when the time would be' [TEV].
c. ποῖος (LN 92.36, 58.30) (BAGD 1.a.α. p. 684): 'which, which one' [LN (92.36)], 'what kind of' [BAGD, LN (58.30)], 'what manner of' [KJV]. This is also combined with καιρός 'time' to mean 'when' [CEV, NLT], 'circumstances' [NJB], 'what circumstances' [NAB, REB, TNT], 'the time' [NRSV], 'how it would come' [TEV].
d. καιρός (LN 67.1) (BAGD 1. p. 394): 'time' [BAGD, BNTC, LN, NIC, WBC; KJV, NIV, NJB, NRSV, REB, TEV], 'times' [NAB], 'occasion' [LN], not explicit [CEV].

QUESTION—What is meant by the phrase τίνα ἢ ποῖον καιρόν 'what/who or what/what kind of time'?
1. It means who and what time [IVP, NIBC, TNTC; CEV, NLT, NRSV]: they searched for who the person was and what time the Spirit was indicating.
2. It means who and what circumstances [TNT]: they searched for who the person was and what circumstances the Spirit was indicating.
3. It means what time and what circumstances [Alf, BAGD, BNTC, ICC, NIC, Sel, TH, WBC; KJV, NAB, NIV, NJB, REB, TEV]: they searched for what time or what circumstances the Spirit indicated. They wanted to know when this salvation would take place and how it would come about [TH].

QUESTION—What did the prophets search?
They searched their own prophecies [EGT, NIC, TNTC, WBC] and those of other prophets written previously [EGT, TNTC]. They searched their own times and circumstances in addition to the other Scriptures [TNTC].

**the Spirit/spirit of Christ in them was-indicating[a]**
LEXICON—a. imperf. indic. act. of δηλόω (LN 33.152) (BAGD p. 178): 'to indicate' [WBC; NRSV, TNT], 'to point to' [BNTC, NIC; NAB, NIV, REB, TEV], 'to make clear' [BAGD], 'to make known, to make plain' [LN], 'to make evident' [LN], 'to reveal' [BAGD; NJB], 'to show' [BAGD], 'to tell' [CEV], 'to signify' [KJV], 'to talk about' [NLT].

QUESTION—What is meant by τὸ πνεῦμα Χριστοῦ 'the Spirit of Christ'?
1. It refers to the Holy Spirit of God [IVP, NIC, NTC, Sel, TG, TH, TNTC]. The terms 'Spirit of God' and 'Spirit of Christ' were both used to refer to the Holy Spirit [TH]. It also implies Christ's pre-existence with God [TG]. The Holy Spirit is the spirit of the pre-existent Christ [NTC]. In Peter's mind the terms Holy Spirit and Spirit of Christ were the same thing as the pre-existent Christ [WBC]. It is a prolepsis, anticipating a future condition or circumstance as though it were a present reality, similar to Hebrews 11:26 where Moses considered the sufferings of Christ [Sel, WBC].
2. It refers to Christ himself in his preincarnate spiritual existence [BNTC, NIBC]. The title Christ is used instead of the name Jesus in all eight references to his sufferings in this epistle to indicate that the Messiah was the suffering servant, whose pre-existent spirit prompted the OT writers [NIBC].
3. It is the spirit from Christ and who witnesses to Christ [NIC]. It is the spirit which Christ has and gives [Alf]. It is the spirit poured out by Christ and which is concerned with glorifying Christ and with the work of Christ in the church [IVP].

**(when he was) predicting[a] the sufferings[b] to[c] Christ and the glories[d] after[e] these.**
LEXICON—a. pres. mid. (deponent = act.) participle of προμαρτύρομαι (LN 33.282) (BAGD p. 708): 'to predict' [**LN**, WBC; NAB, NIV], 'to foretell'

[BNTC, LN; REB, TNT], 'to reveal' [NJB], 'to tell in advance' [NLT], 'to prophesy' [TEV], 'to testify beforehand' [KJV], 'to give testimony beforehand' [NIC], 'to testify in advance' [NRSV], 'to bear witness to beforehand' [BAGD], not explicit [CEV]. The subject of this participle is the Spirit of Christ [BNTC, NIC, WBC; all versions].

b. πάθημα (LN 24.78) (BAGD 1. p. 602): 'sufferings' [BAGD, BNTC, LN, NIC, WBC; all versions except CEV, NLT], 'suffering' [NLT], 'pain' [LN]. This is also translated as a verb phrase: 'how Christ would suffer' [CEV].

c. εἰς with accusative object (LN 90.59, 90.41): 'to, toward, for' [LN (90.59)], 'of' [NIC; KJV, NIV, NJB, TNT], 'in store for' [BNTC], 'intended for' [WBC], 'destined for' [NAB, NRSV], 'that Christ would have to endure' [TEV], 'for, on behalf of' [LN (90.41)], 'in the cause of' [REB], not explicit [CEV]. This is also translated as a possessive: 'Christ's' [NLT].

d. δόξα (LN 87.4, 87.23) (BAGD 1.b.α. p. 203): 'glory' [LN (87.23); all versions except CEV, NLT], 'great glory' [NLT], 'honor' [LN (87.4)], 'great honor' [CEV].

e. μετά with accusative object (LN 67.48): 'after' [LN], 'afterward' [NLT], 'subsequent' [NRSV]. This is also translated as a verb phrase: 'would then be given' [CEV], 'that should follow' [NIC; KJV], 'that would follow' [BNTC, WBC; NAB, NIV, TEV], 'which were to follow' [TNT], 'to follow' [NJB, REB, TNT].

QUESTION—What relationship is indicated by εἰς 'to'?

1. This indicates the one who experienced the sufferings [Alf, BNTC, IVP, NCBC, NIBC, NIC, TG, TNTC, WBC; all versions except REB]: the sufferings that Christ would endure. The sufferings were destined for Christ according to the sovereign will of God [Alf, BNTC, IVP, NCBC, NIBC, NIC, TG, TNTC, WBC; NAB, NRSV].

2. This indicates the one being benefited by the sufferings [REB]: the sufferings are those which Christians would endure for the cause of Christ.

QUESTION—What is the significance of the plural 'glories', and to what does it refer?

The 'sufferings' of both Christ and the believer are plural in this epistle, whereas 'glory' is used with reference to the believer only in the singular, but is used in the plural only with reference to Christ. 'Glories' probably refers to the events of 3:18–22 [WBC].

**1:12** To-whom it-was-revealed[a] that not to themselves but to-you they-were-ministering[b] these (things),

TEXT—Instead of ὑμῖν 'you', some manuscripts have ἡμῖν 'us'. GNT does not mention this alternate reading. The reading 'us' is taken only by KJV.

LEXICON—a. aorist. pass. indic. of ἀποκαλύπτω (LN 28.38) (BAGD 2. p. 92): 'to be revealed' [BAGD, BNTC, LN, NIC, WBC; KJV, NIV, NJB,

NRSV, TNT], 'to be disclosed' [LN; REB], 'to be made fully known' [LN], 'to be told' [CEV, NLT]. This is also translated as a verbal clause: 'they knew by revelation' [NAB], 'God revealed' [TEV].
   b. imperf. act. indic. of διακονέω (LN 35.19) (BAGD 2. p. 184): 'to minister' [BNTC, NIC; KJV], 'to serve' [BAGD, LN; CEV, NIV, NRSV, TNT], 'to provide' [NAB], 'to act as servants' [NJB], not explicit [NLT, REB]. This verb is also translated as a noun: 'ministry' [WBC], 'work' [TEV]. The dative case used to identify the recipients of the ministry or service ('not to themselves but to you') is indicated in some translations by the use of the phrase 'for the benefit of' [WBC; REB, TEV, TNT], and 'for the sake of' [NJB].
QUESTION—What relationship is indicated by ὅτι 'that'?
   It indicates the content of what the prophets were told [BNTC, NIC, WBC; all versions].
QUESTION—What does αὐτά 'these things' refer to?
   It refers to the sufferings and glories of Christ [ICC], which also constitute the message reported by evangelists [Alf, BNTC, NIC, NTC, TNTC].
QUESTION—What is the significance of the use of the imperfect tense 'were ministering'?
   It indicates the ongoing nature of the prophetic ministry through the years for the benefit of those who came later [BNTC, NIC, NTC] and the unity that exists between the old covenant and the new [BNTC, NCBC, NIBC, NTC].

**which now[a] were-announced[b] to-you by/through[c] those having-preached-the-gospel[d] to-you**
LEXICON—a. νῦν (LN 67.39): 'now' [BNTC, NIC, WBC; all versions except CEV], not explicit [CEV].
   b. aorist act. indic. of ἀναγγέλλω (LN 33.197) (BAGD 2. p. 51): 'to announce' [BAGD, LN, NIC, WBC; NJB, NLT, NRSV, REB, TEV, TNT], 'to proclaim' [BAGD, BNTC; NAB], 'to report' [KJV], 'to speak' [NIV], not explicit [CEV]. This phrase is conflated with the following phrase as 'which you have now heard from the messengers who announced the Good News' [TEV].
   c. διά with genitive object (LN 89.76): 'by' [LN; KJV, NAB, NIV, NJB, NLT, TNT], 'through' [BNTC, LN, NIC, WBC; NRSV, REB], 'from' [TEV], not explicit [CEV].
   d. aorist. mid. participle εὐαγγελίζω (LN 33.215) (BAGD 2.a.γ. p. 317): 'to preach the gospel' [NIC; KJV, NAB, NIV, NJB], 'to preach the good news' [BNTC; NLT], 'to bring the gospel' [WBC; REB], 'to preach' [BAGD; CEV], 'to bring the good news' [NRSV, TNT], 'to announce the good news' [TEV], 'to tell the good news, to announce the gospel' [LN].
QUESTION—What is the significance of the word νῦν 'now'?
   It shifts the focus from the OT period to the NT period [NCBC, NTC, WBC], while linking the two [NTC]. Νῦν 'now' is used to call attention to a contrast or change in the situation, 'but now', as opposed to ἄρτι 'at the

present time' found in 1:6 and 1:8 [NIBC]. When combined with the aorist verb, νῦν has the sense of the perfect tense [Alf, ICC, WBC], and is used in this manner in this epistle to refer to the conversion of the readers [WBC].

QUESTION—What relationship is indicated by διά 'through'?
1. It indicates the direct agent of the passive verb [CEV, KJV, NAB, NIV, NJB, NLT, TEV, TNT]: it was announced to you by those who preached the gospel.
2. It indicates intermediate agency, that is, those who evangelized you were the ones the Holy Spirit used to announce the gospel [BNTC, NIC, WBC; NRSV, REB]: it was preached to you through those who preached the gospel.

**by[a] the Holy Spirit sent[b] from heaven,**

TEXT—The word ἐν 'by' does not occur in some manuscripts. It is included by GNT with a C rating, indicating difficulty in deciding whether or not to place it in the text. Inclusion or omission does not appreciably affect the translation of the text because the meaning is carried by the use of the dative case [WBC].

LEXICON—a. ἐν (LN 89.76, 90.6) 'by' [LN, NIC; CEV, NIV, NRSV, TEV, TNT], 'in' [BNTC; NAB, NLT, REB], 'with' [WBC; KJV], 'through' [NJB]. This is also translated with the addition of the phrase 'the power of' as implied information [CEV, NAB, NLT, REB, TEV].
  b. aorist pass. participle of ἀποστέλλω (LN 15.66) (BAGD 1.b.δ. p. 98, 1.c. p. 99): 'to be sent' [BAGD, BNTC, LN, WBC; all versions except KJV], 'to be sent forth' [BNTC], 'to be sent down' [KJV].

QUESTION—What relationship is indicated by ἐν?
1. It indicates means [TH; CEV, NAB, NLT, REB, TEV]: they preached the gospel by means of (the power of) the Holy Spirit.
2. It indicates agency [KJV, NIV, NRSV, TNT]: they preached the gospel through the Holy Spirit.

QUESTION—What does 'sent from heaven' refer to?
It refers to the coming of the Holy Spirit at Pentecost [Alf, IVP, NIBC, NTC, TH], which authenticated the Christian message [NIBC] and empowered the preaching of it [NTC]. It indicates divine origin, that is, that God sent the Holy Spirit [BNTC, TG], but it is not necessarily a reference to Pentecost [BNTC].

**into which (things) (the) angels long[a] to-look.[b]**

LEXICON—a. pres. act. indic. of ἐπιθυμέω (LN 25.12) (BAGD p. 293): 'to long' [BAGD, LN; NAB, NIV, NJB, NRSV, REB, TNT], 'to desire very much' [LN], 'to desire' [BAGD, BNTC, NIC, WBC; KJV], 'to like to' [CEV, TEV]. This is also translated as an adverb modifying the next verb: 'eagerly' [NLT].
  b. aorist act. inf. of παρακύπτω (LN **27.39**) (BAGD 2. p. 619): 'to look' [BNTC, NIC, WBC; KJV, NIV, NRSV, TNT], 'to look in' [BAGD], 'to gain a clear glance' [BAGD], 'to search' [NAB], 'to watch' [NLT], 'to

catch a glimpse' [NJB], 'to glimpse' [REB], 'to know more' [CEV], 'to understand' [TEV], 'to try to learn' [LN], 'to learn about' [**LN**].

**DISCOURSE UNIT: 1:13–2:10** [IVP, TG, TH]. The topic is the basic characteristics of Christian living [IVP], the Christian life [TH], the holy life [TG].

**DISCOURSE UNIT: 1:13–2:3** [NTC, Sel; NIV, NLT]. The topic is holiness [NTC], the first hortatory section [Sel], be holy [NIV], a call to holy living [NLT].

**DISCOURSE UNIT: 1:13–25** [NIC, TNTC, WBC; CEV, NRSV, TEV]. The topic is a call to holiness [NIC], application: you must be holy in all your conduct [TNTC], a new way of life [WBC], chosen to live a holy life [CEV], a call to holy living [NRSV, TEV].

**DISCOURSE UNIT: 1:13–21** [IVP; NAB, NJB]. The topic is hope and obedience [IVP], filial obedience and fear [NAB], the demands of the new life, holiness of the newly baptized [NJB].

**DISCOURSE UNIT: 1:13–16** [Sel, TH, WBC]. The topic is the holiness of the Christian calling [Sel], the holiness of God as the foundation of the Christian life [TH], a life of holiness [WBC].

**1:13** Therefore[a] having-girded-up[b] the loins of your mind[c]

LEXICON—a. διό (LN 89.47): 'therefore' [BNTC, LN, NIC, WBC; NIV, NRSV, REB], 'wherefore' [KJV], 'for this reason' [LN], 'so then' [LN; TEV], 'so' [NAB, NLT, TNT], 'then' [NJB], not explicit [CEV].

b. aorist mid. participle of ἀναζώννυμι (LN 27.55) (BAGD p. 53): 'to gird up' [BAGD, BNTC; KJV]. The phrase 'to gird up the loins of the mind' is translated 'to bind up the loins of the mind' [LN], 'to gird the loins of one's understanding' [NAB], 'to gird oneself for action' [WBC], 'to get one's mind ready for work' [NIC], 'to prepare one's mind for action' [NIV, NRSV] 'to have one's mind ready for action' [**LN**; TEV], 'to be stripped for action' [REB], 'to be ready for action' [NJB] 'to think clearly' [NLT], 'to think straight' [CEV].

c. διάνοια (LN 26.14) (BAGD 2. p. 187): 'mind' [BNTC, NIC, WBC; KJV, NIV, NJB, NRSV, REB, TEV], 'understanding' [NAB], not explicit [CEV, NLT, TNT].

QUESTION—What relationship is indicated by the connective particle διό 'therefore'?

Its position is emphatic [BNTC]. It connects the previous section with the following in a condition-result relationship [TH]. It shifts the focus from the hope of the gospel of the previous section to the ethical responsibilities that naturally follow [IVP, NCBC, Sel, WBC]. The blessings described in the preceding text are the basis for what follows [BNTC, ICC, NIC, TG, TNTC]. What follows is an amplification of the term 'sanctification' found in 1:2 [ICC]. What follows is based on the 'hope' found in 1:3 [IVP].

QUESTION—What is meant by the metaphor 'gird up the loins of your mind'?
It evokes not only the image of tucking the robes into a belt for the purpose of work or mobility familiar to the ancient world, but also the preparation of the people of Israel for the Exodus in Exodus 12:11 [BNTC, ICC, IVP, NCBC, NIBC, NIC, TNTC, WBC]. It speaks of the spiritual alertness that should characterize people of the new covenant [TNTC], and of their preparedness for instant obedience [ICC] or for the coming of Christ [BNTC, EGT]. The Christian is to be prepared for tough work in the mental and spiritual dimension [NCBC] and ought to remove any mental hindrance to Christian service [NTC].

QUESTION—What is meant by the term διάνοια 'mind'?
It does not refer primarily to the intellect [BNTC, NCBC, NIC, WBC]. It refers to the enlightened mind or understanding that results from redemption, as opposed to the ἄγνοια 'ignorance' of the following verse [WBC]. It refers to mental resolve and preparation [NIC], to a person's entire mental and spiritual attitude [BNTC] and conscious relationship with God [NTC]. It is equivalent to 'heart' [EGT]. It is the inner faculty of understanding from which thinking and decisions flow [IVP, LN] and which shapes and guides conduct [NCBC, NIBC].

**being-sober[a] completely[b] hope[c]**

LEXICON—a. pres. act. participle of νήφω (LN 30.25) (BAGD p. 538): 'to be sober' [BAGD, BNTC, LN; KJV, NJB], 'to live soberly' [NAB], 'to be self-controlled' [BAGD; NIV] 'to exercise self-control' [NLT], 'to discipline oneself' [NRSV], 'to be well balanced' [BAGD, NIC] 'to be fully alert' [REB], 'to keep alert' [TEV] 'to be alert' [LN; CEV], 'to be on the alert' [TNT], 'with attention' [WBC].

b. τελείως (LN **78.47**) (BAGD p. 810): 'completely' [BAGD, **LN**; TEV], 'wholly' [LN; TNT], 'totally' [NIC], 'unreservedly' [BNTC], 'all' [CEV, NAB, NJB, NRSV], 'fully' [BAGD; NIV, REB], 'full' [WBC], 'to the end' [KJV], not explicit [NLT].

c. aorist act. impera. of ἐλπίζω (LN 25.59) (BAGD 3. p. 252): 'to hope' [LN; KJV], 'to set one's hope' [BNTC, WBC; NAB, NIV, NRSV, TEV, TNT], 'to put one's hope' [BAGD; CEV, NJB], 'to place one's hope' [NIC], 'to fix one's hope' [REB], 'to look forward to' [NLT], 'to hope for' [LN].

QUESTION—Is νήφοντες 'being sober' used here primarily in a literal sense or in a metaphorical sense?
1. It is metaphorical, expressing the need for clear thinking and judgment, and not being distracted from the hope of Christ's parousia by the cares of life or by persecution [NIC]. It refers to mental discipline, balance and single-minded commitment [NIBC]. It refers to keeping oneself from moral sin and doctrinal error [ICC].
2. It is not necessarily metaphorical, but should simply be taken to mean paying close attention [WBC].

# 1 PETER 1:13

3. It refers to both physical and mental sobriety [Alf, IVP, NCBC, NTC, Sel, TNTC]. That is, don't return to drunkenness and don't be subject to disordered thinking [NCBC], don't be distracted by the 'mental intoxication' of the things of this world [TNTC], or by rashness and confusion [NTC]. It means to be alert to spiritual realities [IVP] or alert and sober in speech and conduct [TH].

QUESTION—What does the adverb τελείως 'completely' modify?
1. It modifies 'sober' [EGT, ICC, WBC; REB]: 'with full attention' [WBC], 'being perfectly sober' [ICC], 'fully alert' [REB].
2. It modifies the imperative 'hope' [Alf, BNTC, LN, NIC, NTC, Sel, TG, TNTC; KJV, NAB, NIV, NJB, NRSV, TEV, TNT].
   2.1 It refers to the manner of hoping: wholeheartedly and eagerly set your hope [BNTC, Sel, TNTC].
   2.2 It refers not to the degree or quality of the hope, but to the object of the hope: set your hope completely on the grace, not on anything else [NIC].

QUESTION—What relationship is indicated by the use of the two participles in conjunction with the imperative ἐλπίσατε 'hope' that follows?

The main emphasis is given to the imperative [BNTC, NTC]. The two participles are a preliminary to 'hope', that is, hope should be characterized by mental alertness and readiness for action [TNTC, WBC]. The participles explain the imperative: the way one hopes is by preparing the mind and being well balanced [NIC].

QUESTION—What is the significance of the use of the aorist imperative here?

This is the first of many aorist imperatives that follow and which are directives that define the future course for the church [WBC]. This exhortation to hope forms a transition point to the rest of the letter, and the many imperatives which follow flow directly from this hope of eternal reward [TNTC]. The aorist tends to make the exhortation more urgent and insistent [BNTC, Sel]. Hope is a prominent concept in this epistle, and the aorist tense here is constative or all inclusive, showing action in its entirety [NTC].

**in the grace[a] being-brought[b] to you**

LEXICON—a. χάρις (LN 88.66) (BAGD 3. b. p. 878): 'grace' [BAGD, BNTC, LN, NIC, WBC; KJV, NIV, NJB, NRSV, TNT], 'gift' [NAB], 'special blessings' [NLT], 'blessing' [TEV], 'how kind God will be' [CEV]. See this word also at 1:2, 10.
b. pres. pass. participle of φέρω (LN 15.166) (BAGD 4. a. β. p. 855): 'to bring' [BAGD, LN; KJV, NJB, NRSV, TNT], 'to be conferred' [NAB], 'to be given' [NIV, TEV], 'to be brought' [NIC, WBC], 'to be conveyed' [BNTC], 'to be yours' [REB], 'to come' [NLT], not explicit [CEV].

QUESTION—How is the word 'grace' used in this context?
1. It is the final eschatological salvation previously spoken of [BNTC, EGT, ICC, NCBC, NIC, NTC, TNTC, WBC]. It refers to the gift of salvation [TG, TH].

# 1 PETER 1:13

   2. It is the daily grace of God by which we live as well as ultimate salvation [NIBC].

QUESTION—What is the significance of the use of a present participial phrase 'being brought to you' in this passage?
   1. Even though it is a present tense form, it is used to refer to the future as in 1:7 [WBC].
   2. It is used to heighten the expectation of future blessings in the present moment [TNTC]. The object of hope will be received in the future, but is already near at hand or on the way [Alf, BNTC, EGT, NCBC, NTC, Sel].
   3. It refers to grace being brought day by day to the believer, culminating in the ultimate return of Christ [NIBC].

**at[a] the revelation[b] of Jesus Christ.**
LEXICON—a. ἐν with dative object (LN 67.33): 'at' [BNTC; KJV, NLT], 'in' [NIC], 'when' [LN], 'by' [NJB]. This preposition is also translated as an adverb 'when' with the following word translated as a verb [WBC; CEV, NAB, NIV, NRSV, REB, TEV, TNT].
   b. ἀποκάλυψις (LN 28.38) (BAGD 3. p. 92): 'revelation' [BNTC, LN, NIC; KJV, NJB], 'revealing' [BAGD], 'return' [NLT]. This noun is also translated as a verb: 'to come' [TNT], 'to be revealed' [WBC; NIV, NRSV, REB, TEV], 'to appear' [CEV, NAB]. See this word at 1:7.

QUESTION—What is meant by 'the revelation of Jesus Christ'?
   1. It refers to a future event as in 1:7 [Alf, BNTC, ICC, NIC, NTC, WBC]. It refers to the second coming of Christ [NCBC, NIBC].
   2. It has both a present and future focus [EGT]. That is, Jesus Christ is being revealed now to the believer, and he will be revealed fully when he returns.

**1:14** As[a] **children of obedience not conforming[b] to the desires[c] (you had) formerly[d] in your ignorance[e]**
LEXICON—a. ὡς (LN 64.12) (BAGD III.1.a. p 898): 'as' [BNTC, LN, NIC, WBC; KJV, NAB, NIV, NJB], 'like' [LN; CEV, NRSV], not explicit [NLT, REB, TEV, TNT].
   b. pres. mid. participle of συσχηματίζω (LN 41.29) (BAGD p. 795): 'to conform' [NIV] 'to be conformed to' [BAGD BNTC, NIC; NRSV], 'to fashion oneself' [KJV], 'to conform one's life' [LN], 'to let your life be controlled by' [CEV], 'to allow yourself to be shaped by' [NJB], 'to let your character be shaped by' [REB], 'to allow your life to be shaped by' [TEV], 'to let your behavior be ruled by' [TNT], 'to yield' [WBC; NAB]. The phrase 'not conforming to the desires you had formerly' is translated 'to slip back into your old ways of doing evil' [NLT]. This verb appears in the NT only here and in Romans 12:2.
   c. ἐπιθυμία (LN 25.20) (BAGD 3. p. 293): 'desires' [BAGD, **LN**, NIC; CEV, NAB, NRSV, REB, TEV, TNT], 'evil desires' [LN; NIV], 'lusts' [LN; KJV], 'impulses' [WBC], 'passions' [BNTC; NJB], 'evil' [NLT].

1 PETER 1:14　　37

d. πρότερος (LN **67.18**) (BAGD 1.b.β. p. 722): 'formerly' [BAGD, BNTC, LN; NRSV], 'former' [NIC; KJV], 'once' [WBC; NAB], 'old (ways)' [NLT], 'old (ignorance)' [NJB]. This adverb is translated by a phrase: 'as they used to be' [CEV]; also in combination with the following noun: 'when you lived in ignorance' [NIV], 'your days of ignorance' [REB], 'when you were still ignorant' [TEV], 'when you were in a state of ignorance' [TNT].

e. ἄγνοια (LN 28.13) (BAGD 2 p. 11): 'ignorance' [BAGD, BNTC, LN, WBC; all versions except CEV, NLT], not explicit [CEV]. The prepositional phrase ἐν τῇ ἀγνοίᾳ ὑμῶν 'in your ignorance' is translated as an adverbial phrase: 'when you were ignorant' [NIC]; as a clause: 'you didn't know any better then' [NLT].

QUESTION—What relationship is indicated by ὡς, 'as'?
1. It indicates the grounds for the exhortations that follow: since you are obedient children, therefore do this [BNTC, EGT, TG, WBC].
2. It describes what they should be like: as obedient children should, do thus and so [IVP, NIBC, NIC; NLT, REB, TEV, TNT].

QUESTION—What is meant by the genitive phrase τέκνα ὑπακοῆς 'children of obedience'?

It means 'obedient children' [NIC, WBC; CEV, KJV, NIV, NJB, NRSV], 'obedient sons' [NAB], or 'obedient people' [NCBC]. It can be considered synonymous with 'genuine believer' [NIC]. The use of the genitive with an abstract noun is a Semitism which has more than an attributive or adjectival function, and emphasizes a specific central characteristic: you are a class or kind of people, characterized by obedience [BNTC, ICC, LN (58.26), NIBC, NIC, TNTC, WBC], who were chosen for obedience [NCBC], whose mother is obedience, and in whom is a spirit of obedience [ICC]. The reference to τέκνα 'children' implies the Father's care for his children [IVP, NIC]. Several translations render this adjectival phrase as an imperative: 'obey God because you are his children' [NLT], 'be obedient to God your Father' [REB], and 'be obedient to God' [TEV, TNT].

QUESTION—What is the function of the participial phrase μὴ συσχηματιζόμενοι 'not conforming'?

In this epistle Peter frequently follows the Hebraic and rabbinical style of expressing rules of conduct through participles functioning as imperatives [BNTC, NCBC, NIBC], and in this instance he uses the participial form with the subjunctive prohibitory particle μή [BNTC]. The participle here should be seen as having the force of an imperative [EGT, TH]. The aorist imperative 'be (holy)' that follows in the next verse influences this participle and makes its imperatival use more clear [NTC, WBC].

QUESTION—What is implied by the use of the plural noun ἐπιθυμίαις 'desires'?

The term can be morally neutral in Greek, but in the NT and particularly in this epistle, it has a negative connotation [BNTC, NCBC, NIBC, NIC, TH]. It refers to licentiousness [ICC], desires for evil things [TG], the urges of fallen man [NIC], the baser appetites that lead men to sin [BNTC], and general self-seeking [WBC]. It is used in contrast to ἐπιποθέω of 2:2, which is the appropriate desire for spiritual nourishment.

QUESTION—What does πρότερον 'formerly' modify?
    1. It modifies ἐπιθυμία 'desires' [Alf, BNTC, LN, NIC, WBC; KJV]. Several versions render it as modifying an implied verb with ἐπιθυμία as the subject or object of the verb phrase: 'desires you had' [NIV, NRSV, TEV, TNT], 'desires you cherished' [REB], 'desires that once shaped you' [NAB], 'impulses that once drove you' [WBC], 'passions which dominated you' [BNTC].
    2. It modifies 'ignorance' [NJB].

QUESTION—What ignorance is referred to here?
It is ignorance of God [Alf, BNTC, NIBC, Sel, TNTC], of his ways [TNTC], and of his laws [NIBC, NTC]. It is ignorance of the gospel [TG, TH], of Christ [TG], or of God as revealed in Christ [TH].

**1:15** but[a] like[b] the holy[c] (one) having-called-you[d]

LEXICON—a. ἀλλά (LN 89.125): 'but' [BNTC, LN, NIC, WBC; KJV, NIV, NJB], 'instead' [LN; NRSV, TEV], 'rather' [NAB], 'but now' [NLT], not explicit [CEV, REB, TNT].
    b. κατά with accusative object (LN 89.8) (BAGD II.5.a.α. p. 407): 'like' [WBC; REB], 'as' [BNTC; KJV, NJB], 'just as' [NIC; NIV, NLT, TEV], 'in accordance with' [BAGD, LN], 'after the likeness of' [NAB], 'after the model of' [NJB], not explicit [CEV].
    c. ἅγιος (LN **88.24**) (BAGD 1.b.δ. p. 9): 'holy' [BAGD, BNTC, LN, NIC, WBC; all versions].
    d. aorist act. participle of καλέω (LN 33.312) (BAGD 2. p. 399): 'to call' [BAGD, BNTC, LN, NIC, WBC; all versions except CEV, NLT], 'to choose' [CEV, NLT]. This participle is translated as a past indicative active verb [BNTC, WBC; all versions except NJB], as a present indicative active verb [NJB] and as a present participle [NIC].

QUESTION—What relationship is indicate by ἀλλά 'but'?
It is contrastive and is used as an adversative conjunction to introduce a conditional clause [TH]. It indicates a strong contrast, shifting from the negatives of the preceding verse to the positive commands that follow [Alf, NCBC, NTC, TNTC].

QUESTION—What relationship is indicated by the preposition κατά 'like'?
    1. It is used as a conjunction in a verb phrase with ἅγιον 'the holy one' serving as the predicate nominative of the implied verb 'to be': just as or in the same way that the one who calls you (is) holy [BNTC, EGT, NIC, TNTC; KJV, NIV, NLT, NRSV, REB, TEV, TNT].
    2. It is used as a preposition. Τὸν ἅγιον 'the holy one' is the object of the preposition and is modified by the participle καλέσαντα 'the one having called': like the holy one who called you [Alf, ICC, WBC; NAB, NJB], or according to the holiness of the one who called you [TH].

QUESTION—What is meant here by καλέω 'to call'?
It is God's invitation to believe in Christ and become part of the Christian community [TH]. The call is the divine initiative in saving men and making them his own [BNTC]. It is a divine summons out of darkness and worldliness [NIC, TNTC] into relationship with God as his own people [BNTC, NCBC, NIC, TNTC], to receive and express a new nature [NIBC] and become like God himself [TNTC]. It is the basis for holiness [NTC, WBC]. It is the invitation to become a pilgrim [ICC, NIBC], moving on a path to glory as well as suffering [ICC].

**be[a] holy yourselves[b] also[c] in all[d] (your) conduct,[e]**
LEXICON—a. aorist pass. (deponent = act.) impera. of γίνομαι (LN 13.3): 'to be' [BNTC, LN, WBC; KJV, NIV, NJB, NRSV, REB, TEV], 'to become' [NIC; NAB]. This imperative is translated 'you must be' [NLT, TNT], and the entire clause is translated 'always live as God's holy people should' [CEV].
  b. αὐτοί (LN 92.37): 'yourselves' [BNTC, LN, NIC; NAB, NJB, NRSV], 'ye' [KJV], not explicit [WBC; CEV, NIV, NLT, REB, TEV, TNT].
  c. καί (LN 89.93): 'also' [LN, NIC], 'too' [BNTC; TNT], 'so' [KJV, NIV], 'now' [NLT], not explicit [CEV, NJB, NLT, NRSV, REB, TEV].
  d. πᾶσα (LN 59.23): 'all' [LN; NIV, NJB, NRSV, REB, TEV], 'every' [LN; TNT], 'all manner' [KJV], 'every aspect' [NAB] 'everything' [NLT], 'always' [CEV].
  e. ἀναστροφή (LN 41.3) (BAGD p. 61): 'conduct' [BAGD, BNTC, LN, WBC; NAB, NJB, NRSV, REB], 'behavior' [LN], 'life-style' [NIC], 'conversation' [KJV]. The phrase 'all (your) conduct' is translated 'all you do' [NIV], 'all that you do' [TEV], 'everything you do' [NLT], 'every part of your life' [TNT].

QUESTION—What is the significance of the use of the aorist imperative γίνομαι?
  1. Γίνομαι is used in the sense of becoming [ICC, NIC; NAB]. Become holy if you are not already, or become more holy than you already are.
  2. Γίνομαι is used as synonym for the verb 'to be' [EGT, NTC, WBC; all versions except NAB], and substitutes for it because the Greek verb 'to be' has no aorist tense [NTC]. It can mean 'to be' in the sense of having certain acquired characteristics [LN]. The aorist imperative is used here because it is all-inclusive [NTC] and it indicates the completeness with which the holiness is to be put on [Alf]. It means to make holiness your characteristic once for all [WBC].

QUESTION—What is the function of αὐτοί 'yourselves' in this verse?
It is used for emphasis [NTC]. It is used here and in 2:5 to mark the shift from the singular, referring to titles or attributes of God, to the plural, referring to God's people [WBC].

QUESTION—What relationship is indicated by καί 'also'?
It is conjoining, indicating an additive relation: God is holy, so you be holy also [BNTC, LN, NIC; TNT]. Many versions leave it untranslated.

QUESTION—What is the holiness to which they are called?
It means belonging to God and also being separated from the world by how one lives [IVP]. It is freedom from sin coupled with absolute moral purity [BNTC] in imitation of God's absolute purity [NTC]. It is a positive idea of separation to God and from sin rather than just a negative idea of separation from the world [NCBC, NIBC]. It can refer either to separation to God or to moral and ethical integrity, but here it primarily refers to ethical conduct [TH]. It has a distinctively moral sense of separation from evil to a righteous life that reaches every part of the personality [TNTC]. It has the sense of positive ethical virtues of purity, reverence, and goodness in all of life [WBC]. The concept of holiness forms the foundation for all subsequent ethical teaching of this epistle [Sel].

QUESTION—What is meant by πάσῃ ἀναστροφῇ 'all your conduct'?
Ἀναστροφή occurs 13 times in the NT, and six of those are in this epistle, this being the first [NTC]. Its frequency emphasizes the importance of everyday conduct in society [NIBC]. It refers to holiness expressed in the whole of life [NCBC], and to all personal and social conduct everywhere [TH, WBC], but especially in the context of public behavior [IVP].

**1:16** for[a] it-is-written[b] "You-shall-be[c] holy, for[d] I am holy."

TEXT—Some manuscripts include ὅτι 'that' after 'it is written' to mark the discourse content that follows. GNT includes this variant in brackets but does not rate it. Its inclusion or exclusion does not affect the meaning of the passage, and is virtually untranslatable in English [WBC].

TEXT—The verb εἰμί 'to be' in the statement 'I am holy' does not occur in many manuscripts. GNT includes this variant in brackets but does not rate it. Its inclusion or exclusion does not affect the meaning of the passage in Greek, though it must be supplied in English translations.

LEXICON—a. διότι (LN 89.26) (BAGD 3. p. 199): 'for' [BAGD, NIC, WBC; NIV, NLT, NRSV], 'because' [KJV], 'since' [BNTC; NJB], 'that's why' [CEV] 'because of' [LN], 'on account of' [LN], not explicit [TEV]. The clause 'for it is written' is translated 'remember' [NAB, TNT], 'does not scripture say?' [REB].

  b. perf. pass. indic. of γράφω (LN 33.61) (BAGD 2.c. p. 166): 'to be written' [BAGD, BNTC, LN, NIC, WBC; KJV, NIV, NRSV]. This verb is also translated as a phrase: 'the scriptures say' [CEV], 'scripture says' [NAB, NJB, TEV, TNT], 'does not scripture say' [REB], 'he himself has said' [NLT].

  c. fut. indic. act. of εἰμί (LN 13.1): 'to be' [BNTC, LN, NIC, WBC; all versions]. This is consistently treated as an imperative [BNTC, NIC, WBC; all versions], corresponding to the same usage in Matthew 5:48 which some commentators consider to be a parallel passage drawn by

Christ from the same source in Leviticus [Alf, EGT, ICC, NIC]. The imperative is translated 'be holy' [NIC, WBC; KJV, NAB, NIV, NJB, TEV], 'you shall be holy' [NRSV, REB], 'you must be holy' [CEV, NLT, TNT], 'you are to be holy' [BNTC].

d. ὅτι (LN 89.33): 'for' [BNTC, LN; KJV, NAB, NJB, NRSV, REB, TNT], 'because' [LN, NIC, WBC; NIV, NLT, TEV], 'since' [LN], not explicit [CEV].

QUESTION—What relationship is indicated by διότι 'because'?

The Scripture is the grounds for saying that God is holy [Alf], and the fact of God's holiness combined with the authority of the scriptural command to imitate his holiness is the basis for the exhortation to be holy [Alf, TNTC]. That is, God is holy because the Scripture says so, and because he is holy and commands holiness, you should be holy.

QUESTION—What is implied by γέγραπται 'it is written'?

It is a formula used to introduce a quotation from the OT [NCBC, NIBC, WBC] and is typical in the NT [TH]. The use of the perfect tense indicates enduring resultant effect [NTC] or continuing validity [TNTC]. Peter bases the authority of what he has said on the recognized authority of what has been written [BNTC, NIBC, NIC]. The passage quoted is from Leviticus 19:2.

QUESTION—What relationship is indicated by ὅτι 'for'?

It indicates the grounds for the preceding command [BNTC, NIC, TNTC, WBC; all versions]: God's people are to be holy because he is holy.

QUESTION—Is there any distinction between ἅγιος 'holy' in how it applies to God and how it applies to people in this verse?

The intrinsic holiness of God is that from which human holiness is derived and on which it is based [BNTC, NTC, TNTC]. To be holy is to be separate from what is profane or evil, whether spoken of God or man [BNTC, TH]. It is also used to describe any person, place or thing that is dedicated for God's possession or use [NTC].

**DISCOURSE UNIT: 1:17–21** [TH, WBC]. The topic is the sacrifice of Christ as a reason for proper conduct [TH], a life of reverence [WBC].

**1:17** If/since[a] you call-upon-(as)/call[b] Father the (one) impartially[c] judging[d] according-to[e] the work[f] of each[g] (person)

LEXICON—a. εἰ (LN 89.30): 'if' [WBC; KJV, NJB, NRSV, REB, TNT], 'since' [BNTC, LN, NIC; NIV], not explicit [CEV, NAB, NLT, TEV].

b. pres. mid. indic. of ἐπικαλέω (LN 33.131, 33.176) (BAGD p. 294): 'to call upon' [BAGD, LN (33.176)], 'to call on' [KJV, NIV], 'to invoke' [BNTC, WBC; NRSV], 'to address' [NJB], 'to pray to' [NLT], 'to say' [CEV, REB], 'to call upon in prayer' [NAB, TNT], 'to call when you pray' [TEV], 'to call' [LN (33.131), NIC], 'to name' [LN (33.131)].

c. ἀπροσωπολήμπτως (LN **88.240**) (BAGD p. 102): 'impartially' [BAGD, BNTC, **LN**, WBC; NIV, NRSV, REB, TNT], 'without respect of persons'

[KJV], 'justly' [NAB], 'without favoritism' [NIV, NJB], 'does not have favorites' [CEV], 'has no favorites' [NLT], 'by the same standard' [TEV].
- d. pres. act. participle of κρίνω (LN 56.20) (BAGD 4.b.α. p. 452): 'to judge' [BAGD, BNTC, NIC, WBC; all versions except NLT], 'to judge or reward' [NLT], 'to act as judge' [LN].
- e. κατά with accusative object (LN 89.8): 'according to' [NIC, WBC; KJV, NJB, NLT, NRSV, TEV, TNT], 'on the basis of' [NAB, REB], 'in accordance with' [LN], 'by' [CEV], 'in the light of' [BNTC], not explicit [NIV].
- f. ἔργον (LN 42.11) (BAGD 1.c.β. p.308): 'work' [WBC; KJV, NIV], 'deed' [BAGD, LN], 'deeds' [NIC; NJB, NRSV, TNT], 'act' [LN], 'actions' [NAB], 'what they do' [CEV], 'what they have done' [REB], 'what each one has done' [BNTC; TEV], 'what you do' [NLT].
- g. ἕκαστος (LN 59.27): 'each' [BNTC, LN], 'all people' [CEV], 'every man' [KJV, TNT], 'each one' [NAB], 'each one's' [NIC], 'each man' [NIV], 'each individual' [NJB], 'each person's' [WBC], 'you' [NLT], 'all people' [NRSV, TEV], 'everyone' [REB].

QUESTION—What relationship is indicated by καὶ εἰ 'and if'?
1. It indicates the grounds for the exhortation that follows: since you do call on the Father who is an impartial judge, you should therefore conduct your lives in fear. [Alf, BNTC, NCBC, NIC, NTC, TG, TNTC, WBC; NAB, NIV, NLT, TEV].
2. It is translated 'if' without indication of whether it is to be understood as conclusive ('if, as you already do') or conditional ('if, as you may or may not do') [KJV, NJB, NRSV, REB, TNT].

QUESTION—What is implied by the use of ἐπικαλεῖσθε 'call upon/call' in the middle voice?
1. The active voice form means to address [LN, TNTC], but the middle voice is not used that way in the NT [TNTC]. It means to call upon or invoke (as in prayer) [Alf, BAGD, BNTC, EGT, ICC, IVP, LN, NCBC, NTC, Sel, TG, TH, TNTC, WBC; KJV, NAB, NIV, NLT, NRSV, TNT]: since you call upon him.
2. The verb is translated with the same sense as the active voice, 'to call' or 'to name' [NIC; CEV, NJB, REB, TEV]: since you call him Father.

QUESTION—What is the significance, if any, of the lack of the definite article with πατήρ 'father'?
1. Other nouns in this epistle lack the definite article in Greek, but the article is supplied for English translation. Πατήρ is a word that can readily be used without the definite article without changing the meaning (as in 1:2) [ICC]. The definite article is to be supplied; God is 'the father' [ICC; KJV, NLT].
2. The article is not supplied, God is 'father', 'a father' or is invoked 'as father' [BNTC, EGT, IVP, NIC, NTC, Sel, TNTC, WBC; NAB, NIV, NJB, NRSV, REB, TEV, TNT].

# 1 PETER 1:17

QUESTION—What is implied by the use of the present participle κρίνοντα 'judging'?
1. It indicates continued action [NTC]. It occurs continually, as present judgment and discipline in this life [TNTC]. The present tense shows God's essential function as judge, and does not refer to any particular event in the past or future [TH]. It is translated as a present indicative active verb [BNTC, NIC, WBC; all versions except NLT].
2. It speaks of the judgment at the end of all things [NIBC]. It is translated as a future indicative active verb [NLT].

QUESTION—What aspect of God is given prominence in this clause, his role as father or as judge?
1. The prominence is given to God's role as father: you invoke the impartial judge as father [IVP, Sel]. This is because the father in the Jewish culture was highly revered and had a judicial role and authority in the family [IVP, Sel]. Presumably this fact would be understood even if the readers were mostly Gentiles.
2. The prominence is given to God's role as judge: you invoke as father one who is the impartial judge [BNTC, ICC, WBC; and probably Alf, NTC]. Just as in 1:15–16 where God's intrinsic holiness is primary to the argument and the personal calling is secondary, so also in this verse his impartial judging is given prominence over the special relationship of father to child [WBC].

QUESTION—What is the significance of the use of the singular ἔργον 'work' as opposed to 'works'?
1. It is singular because it speaks of the whole of one's life [NTC, TNTC]. It is equivalent to ἀναστροφή 'conduct, behavior, life-style' of the previous verse [WBC]. It is translated as a singular noun [BNTC, WBC; KJV, NIV] and as a verb phrase with the verb 'to do' [CEV, NLT, REB, TEV].
2. It is treated as plural: people will be judged for their works, actions, or deeds [NIC; NAB, NJB, NRSV, TNT].

**conduct-yourselves[a] in[b] reverent-fear[c] (during) the time[d] of your exile,[e]**
LEXICON—a. aorist pass. impera. of ἀναστρέφω (LN 41.3) (BAGD 2.b.β. p. 61): 'to conduct oneself' [BNTC, LN; NAB], 'to behave' [LN], 'to live' [BAGD, LN; CEV, NRSV, REB] 'to spend one's life' [TEV], 'to spend (time)' [WBC], 'to live out' [NIC; NJB, TNT], 'to pass (the time)' [KJV], 'to live one's life' [NIV].
b. ἐν with dative object (LN 89.84): 'in' [NIC, WBC; all versions except CEV, NAB], 'with' [BNTC, LN], not explicit [CEV, NAB].
c. φόβος (LN 53.59) (BAGD 2.a.α. p. 863, 2.b.α. p. 864): 'reverent fear' [WBC; NIV, NLT, NRSV], 'fear' [BAGD, BNTC, NIC; KJV], 'reverence' [BAGD, LN; TEV, TNT], 'respect' [BAGD], 'awe' [LN; REB], 'reverent awe' [NJB]. This noun is also translated as a verb: 'to honor' [CEV]; as an adverb: 'reverently' [NAB].

d. χρόνος (LN 67.78) (BAGD p. 888): 'time' [BAGD, LN; KJV, NJB, NLT, NRSV, REB, TNT], 'allotted time' [WBC], 'for the duration of' [BNTC], 'period' [NIC]. This noun is also translated as an adverb: 'while' [CEV], 'during' [NAB]; conflated with ἀναστράφητε: 'to live your lives' [NIV], 'to spend the rest of your lives' [TEV].
e. παροικία (LN 85.79) (BAGD 1.b. p. 629): 'exile' [NJB, NRSV], 'time of residence' [LN], 'stay' [BAGD, LN], 'temporary stay' [BNTC], 'sojourning' [NIC; KJV], 'sojourn' [NAB]. This noun is also translated as a prepositional phrase: 'on earth' [REB]; as an adverbial phrase: 'as strangers here' [NIV], 'here on earth', [TEV], 'as strangers here on earth' [CEV], 'exile here on earth' [TNT], 'as foreigners here on earth' [NLT], 'wherever you are' [WBC].

QUESTION—What relationship is indicated by ἐν 'in'?
This word is often used to indicate manner [LN], and here it indicates the manner in which the readers' lives are to be conducted, that is, 'in fear', 'with fear', or 'reverently' [BNTC, NIC, WBC; all versions].

QUESTION—What is meant by φόβος 'fear'?
It refers to a godly fear or awe, even a healthy dread of judgment, because God does not show favoritism even to his own children [BNTC]. It is fear of his discipline [TNTC], reverential awe in view of his judgment [NIC], a respectful, reverential fear [NTC, TG, WBC]. It is not dread but respect [NTC], nor is it abject fear [NCBC]; it is a filial fear [NCBC, NIBC]. It is a fear mixed with awe and gratitude [NCBC, Sel]. It is the awe and respect as of worship spread to all of life [Sel, TG].

QUESTION—What is meant by the metaphor παροικία 'exile'?
It is used in the same sense as παρεπιδήμοις 'aliens' of 1:1 [BNTC, NIBC, Sel, TNTC], referring to pilgrims who really don't belong [Sel], to those who are strangers to this world [NTC], who lack the rights of citizens [BNTC, NIC], and who live in a temporary existence away from their true home [TH].

**1:18** knowing[a] that not with perishable[b] (things), (as) with silver or gold, you were-redeemed[c]

LEXICON—a. perf. act. participle of οἶδα (LN 28.1): 'to know' [BNTC, LN, NIC, WBC; all versions except NAB, REB], 'to know well' [REB], 'to realize' [NAB]. The perfect tense of this Greek verb carries a present tense meaning.
b. φθαρτός (LN 23.125) (BAGD p. 857): 'perishable' [BAGD, BNTC, LN, NIC, WBC; NIV, NJB, NRSV], 'corruptible things' [KJV], 'destructible' [TNT], 'diminishable' [NAB], 'of passing value' [REB]. This adjective is also translated by a verb phrase: 'that don't last forever' [CEV], 'that can be destroyed' [NLT, TEV]. See 1:4 for this word in its negated form ἄφθαρτος 'incorruptible'.
c. aorist pass. indic. of λυτρόω (LN 37.128) (BAGD 1.b. p. 482): 'to be redeemed' [BAGD, WBC; KJV, NIV], 'to be ransomed' [BAGD, BNTC,

NIC; NRSV], 'to be set free' [LN; TNT], 'to be liberated' [LN], 'to be delivered' [LN; NAB], 'to be rescued' [CEV]. This verb is also translated as a verb phrase: 'to pay the price of your ransom' [NJB], 'to pay a ransom to save you' [NLT], 'to buy your freedom . . . to set you free' [REB], 'what was paid to set you free' [TEV].

QUESTION—What relationship is indicated by the participle εἰδότες 'knowing'?

It gives the grounds for all the preceding exhortations enumerated in 1:13–17 in which Christians are called to hope and holy living [NIC]. Fear of his judgment as well as gratitude and wonder for what he has done in redemption are the grounds for awe of God [NIC]. The holiness of God, fear of his judgment, and recognition of the great cost of redemption are the grounds for moral earnestness [BNTC] and for fear of God [ICC]. Recognition of what God has accomplished in redemption is the grounds for Christian conduct [IVP, NCBC]. This passage gives further grounds for the fear of God in addition to what has been said before [Alf, Sel, TH]. Recognition of the great cost of redemption is the grounds for the fear of God's discipline in 1:17 and for the desire to please God [TNTC].

QUESTION—What is meant by the word 'perishable' with reference to gold and silver?

Even the most durable and precious things of this world can lose their value or can be destroyed [IVP, NIC, NTC, TH, TNTC], and have no benefit for spiritual deliverance [BNTC]. The focus here is not so much on the possible physical perishability of precious metals as on the enormous value of the price paid for redemption in contrast to the treasures of this world which are worthless by comparison [ICC, NIBC, NTC, Sel].

QUESTION—Who is the implied agent of the passive verb ἐλυτρώθητε 'redeemed'?

1. God is the agent [NIC, TG, TH, WBC]. Christ is the ransom paid [WBC].
2. Christ is the agent and God is the recipient of the ransom payment [BNTC].

QUESTION—What is meant by ἐλυτρώθητε 'redeemed'?

It means to liberate and restore [NIBC] or to set free [TG, TH]. The redemption of Christians is likened to the exodus from Egypt [ICC, IVP, NIC, NTC, Sel]. The word implies a redemption by payment of a ransom price; that is, our redemption came at the cost of the sacrifice of Christ [Alf, BNTC, ICC, TNTC, WBC]. However, the metaphor of purchase cannot be stretched to the point of asking who receives the payment, which is beyond the scope of its intended meaning [ICC, NCBC, NIBC, NTC, TG, TH]. The word implies deliverance or setting free as well as the concept of redemption by a purchase [NCBC].

**from[a] your futile[b] way-of-life[c] handed-down-from-(your)-ancestors[d]**

LEXICON—a. ἐκ with genitive (LN 89.121): 'from' [BNTC, LN, NIC, WBC; all versions].

b. μάταιος (LN 65.37) (BAGD p. 495): 'futile' [BAGD, BNTC, LN; NAB, NJB, NRSV], 'futility' [REB], 'empty' [BAGD, LN, NIC, WBC; NIV, TNT], 'useless' [BAGD, LN; CEV], 'vain' [KJV], 'worthless' [TEV].
   c. ἀναστροφή (LN 41.3) (BAGD p. 61): 'way of life' [BAGD, NIC, WBC; CEV, NAB, NIV, NJB, TNT], 'manner of life' [TEV], 'life' [NLT], 'conduct' [BAGD, LN], 'mode of conduct' [BNTC], 'behavior' [BAGD, LN], 'conversation' [KJV], 'ways' [NRSV, REB]. See this word at 1:15.
   d. πατροπαράδοτος (LN **33.240**) (BAGD p. 637): 'handed down from your ancestors' [LN, NIC; NJB], 'handed down by your ancestors' [TEV], 'handed down to you from your forefathers' [NIV], 'inherited' [BAGD], 'inherited from your ancestors' [BNTC; NLT, NRSV], 'you learned from your ancestors' [CEV], 'received by tradition from your fathers' [KJV], 'your fathers handed on to you' [NAB], 'your fathers had passed on to you' [TNT], 'that was your heritage' [WBC], 'traditional' [REB].

QUESTION—What is implied by the use of the word μάταιος 'futile'?

It refers to the vanity of idolatry [BNTC, NIBC], to life without the worship of the true God due to ignorance or apostasy [Sel]. It means that which is devoid of hope [NIC, TH]. It means that their way of life was not worthwhile [TG], and was purposeless, in that nothing good issued from it [IVP].

QUESTION—What is being referred to by πατροπαράδοτος 'the way of life handed down from your ancestors'?

It refers to idolatrous pagan religion [EGT, NIBC], and deeply cherished family religious traditions [NIBC]. It refers not only to religion but to the entire pagan lifestyle and culture [ICC, NIC, TG, WBC], which was transmitted by family, political leaders, and philosophers [ICC]. Conformity to the tradition was expected and failure to conform was considered to be a betrayal of one's own culture and heritage [ICC, NIC, TNTC].

**1:19** but[a] with (the) precious[b] blood[c] of Christ as[d] of a lamb[e] without-blemish[f] and spotless,[g]

LEXICON—a. ἀλλά (LN 89.125): 'but' [BNTC, LN, NIC, WBC; KJV, NAB, NIV, NJB, NRSV], 'instead, on the contrary' [LN], not explicit [CEV, NLT, REB, TEV, TNT].
   b. τίμιος (LN 65.2) (BAGD 1.b. p. 818): 'precious' [BAGD, BNTC, LN, NIC, WBC; all versions except NAB, TEV], 'valuable' [LN], 'of great worth or value' [BAGD], 'costly' [TEV], 'beyond all price' [NAB].
   c. αἷμα (LN 8.64, 23.107) (BAGD 2.b. p. 23): 'blood' [BAGD, BNTC, LN (8.64), NIC, WBC; all versions except NLT, TEV], 'lifeblood' [NLT], 'costly sacrifice' [TEV], 'death' [LN (23.107)].
   d. ὡς (LN 64.12) (BAGD III.1.a. p. 898): 'as' [BAGD, BNTC, LN], 'like' [LN, NIC, WBC; NRSV, REB, TEV], not explicit [CEV, NAB, NIV, NLT, TNT].
   e. ἀμνός (LN 4.24) (BAGD p. 46): 'lamb' [BAGD, BNTC, LN, NIC, WBC; all versions except NLT, TNT], 'sacrificial lamb' [TNT], 'Lamb of God' [NLT].

f. ἄμωμος (LN **79.61**) (BAGD 1. p. 47): 'without blemish' [BNTC, LN, NIC; KJV, NIV], 'unblemished' [BAGD; TNT], 'without defect' [**LN**; NRSV, TEV], 'without mark' [REB], 'spotless' [CEV, NAB], 'blameless' [NJB], 'sinless' [NLT], 'faultless' [WBC].

g. ἄσπιλος (LN **79.59**) (BAGD 1. p. 117): 'spotless' [BAGD, LN; NJB, NLT, TNT], 'without stain' [BNTC, LN], 'without blemish' [BAGD; NRSV, REB], 'innocent' [CEV], 'without spot' [**LN**; KJV], 'unblemished' [NAB], 'without defect' [NIC; NIV], 'without flaw' [TEV], 'flawless' [WBC].

QUESTION—What relationship is indicated by ἀλλά 'but'?

This word is used to indicate emphatic contrast between two objects [BNTC, ICC, NIC, NTC, WBC; KJV, NAB, NIV, NJB, NRSV]: not this but that. The contrast extends both to the nouns as well as their adjectives [BNTC, EGT, ICC, NTC, Sel, WBC].

QUESTION—Is there any significance in the lack of the definite article with αἷμα 'blood'?

The definite article is supplied in many English translations [BNTC, NIC; CEV, KJV, NAB, NIV, NLT, NRSV, TEV, TNT]. Some translations do not include it [WBC; NJB, REB]. Its exclusion may have nothing to do with the meaning [NTC]. The omission of the article strengthens the contrast between corruptible silver and gold and the blood of Christ by balancing both sides of the comparison: not with corruptible metal but with precious blood [Alf, ICC].

QUESTION—What relationship is indicated by ὡς 'as'?

1. This is used to compare the blood of Christ with the blood of a spotless lamb [BNTC, NIC, WBC; KJV, NJB, NRSV, REB].
2. This is used to compare Christ himself with a spotless lamb [TEV, TNT] or to identify Christ as such a lamb [CEV, NAB, NIV, NLT].

QUESTION—What is the distinction between ἄμωμος 'without blemish' and ἄσπιλος 'spotless'?

Ἄμωμος means to be 'without blemish or defect' [LN (**79.61**)]. It is used in the LXX of Leviticus 22:21 to describe the quality of a sacrificial lamb, which is to be 'without blemish' [Sel]. It is used here in a moral sense of blamelessness [WBC] or faultlessness [BNTC]. The second term, ἄσπιλος, means to be 'spotless or without stain' [LN (**79.59**)], and denotes physical or moral cleanliness and perfection [WBC]. It is added here for rhetorical effect [WBC] and reinforces and emphasizes the first word [BNTC, NIC]. Taken together the two words mean total perfection [NIBC, Sel].

**1:20** having-been-chosen[a] before[b] (the) foundation[c] of (the) world[d]

LEXICON—a. perf. pass. participle of προγινώσκω (LN **28.6**, 30.100) (BAGD p. 703): 'to be chosen' [CEV, NAB, NIV, TEV, TNT], 'to be chosen beforehand' [BAGD, LN (30.100)], 'to be selected in advance' [LN (30.100)], 'to be chosen in advance' [NIC], 'to be predestined' [BNTC; REB], 'to be destined' [NRSV], 'to be foreordained' [KJV], 'to be

marked out' [NJB]. 'to be known already' [LN (**28.6**)], 'to be foreknown' [WBC]. This participle is also translated as an active verb with God as the agent and Christ as the object: 'God chose him for this purpose' [NLT].
    b. πρό (LN 67.17) (BAGD 2. p. 701): 'before' [BAGD, BNTC, LN, NIC, WBC; all versions except NLT], 'long before' [NLT].
    c. καταβολῆ (LN 42.37) (BAGD p. 409): 'foundation' [BAGD, BNTC, NIC; KJV, NAB, NRSV, REB], 'creation' [LN, WBC; NIV, TEV], 'beginning' [BAGD]. This noun is also translated as a verb: 'to be made' [NJB, TNT], 'to be created' [CEV], 'to begin' [NLT].
    d. κόσμος (LN 1.39) (BAGD 2. p. 446): 'world' [BAGD, BNTC, LN, NIC, WBC; all versions].

QUESTION—What is meant by προεγνωσμένου 'chosen'?
It indicates that Christ was chosen or appointed beforehand to the task of redemption [BNTC, IVP, NIC, NTC, Sel, TG, TH, TNTC, WBC], God being the implied agent [BNTC, ICC, IVP, NCBC, NIBC, NIC, NTC, TH, TNTC, WBC; NLT]. It implies his pre-existence [EGT, NTC]. See the noun form of this word at 1:2.

**but[a] having-been-revealed[b] in[c] (the) last[d] of-the-times[e] for[f] you**
LEXICON—a. δέ (LN 89.136): 'but' [BNTC, LN, NIC, WBC; CEV, KJV, NIV, NRSV, REB], 'and' [NAB, NJB, TEV, TNT].
    b. aorist pass. participle of φανερόω (LN 24.19) (BAGD 2.b.β. p. 853): 'to be revealed' [NIC; NAB, NIV, NJB, NRSV, REB, TEV, TNT], 'to appear' [BAGD, LN, WBC], 'to be manifest' [KJV], 'to be made manifest' [BNTC], 'to come' [CEV], 'to be made visible, to cause to be seen' [LN], 'to be shown' [BAGD]. This participle is also translated as a verb phrase: 'to be sent to the earth for all to see' [NLT].
    c. ἐπί with genitive (LN 67.33) (BAGD I.2. p. 286): 'in' [WBC; KJV, NAB, NIV, NLT, REB, TEV, TNT], 'at' [BAGD, BNTC, NIC; NJB, NRSV], 'not until' [CEV], 'when, at the time of' [LN], 'in the time of' [BAGD].
    d. ἔσχατος (LN 61.13) (BAGD 3.b. p. 314): 'last' [BAGD, LN, WBC; CEV, KJV, NAB, NIV, REB, TEV, TNT], 'final' [LN; NJB, NLT], 'end' [BNTC, NIC; NRSV].
    e. χρόνος (LN 67.78) (BAGD p. 888): 'of the times' [BNTC, NIC], 'times' [KJV, NIV], 'time' [BAGD, LN], 'period of time' [BAGD, LN; REB], 'of the ages' [WBC; NRSV], 'days' [CEV, NAB, NLT, TEV, TNT], 'point of time' [NJB]. See this word at 1:17.
    f. διά with accusative (LN 90.38): 'for' [BNTC, NIC, WBC; all versions except CEV], 'for the sake of, on behalf of, for the benefit of' [LN], 'because of' [CEV]. The phrase δι᾽ ὑμᾶς 'for you' is translated 'for your sake' [BNTC, NIC, WBC; NAB, NIV, NJB, NRSV, REB, TEV], 'for your sakes' [TNT], and 'for you' [KJV, NLT].

QUESTION—What relationship is indicated by δέ 'but'?
This is part of the μέν ... δέ construction in which the affirmative enclitic particle μέν remains untranslated, but which marks the clause that contains it

# 1 PETER 1:20

as the first segment of a paired contrast with the clause that contains the negative enclitic particle δέ: προεγνωσμένου μὲν πρὸ καταβολῆς κόσμου, φανερωθέντος δέ 'chosen before the foundation of the world, but revealed . . .' [WBC]. It serves to heighten the contrast between the two balanced clauses [NTC].

QUESTION—What is meant by δι' ὑμᾶς 'for you'?

These readers are being told that they are at the focal point of God's redemptive plan in the unfolding of history [BNTC, Sel, TH, TNTC]. The purposes of God were formed and executed with them in mind, though Christ came so that all people might believe [IVP]. Theirs is the highest privilege [NTC] despite their status as 'strangers' [Sel]. It indicates that God's actions are intended to have an effect in the lives of people [NCBC]. Δι' ὑμᾶς has a function similar to εἰς ὑμᾶς ('for you') in 1:4, which is to mark movement from general doctrine to specific personal application for the readers [WBC]. It personalizes for the reader the reason for God's redemptive acts, and thereby deepens the sense of obligation to personal holiness and reverence [ICC].

QUESTION—What is implied by the use of φανερωθέντος 'revealed'?

It is a reference to the incarnation or first coming of Christ [NIBC, NTC, TG]. It implies the pre-existence of Christ [BNTC, ICC, IVP, NCBC, NIBC, NIC, WBC]. God is the agent of the revealing [NTC, TH].

QUESTION—What is meant by ἐπ' ἐσχάτου τῶν χρόνων 'in the last of the times'?

'Times' refers to epochs or periods of history as God sees it [Sel], and the present age is the last of the periods of time determined by God [NIC, WBC]. The final period of history is that marked by the first coming of Christ [BNTC, IVP, NTC, TH] and which will culminate with his second coming [NTC, TH]. It is the final period in which the world will end [IVP, NCBC, NIC, NTC]. It is variously translated as 'these last days' [CEV, NAB, TEV, TNT], 'the end of the times' [BNTC, NIC], 'these last times' [KJV, NIV], 'these final days' [NLT], 'the last of the ages' [WBC], 'the final point of time' [NJB], 'the end of the ages' [NRSV], or 'this last period of time' [REB].

**1:21** the ones (who) through[a] him (are) believers[b] in[c] God, the one having-raised[d] him from (the) dead and having-given[e] him glory,[f]

LEXICON—a. διά with genitive object (LN 90.4): 'through' [BNTC, LN, NIC, WBC; all versions except CEV, KJV], 'by' [LN; KJV], not explicit [CEV].

b. πιστός (LN 31.86) (BAGD 2. p. 665): 'believers' [WBC; NAB], 'one who trusts in' [LN], 'trusting' [BAGD, LN], 'believing, faithful' [BAGD]. This pronominal adjective is also translated as a verb phrase: 'to have faith' [BNTC; CEV, NJB], 'to believe' [NIC; KJV, NIV, TEV, TNT], 'to come to trust' [NLT, NRSV, REB].

c. εἰς with accusative object: 'in' [BNTC, LN, WBC; all versions], 'on' [NIC].
d. aorist active participle ἐγείρω (LN 23.94) (BAGD 1.a.β. p. 214): 'to raise' [BAGD, BNTC, NIC, WBC; all versions], 'to raise to life, to make live again' [LN].
e. aorist act. participle of δίδωμι (LN 57.71): 'to give' [BNTC, LN, NIC, WBC; all versions except CEV, NIV]. The phrase 'to give glory' is translated 'to glorify' [NIV], 'to honor in a glorious way' [CEV].
f. δόξα (LN 87.4, 87.23) (BAGD 1.b.α. p. 203): 'glory' [BAGD, BNTC, LN (87.23), NIC, WBC; KJV, NAB, NJB, NRSV, REB, TEV], 'great glory' [NLT], 'a position of great honor' [TNT], 'honor, respect, status' [LN (87.4)]. See this word at 1:11.

QUESTION—What is the function of δι' αὐτοῦ 'through him' in this passage?

It provides a link between the preceding clause and what follows; Christ's coming was δι' ὑμᾶς 'for you' because you became believers δι' αὐτοῦ 'through him' [WBC]. The phrase δι' αὐτοῦ 'through him' indicates the difference between Judaism and Christianity which focuses on Christ's redemptive work as the grounds and means of faith [Sel]. It is δι' αὐτοῦ 'through him' that they have relationship with God because of what God did in his death and resurrection [NCBC, NIC]. Jesus is the causative agent of their faith in God [TG], although not in the same sense as believing through the agency of Paul or Apollos [ICC]. It is not only through his manifestation that they believe, but also through him personally as the medium of faith in God [Alf].

QUESTION—What relationship is indicated by the use of εἰς θεόν 'in God' with the pronominal adjective πιστούς 'believers'?

While πιστούς could be understood as describing the readers passively as 'trustworthy' or 'faithful', the presence of εἰς θεόν 'in God' makes God the object of active faith; they believe in God [ICC, TNTC, WBC]. Just as δι' αὐτοῦ 'through him' differentiates Christianity from Judaism, so also εἰς θεόν 'in God' marks for the readers the difference between Christianity and pagan religion, in that the faith that comes through Christ is a faith in God [Sel].

**so-that[a] your faith[b] and hope[c] are[d] in God.**

LEXICON—a. ὥστε (LN 89.52, 89.61) (BAGD 2.a.β. p. 900): 'so that' (indicating purpose) [LN (89.61), WBC], 'in order to' [LN (89.61)], 'so that' (indicating result) [BNTC, LN (89.52), NIC; NRSV], 'and so' [LN (89.52); NIV, REB, TEV], 'then' [NAB], not explicit [NLT]. Purpose is also indicated by verb phrases: 'that's why' [TEV], 'that (it) might be' [KJV], and 'for this very purpose—that (it) should be' [NJB].
b. πίστις (LN 31.85) (BAGD 2.a. p. 662): 'faith' [BAGD, BNTC, LN, NIC, WBC; all versions], 'trust' [BAGD], 'confidence in God' [BAGD]. See this word at 1:7.

c. ἐλπίς (LN 25.59) (BAGD 2.b. p. 253): 'hope' [BAGD, BNTC, LN, NIC, WBC; all versions]. See this word at 1:3.
d. pres. act. inf. of εἶναι (LN 13.1): 'to be' [LN, NIC; NIV], 'to be fixed (on)' [BNTC; REB, TEV], 'to be set (on)' [NRSV], 'to be centered (in)' [NAB]. This is also translated with adverbs: 'might be' [WBC; KJV], 'should be' [NJB]; as a verb phrase with faith and hope as the subject: 'can be placed confidently' [NLT]; as the object: 'you have put' [CEV], or 'you have' [TNT].

QUESTION—What is the glory that was given to Christ?

Glory was given to Christ when God showed his favor by vindicating him through resurrection [EGT, NIC, WBC]. The readers await this same vindication from their present sufferings [WBC]. Glory was given to Christ through his ascension [EGT], through his exaltation to a place of honor and power [TG, TH] and by giving him a name above all others [ICC, NTC]. Christ has been raised to the place of supreme honor and shares the Father's glory [IVP].

QUESTION—What relationship is indicated by ὥστε 'so that'?

1. It indicates simple consequence or result [Alf, BNTC, TG, TH; NLT, REB, TEV; and probably NIC, NTC; NAB, NIV, NRSV]: God raised Jesus from the dead, and as a result you have faith and hope. The clause that follows ὥστε 'so that' is an amplification of the clause that follows δι' αὐτοῦ 'through him', so ὥστε is translated 'through him', that is, through him you believe in God, so that (it is 'through him' that) you have faith and hope in God [TNT].
2. It indicates purpose [IVP, Sel, WBC; CEV, KJV, NJB, TEV]: God raised Jesus from the dead in order that you might have faith and hope. This word taken with δι' αὐτοῦ 'through him' indicates God's purpose carried out through Christ as an intermediary agent; Christ's coming was to lead people to have faith in God, which was accomplished through God's action of raising Christ from the dead and giving him glory [CEV]. The clause that follows ὥστε 'so that' further explains the δι' ὑμᾶς 'for your sake' of the previous verse, indicating that what God did for the sake of the readers in manifesting Christ was to give them faith and hope [IVP, WBC]. The use of ὥστε with an infinitive, as we find here, normally indicates intent, as opposed to using ὥστε with an indicative verb, which normally indicates simple result [Sel]. The hortatory nature of the broader passage fits better with the expression of purpose on the part of God; God did these things through Christ because he intended for you to have faith and hope, so therefore you should respond to him in faith and hope [Sel; probably KJV, NJB].

QUESTION—What distinction is there between faith and hope?

Faith and hope are closely intertwined [Sel], being very close to the same thing [NCBC, NIC] or two aspects of the same thing [BNTC, ICC]. Both faith and hope orient to the future, both are directed toward God in response to what he has done in Christ, and both govern a believer's conduct now

[WBC]. A believer's faith rests on the fact of Christ's resurrection [Alf, NTC], his hope rests on the fact of Christ's glorification [Alf], and he hopes for a share of Christ's glory at his own resurrection [NTC]. Here hope means confidence, as it is patient faith that lays hold of Israel's hope [EGT]. Faith is trust in God and hope is confidence in the fulfillment of God's promises [TG, TH]. Faith is assurance and trust, and hope is the expectation of resurrection and glory [BNTC].

**DISCOURSE UNIT: 1:22–2:3** [IVP, TH; NJB]. The topic is love and purity [IVP], proper relationships among believers [TH], regeneration by the word [NJB].

**DISCOURSE UNIT: 1:22–25** [Sel, WBC; NAB]. The topic is Christian holiness as the fruit of God's word and grace [Sel], a life of genuine love [WBC], brotherly love [NAB].

**1:22** Having-purified[a] your souls by[b] obedience[c] to the truth[d] resulting-in[e] sincere[f] brotherly-love,[g]

TEXT—Some manuscripts include διὰ πνεύματος 'through the spirit' after τῆς ἀληθείας 'to the truth'. GNT omits this with an A rating, indicating that the text is certain. It is included only by KJV.

LEXICON—a. perf. act. participle of ἁγνίζω (LN 88.30) (BAGD 1.b. p. 11): 'to purify' [BAGD, BNTC, LN, NIC, WBC; all versions except NLT], 'to cleanse' [NLT]. The perfect participle is indicated by 'now that' [BNTC, WBC; NIV, NRSV, REB, TEV, TNT], 'since' [NIC; NJB], and 'seeing' [KJV].

b. ἐν with dative (LN 90.10): 'by' [LN, NIC, WBC; NAB, NIV, NJB, NRSV, REB, TEV, TNT], 'through' [BNTC], 'in' [KJV].

c. ὑπακοή (LN 36.15) (BAGD 1.b. p. 837): 'obedience' [BAGD, BNTC, LN, NIC, WBC; NAB, NJB, NRSV, REB, TEV]. This noun is also translated as a verb: 'to obey' [CEV], 'to accept' [NLT]; as a participle: 'obeying' [KJV, NIV, TNT]. See this word at 1:2.

d. ἀλήθεια (LN 72.2) (BAGD 2.b. p. 36): 'truth' [BAGD, BNTC, LN, NIC, WBC; all versions except NLT], 'the truth of the Good News' [NLT].

e. εἰς with accusative object (LN 89.48, 89.57): 'with the result that, so that as a result' [LN (89.48)], 'for' [BNTC, WBC; NAB], 'unto' [KJV], 'for the purpose of, in order to' [LN (89.57)], not explicit [CEV]. This word is translated by a verb phrase: 'so that you have' [NIC; NIV, NRSV], 'so that you can experience' [NJB], 'now you can have' [NLT], 'until you feel' [REB], 'and have come to have' [TEV], 'and (truly love one another)' [TNT].

f. ἀνυπόκριτος (LN **73.8**) (BAGD p. 76): 'sincere' [BNTC, LN, NIC; NIV, NLT, REB, TEV], 'with no insincerity or hypocrisy' [BAGD], 'genuine' [**LN**; NAB, NJB, NRSV], 'pure' [WBC], 'sincerely' [CEV], 'unfeigned' [KJV], 'truly' [TNT].

# 1 PETER 1:22 53

g. φιλαδελφία (LN 25.34) (BAGD p. 858): 'brotherly love' [BAGD], 'affection for a fellow believer' [LN], 'brotherly affection' [WBC], 'love of your brothers' [BNTC; NAB], 'love of the brethren' [KJV], 'love of brothers' [NJB], 'love as brothers' [NLT], 'love for your brothers' [NIV], 'love for your fellow Christians' [NIC], 'love for your fellow believers' [LN; TEV], 'affection towards your fellow-Christians' [REB], 'mutual love' [NRSV, TNT], 'love' [CEV].

QUESTION—What relationship is indicated by the perfect participle ἡγνικότες 'having purified'?

It is the grounds for the exhortation that follows [Alf, EGT, TH]. It indicates a past event with lasting present effect [NCBC, NIBC, NTC, TH]. It represents an on-going process [NIBC], a current state or condition by virtue of submission to the gospel [NIC]. It means that post-conversion growth resulted in a process of purification [TNTC]. Since Peter has previously used aorist and present participles as imperatives by linking them to an aorist imperative (1:13–14), he now uses the perfect participle to indicate that this is not a command, but is something that they have already done [WBC].

QUESTION—What is the purification referred to?

1. It refers to their initial conversion [IVP, NCBC, WBC], to their baptism [EGT], or to conversion and baptism [BNTC, NIC, Sel, TG]. It is accomplished at conversion by the sprinkling of the blood of Christ [WBC].
2. It refers to an ongoing process [Alf, ICC, NTC, TNTC].
3. It refers to a past event of conversion as well as an ongoing process [NIBC].

QUESTION—What is meant here by ψύχη 'soul'?

It refers to the inward nature of the person [TNTC]. It refers to the whole person or self as in 1:9 [BNTC, NCBC, NIC, TG, TH]. It is the center of personality [Alf]. It refers to one's entire life and conduct [WBC]. It is synonymous with 'yourself' [NAB, NIV, NJB, TEV].

QUESTION—What relationship is indicated by ἐν 'by'?

It indicates means [TNTC]: you are purified by obedience. It indicates the sphere within which the process of purification occurs by habitual obedience [Alf].

QUESTION—What is the obedience referred to?

1. It refers to initial submission to the gospel message [BNTC, IVP, NIC, WBC; NLT] or to submission to the gospel message and its ethical teachings [Sel]. It refers to offering oneself for baptism [NCBC].
2. It refers to an ongoing process [Alf, ICC]. It is a process of active obedience [TH], especially to the commands to holiness given in preceding verses [TNTC].
3. It refers to conversion as well as to a continuing process of obedience [NIBC].

QUESTION—What is the truth that is referred to?
   It is the message of the gospel which they believed and accepted [Alf, BNTC, EGT, NCBC, NIC, NTC, Sel, TH, WBC; NLT], the gospel and its demands [TG], the gospel and all Christian teaching [TNTC], the gospel and God's Word [NIBC]. It is the words of the prophets spoken by the Spirit of Christ and which lead to new birth [ICC].
QUESTION—What relationship is indicated by εἰς 'resulting in'?
   1. It indicates simple result [ICC, NIC, NTC, TH, TNTC; CEV, KJV]: you love because your souls have been purified.
   2. It indicates possibility [TG; NJB, NLT]: you can love because your souls have been purified.
   3. It indicates purpose [BNTC, NCBC, WBC]: your souls were purified in order that you would love.

## love[a] one-another fervently[b] from[c] a pure[d] heart[e]

TEXT—The word καθαρᾶς 'pure' does not occur in some manuscripts. It is included by GNT with a C rating, indicating difficulty in deciding whether or not to place it in the text. It is included only by KJV and NIC, and is omitted or not translated by BNTC, WBC, CEV, NAB, NIV, NJB, NLT, NRSV, REB, TEV, TNT.

LEXICON—a. aorist act. imperative of ἀγαπάω (LN 25.43) (BAGD 1.a.α. p. 4): 'to love' [BAGD, BNTC, LN, NIC, WBC; all versions].
   b. ἐκτενῶς (LN **25.71**) (BAGD p. 245): 'fervently' [BAGD, NIC; KJV], 'earnestly' [LN; TEV], 'strenuously' [BNTC], 'deeply' [NIV, NRSV], 'intensely' [NJB, NLT], 'with all your strength' [REB], 'constantly' [BAGD; NAB], 'unremittingly' [WBC]. This adverb is also translated as an adjective: '(let it be) earnest' [TNT]; as an imperative: 'keep on (loving)' [CEV].
   c. ἐκ with genitive (LN 89.85, 90.16): 'from' [BNTC, LN (89.85, 90.16), NIC, WBC; NAB, NIV, NJB, NRSV, TNT], 'with' [LN (89.85); CEV, KJV, NLT, TEV], not explicit [REB].
   d. καθαρός (LN 53.29) (BAGD 3.b. p. 388): 'pure' [BAGD, LN, NIC; KJV], not explicit BNTC, WBC; CEV, NAB, NIV, NJB, NLT, NRSV, REB, TEV, TNT.
   e. καρδία (BAGD 1.b.α. p. 403): 'heart' [BAGD, BNTC, LN, NIC, WBC; all versions except REB], 'inner self' [LN]. The phrase ἐκ καρδίας 'from the heart' is translated 'wholeheartedly' [REB].

QUESTION—What is the function of the aorist imperative ἀγαπήσατε 'love'?
   It is the main verb of this verse and the verse following [NTC]. It forms the heart of this section [NCBC, Sel]. It is ingressive; that is, begin doing this and keep on doing it [BNTC, NTC].
QUESTION—Is there any distinction in meaning between φιλαδελφία 'brotherly love' and ἀγαπάω 'love'?
   1. They are used more or less synonymously [ICC, NCBC, NIC, TG, WBC].

2. Brotherly love is a reciprocal love, whereas ἀγαπάω indicates a non-reciprocal love, which can cause the brotherly love to grow and flourish [IVP]. The difference between brotherly love and agape love is the difference between liking and loving deeply [NTC]. Brotherly love is love for other Christian brothers, whereas ἀγαπάω 'love' is universal charity [Sel]. There is a progression from φιλαδελφία 'brotherly love' to ἀγαπάω 'love', but with much overlap between the two [TNTC]. The φιλαδελφία love was a love of other believers [Alf, BNTC, EGT, ICC, NCBC, NIBC, NIC, NTC, Sel, TG, TH; REB, TEV], and not of all people in general [BNTC, ICC, NCBC].

QUESTION—What relationship is indicated by ἐκ 'from'?

The answer to this will depend on the view taken regarding the textual question of whether or not 'pure' is to be included in the text. If 'pure' is accepted as part of the text, the ἐκ would indicate the source of the love, which is purity of heart [LN (90.16)]. For those versions and commentators not taking 'pure' as a part of the text, ἐκ could be used either to indicate the source of the love or as a marker of manner indicating how the believers are to love; that is, don't love superficially or in word only, but love from the heart [LN (89.85)]. 'From the heart' corresponds to 'without hypocrisy' of the previous clause, both indicating the manner in which they should love [WBC].

QUESTION—What is meant by ἐκτενῶς 'fervently'?
1. It has a temporal focus; that is, the love should be unremitting and enduring throughout time [NCBC, WBC; CEV, NAB].
2. It indicates manner, as of energy, intensity, or fervor [Alf, BNTC, EGT, IVP, NCBC, NIC, Sel, TG, TH, TNTC; KJV, NIV, NJB, NLT, NRSV, REB, TEV, TNT].

**1:23** having-been-born-again[a] not of[b] perishable[c] seed[d] but[e] (of) imperishable[f]

LEXICON—a. perf. pass. participle of ἀναγεννάω (LN 13.55) (BAGD p. 51): 'to be born again' [KJV, NIV, NLT, REB, TEV, TNT], 'to be born anew' [WBC; NRSV], 'to be born afresh' [BNTC], 'to be re-born' [NIC], 'to be caused to be born again' [BAGD, LN], 'to be begotten again' [BAGD]. This participle is also translated as a substantive: 'your rebirth' [NAB], 'your new birth' [NJB]; as a verbal clause with God as the agent of the active verb: 'God has given you new birth' [CEV]. See this word at 1:3.

b. ἐκ with genitive object (LN 90.16): 'of' [NIC; KJV, NIV, NRSV, REB], 'from' [BNTC, LN, WBC; NAB, NJB, NLT], 'through' [TEV], 'by' [LN], not explicit [CEV].

c. φθαρτός (LN 23.125) (BAGD p. 857): 'perishable' [BAGD, BNTC, LN, NIC, WBC; NIV, NJB, NRSV], 'corruptible' [KJV], 'destructible' [NAB], 'mortal' [LN; REB, TEV, TNT], not explicit [CEV, NLT]. See the negated form of this word at 1:4.

# 1 PETER 1:23

d. σπορά (LN **10.23**) (BAGD p. 763): 'seed' [BAGD, BNTC, NIC, WBC; KJV, NAB, NIV, NJB, NRSV], 'planting of seed' [WBC], 'sowing' [BAGD], 'parentage' [LN]. Some translate this as a metonymy, referring to the parentage that begets the new life [LN; REB, TEV, TNT] or to the new life that is begotten [NLT].

e. ἀλλά (LN 89.125): 'but' [BNTC, NIC, WBC; all versions except CEV, TEV], 'not' [TEV], not explicit [CEV].

f. ἄφθαρτος (LN 23.128) (BAGD p. 125): 'imperishable' [BAGD, BNTC, LN, NIC, WBC; NIV, NJB, NRSV], 'incorruptible' [BAGD; KJV], 'indestructible' [NAB], 'immortal' [BAGD, LN; REB, TEV, TNT], not explicit [CEV, NLT]. See this word at 1:4.

QUESTION—What relationship is indicated by the perfect participle ἀναγεγεννημένοι 'having been born again'?

It indicates the grounds for the exhortation to love given in the previous verse [Alf, NIBC, NTC, TH]. It extends the thought begun with the same word in 1:3 by indicating that believers are born into a permanent brotherhood of loving fellowship and therefore ought love one another [ICC, TNTC]. It creates a sense of balance with the previous verse by indicating God's role and action in regeneration [NIC].

QUESTION—What relationship is indicated by ἐκ 'from'?

It indicates source or origin [Alf, NIBC, Sel, WBC]. The source or origin of rebirth is God [Alf] or the grace of God [Sel].

QUESTION—What is meant by σπορά 'seed' in this context?

1. It refers to the seed that is sown, which is the word of God [Alf, NTC, TNTC]. It refers to the sowing of the seed, which is the word of God, not to the seed itself [WBC].
2. It refers to origin or parentage [TG, TH]. Sowing seed refers to the believer's origin or source, which is God's grace, with the word of God being the means of regeneration [Sel]. It is the direct action of God in producing new birth in man by means of the word of God, but is not equivalent to the word of God [NCBC]. It refers to God's divine nature living in his children and which comes through the word of God [NTC].

QUESTION—What relationship is indicated by οὐκ...ἀλλά 'not... but'?

It indicates emphatic contrast; not mortal seed, but immortal seed [BNTC, NIC, WBC; all versions]. It connects the thought with 1:18–19 where it is used in the same manner to contrast the perishable and the imperishable [NIC, WBC].

**through[a] (the) living[b] and enduring[c] word[d] of God.**

TEXT—Some manuscripts include εἰς τὸν αἰῶνα 'forever' after μένοντος 'enduring'. GNT does not mention this reading. Only KJV includes it.

LEXICON—a. διά (LN 90.8): 'through' [BNTC, LN, WBC; NAB, NIV, NRSV, REB, TEV, TNT], 'by' [CEV, KJV], 'by means of' [LN, NIC], 'with' [LN], 'it comes from' [NLT], not explicit [NJB].

## 1 PETER 1:23

b. pres. act. participle of ζάω (LN 23.88) (BAGD 4.b. p. 337): 'to live' [BNTC, NIC, WBC; all versions], 'to be alive' [LN]. See this word at 1:3.

c. pres. act. participle of μένω (LN 13.89) (BAGD 1.c.β. p. 504): 'to endure' [NIC, WBC; NAB, NIV, NJB, NRSV, REB], 'to abide' [BAGD, BNTC; KJV], 'to remain' [BAGD, LN], 'to continue' [BAGD, LN], 'to continue to exist' [LN], 'to remain forever' [TNT], 'eternal' [NLT, TEV], not explicit [CEV].

d. λόγος (LN 33.98) (BAGD 1.b.β. p. 478): 'word' [BAGD, BNTC, LN, NIC, WBC; all versions except CEV], 'message' [CEV].

QUESTION—What relationship is indicated by διά 'through'?

It refers to the instrumentality of the word of God as the means of regeneration [NIBC, Sel, WBC]. It indicates that the word of God is the vehicle of regeneration but not the begetting principle itself [Alf, NCBC, NTC]. It is used to connect the δι' ἀναστάσεως Ἰησοῦ Χριστοῦ 'through the resurrection of Jesus Christ' of 1:3 and the δι' αὐτοῦ 'through him' of 1:21 to 'through the living and eternal word of God' which refers to God's promises fulfilled in the incarnation of Christ and the consequent proclamation of the gospel [Sel].

QUESTION—What do 'living and enduring' modify?

1. They modify 'word'; believers are reborn through the word of God that is living and enduring [Alf, BNTC, ICC, IVP, NCBC, NIBC, NIC, NTC, Sel, TG, TNTC; all versions].
2. They modify God; believers are reborn through the word of the living and eternal God [EGT, WBC].

QUESTION—What is meant by λόγου θεοῦ 'the word of God'?

It is the Gospel message that was preached [BNTC, IVP, NCBC, TG]. It refers to God's promises fulfilled through Christ's incarnation and the resulting salvation offered because of it [Sel]. It means God's words generally, which would include the proclaimed gospel or the written word in the Scripture [NIBC, TNTC]. It means God's word in the widest, most general and abstract sense [Alf]. It is the 'truth' of the previous verse, the word spoken by Christ's spirit through the prophets and which gives new birth and purifies the soul when obeyed [ICC].

**1:24** For[a] all[b] flesh[c] (is) like[d] grass[e]

LEXICON—a. διότι (LN 89.26) (BAGD 3. p. 199): 'for' [BAGD, BNTC, NIC, WBC; KJV, NAB, NIV, NJB, NRSV, TNT], 'because of' [LN]. This is also translated as a verb phrase: 'as the scripture says' [TEV], 'as scripture says' [REB], 'as the prophet says' [NLT], 'the scriptures say' [CEV].

b. πᾶσα (LN 59.23): 'all' [BNTC, LN, NIC, WBC; all versions except CEV, NLT], not explicit [CEV, NLT].

c. σάρξ (LN **9.11**) (BAGD 3. p. 743): 'flesh' [BNTC, NIC; KJV, NRSV] 'people' [**LN**; NLT], 'human beings' [LN], 'mankind' [NAB, TEV,

TNT], 'mortals' [REB], 'humanity' [WBC; NJB], 'men' [NIV], 'humans' [CEV].
  d. ὡς (LN 64.12) (BAGD II.3.b. p. 897): 'like' [BNTC, LN, NIC, WBC; CEV, NIV, NLT, NRSV, REB, TEV, TNT], 'as' [BAGD, LN; KJV], not explicit [NAB, NJB]. NAB, NJB leave out 'like' or 'as' and treat the statement as metaphor instead of simile, 'all humanity is grass' [NJB], 'all mankind is grass' [NAB].
  e. χόρτος (LN 3.15) (BAGD p. 884): 'grass' [BAGD, BNTC, LN, NIC, WBC; all versions].

QUESTION—What relationship is indicated by διότι 'for'?
  It is used as a shortened form of 'for it is written' to introduce a Scripture quotation [ICC, NTC, TG, TH, WBC; CEV, NLT, REB, TEV]. It is a loose conjunction with no causal relationship inferred [WBC]. It introduces Scriptural support for what was said in the previous verse [Alf, IVP, NCBC, NIBC, TNTC].

QUESTION—What is meant by σάρξ 'flesh'?
  It refers to all human existence or all mankind [BNTC, IVP, NIBC, NTC, TG, TH, TNTC, WBC], especially with regard to frailty, mortality, or transience [NIBC, NTC, Sel]. It refers to all creatures [TG] or all perishable things [Sel]. It refers to man in his life of body and soul [Alf].

QUESTION—What relationship is indicated by ὡς 'like'?
  It indicates a simile [BNTC, NIC, WBC; all versions except NAB, NJB]. Those that omit ὡς translate this clause as a metaphor following the LXX of Isaiah 40:6-8, where it is also lacking [NAB, NJB].

QUESTION—What is the verb in this clause?
  The Greek does not have a verb, following the LXX quotation which, in turn, is a translation of the Hebrew, which lacks a verb. Most English translations supply 'is' [BNTC, NIC, WBC; KJV, NAB, NJB, NRSV, TNT] or 'are' [NIV, NLT, REB, TEV] as the understood verb, and CEV supplies 'wither' as the understood verb.

**and all glory[a] of-it like[b] (the) flower[c] of-grass; the grass withers[d] and the flower falls[e];**

TEXT—Instead of αὐτῆς 'of it', some ancient manuscripts have ἀνθρώπου 'of man'. GNT does not mention this alternative. Only KJV, NAB, TNT use this reading.

LEXICON—a. δόξα (LN 79.18) (BAGD 2. p. 204): 'glory' [BNTC, LN, NIC, WBC; all versions except NJB, NLT], 'beauty' [NJB, NLT], 'magnificence' [BAGD], 'splendor' [BAGD, **LN**].
  b. ὡς (LN 64.12) (BAGD II.3.b. p. 897): 'like' [BNTC, LN, NIC, WBC; all versions except KJV, NLT], 'as' [BAGD, LN; KJV, NLT].
  c. ἄνθος (LN 3.56) (BAGD 1. p. 67): 'flower of grass' [BNTC; KJV, NRSV], 'flower of the grass' [NIC], 'flower of the field' [NAB, REB], 'flowers of the field' [NIV], 'flower' [BAGD, LN], 'blossom' [BAGD], 'wild flower' [WBC; NJB], 'wild flowers' [CEV, NLT, TEV, TNT].

# 1 PETER 1:24

d. aorist pass. indic. of ξηραίνω (LN 79.82) (BAGD 2.a. p. 548): 'to wither' [BAGD, BNTC, LN, WBC; all versions except CEV], 'to dry up' [BAGD, LN, NIC; CEV]. This is translated as present tense by NIC, WBC and all versions, and as perfect tense by BNTC.

e. aorist act. indic. of ἐκπίπτω (LN **15.120**) (BAGD 1. p. 243): 'to fall' [**BNTC, LN**, NIC; NIV, NRSV, REB, TEV, TNT], 'to fall away' [WBC; KJV, NLT], 'fall off' [BAGD, LN], 'to fall to the ground' [CEV], 'to wilt' [NAB], 'to fade' [NJB]. This is translated as present tense by NIC, WBC and all versions, and as perfect tense by BNTC.

QUESTION—What is the function of the aorist tense of the two verbs ἐξηράνθη 'to wither' and ἐξέπεσεν 'to fall off'?

They are gnomic or timeless aorists [ICC, NTC, WBC]. This construction is used for proverbial expressions or universally observed occurrences, and is used in the LXX to translate the Hebrew perfect of the Isaiah passage, which is used the same way [WBC]. Fact is being related as a story [Alf]. It is used to express vividness [BNTC]. In intent and meaning it is present tense [BNTC, NIC, NTC, TG, TH, WBC; all versions].

**1:25** but<sup>a</sup> the word<sup>b</sup> of (the) Lord<sup>c</sup> endures<sup>d</sup> forever.<sup>e</sup>

LEXICON—a. δέ (LN 89.124): 'but' [BNTC, LN, NIC, WBC; all versions].

b. ῥῆμα (LN 33.98) (BAGD 1. p. 735): 'word' [BAGD, LN, NIC; all versions except CEV], 'message' [LN], 'utterance' [BNTC]. This is also translated as a verb phrase: 'what the Lord has said' [WBC; CEV].

c. κύριος (LN 12.9) (BAGD 2.a. p. 459): 'the Lord' [BNTC, WBC; all versions], 'our Lord' [NIC], 'lord' [BAGD, LN].

d. pres. act. indic. of μένω (LN 13.89) (BAGD 1.c.β. p. 504): 'to endure' [WBC; KJV, NAB, NRSV, REB], 'to remain' [BAGD, LN, NIC; NJB, TEV, TNT], 'to continue to exist' [LN], 'to last' [BAGD; NLT], 'to abide' [BNTC], 'to stand' [CEV, NIV]. See this word at 1:23.

e. αἰών (LN 67.95) (BAGD 1.b. p. 27): 'forever' [BNTC, LN, WBC; all versions except REB], 'for evermore' [REB], '(to) eternity' [BAGD], 'always' [LN], 'eternally' [LN, NIC].

QUESTION—What relationship is indicated by δέ 'but'?

It is contrastive [BNTC, NIC, WBC; all versions].

QUESTION—Is there any distinction between the λόγος 'word' of the previous verse and the ῥῆμα 'word' of this verse?

The ῥῆμα 'word' is an utterance [Alf, BNTC]. Ῥῆμα is a specific actual word, whether spoken or written, whereas λόγος is a message, whether spoken or written [TNTC]. Λόγος was a term that came to have a special meaning among early Christians, which was the preached message about Christ, the Gospel [NCBC].

1. In this context the two terms are used as functional synonyms with no difference of meaning intended [BNTC, NIBC, NIC, NTC, TNTC; all versions]. Both refer to the word of the gospel message, as opposed to God's creative word or his word through the prophets [NIC]. Peter's

choice of ῥῆμα here may simply be due to the fact of the quotation from the LXX which uses it [Alf].
2. The ῥῆμα refers to God's promise, whereas λόγος refers to God's promise fulfilled in Christ's incarnation and the preaching of the gospel [Sel].

QUESTION—Who is being referred to as κύριος 'Lord'?
    1. It refers to Christ [Alf, BNTC, ICC, NCBC, NIBC, NIC, NTC, WBC].
      1.1 It is an intentional shift by the author from the wording of the LXX of Isaiah 40:8, which uses 'God' instead of 'Lord'. This is done to indicate the deity of Christ [BNTC, NCBC, NIBC, NIC, NTC]. It is changed for the sake of the application that follows [Alf].
      1.2 It refers to Christ, although the shift may be unintentional because the version of the LXX that Peter quoted from may have read this way [WBC].
    2. It refers to God [TG].

**And<sup>a</sup> this is the word<sup>b</sup> that-was-preached<sup>c</sup> to you.**

LEXICON—a. δέ (LN 89.94): 'and' [LN, NIC; KJV, NIV, NJB, NLT, REB], 'now' [NAB], not explicit [BNTC, WBC; CEV, NRSV, TEV, TNT].
    b. ῥῆμα (LN 33.98) (BAGD 1. p. 735): 'word' [BAGD, LN, NIC; NIV], 'message' [LN], 'what the Lord has said' [CEV]. This word is also translated in light of the verb that follows as 'the good news' [BNTC; NJB, NLT, NRSV, TEV, TNT], 'the gospel' [NAB, REB], 'the message of the gospel' [WBC] or conflated with the verb and translated 'the word which by the gospel is preached' [KJV], 'the good news that has been brought' [NJB].
    c. aorist pass. participle of εὐαγγελίζω (LN 33.215) (BAGD 2.b.α. p. 317): 'to preach' [BAGD, BNTC, NIC; KJV, NAB, NIV, NLT, REB, TNT], 'to tell the good news, to announce the gospel' [LN], 'to announce' [NRSV], 'to proclaim' [WBC; TEV]. This verb is translated as a substantive and made the subject of the sentence: 'our good news to you' [CEV].

QUESTION—What relationship is indicated by δέ 'and'?
    It is conjoining [Alf, NIC; KJV, NAB, NIV, NJB, NLT, REB]. It connects the general truth of what was said previously to the particular that follows [Alf].

QUESTION—What is implied by εἰς ὑμᾶς 'to you'?
    1. It is equivalent to the dative ὑμῖν 'to you' [ICC].
    2. It means 'intended for you' [NCBC], or 'addressed to and distributed among' you [Alf]. It is used in the sense of 'purposed for you', as it is in 1:4 and 10, and as δι' ὑμᾶς in 1:20. Coupled with 12 other uses of this pronoun in other cases throughout this chapter, Peter is trying to build within the readers a sense of identity as the recipients of God's great gifts and their consequent responsibility [WBC].

**DISCOURSE UNIT: 2:1–10** [NIC, TNTC, WBC; CEV, NAB, NRSV, TEV]. The topic is Christian identity [NIC], how to advance in holiness [TNTC], a chosen priesthood [WBC], a living stone and a holy nation [CEV], growth in holiness [NAB], a living stone and a chosen people [NRSV], the living stone and the holy nation [TEV].

**DISCOURSE UNIT: 2:1–3** [Sel, WBC]. The topic is a call to renounce evil and persevere in the life of grace [Sel], receiving the word [WBC].

**2:1** Therefore[a] having-put-away[b] all[c] malice[d]

LEXICON—a. οὖν (LN 89.50): 'therefore' [BNTC, LN, NIC, WBC; NIV, NRSV], 'wherefore' [KJV], 'so' [NAB, NLT], 'then' [NJB, REB, TEV, TNT], not explicit [CEV].
  b. aorist mid. participle of ἀποτίθημι (LN 85.44) (BAGD 1.b. p. 101): 'to put away' [LN], 'to remove' [LN], 'to put off' [BNTC], 'to strip away' [NAB], 'to lay aside' [BAGD; KJV], 'to rid oneself of' [BAGD; NIV, NJB, NRSV, TEV, TNT], 'to get rid of' [NIC, WBC; NLT], 'away with' [REB]. This participle is translated as a series of imperatives in combination with the list of vices that follows it, 'stop being … quit trying to fool … start being … .don't be … don't say' [CEV], 'so get rid of … don't just pretend … be done with' [NLT]. It is also translated as an imperative 'rid yourselves' with the first vice and by the phrase 'no more' with all the other vices [TEV].
  c. πᾶς (LN 59.23) (BAGD 1.a.β. p. 631): 'all' [BAGD, BNTC, LN, NIC, WBC; all versions except CEV, NAB], 'every' [BAGD, LN], 'every kind of' [BAGD], 'everything' [NAB], not explicit [CEV].
  d. κακία (LN 88.199, 88.105) (BAGD 1.b. p. 397): 'malice' [BAGD, NIC, WBC; KJV, NIV, NRSV], 'ill will' [BAGD; TNT], 'hateful feeling' [LN (88.199)], 'spite' [NJB], 'malicious behavior' [NLT], '(everything) vicious' [NAB], 'wickedness' [BNTC, LN (88.105); REB], 'evil' [TEV]. The phrase 'having put away malice' is translated 'stop being hateful' [CEV].

QUESTION—What relationship is indicated by οὖν 'therefore'?
  1. It resumes the exhortations that began in 1:13 [EGT].
  2. It refers back to the section just before it (1:22–25) about how reborn people should live [NTC].
  2.1 It follows from 1:22–23 about how reborn people should put away sins, grow, and love each other [NCBC]. It refers to repentance, conversion, and regeneration in 1:22–23 as a basis for exhortation about how to live as believers [NIC]. It assumes the general cleansing referred to in 1:22–23, but goes on to outline specific vices that must be removed if they are present [WBC].
  2.2 It refers back to 1:22 and states how to go about carrying out the exhortation to love [BNTC, IVP, TH, TNTC].
  2.3 It refers back to 1:23 about how to live the new life implanted within [Alf, ICC, TG].

QUESTION—What is the function of the aorist participle ἀποθέμενοι 'having put away'?
1. The participle is used as an imperative due to dependence on the aorist imperative that follows [EGT, ICC, IVP, NCBC, NIBC, NTC, TNTC, WBC; all versions]. Fulfillment of this imperative is the basis for being able to obey the following one of longing for the pure spiritual milk [IVP, NCBC].
    1.1 It implies a continuous or on-going process of turning away from these vices [IVP, NCBC].
    1.2 It implies a once-and-for-all action of breaking with the vices of the past [NIBC].
2. It is used as a participle representing an action completed in the past [Alf, BNTC, NIC]: having already put off these vices, now do this.

QUESTION—What is meant by the metaphor ἀποθέμενοι 'having put away'?
This verb is used of removing old clothing, and in this sense it means to shed these vices as one removes old or dirty clothing [BNTC, IVP, NCBC, NIBC, NIC, NTC, TH; NAB]. This verb is also used of washing dirt from the body, so in this sense it can mean to cleanse oneself of these vices as one washes away dirt or filth [EGT, ICC, NCBC, TH, WBC].

QUESTION—What is meant by κακία 'malice'?
1. It means wickedness or evil in general [BNTC, ICC; REB, TEV]. It refers to all the wickedness of the pagan world [Sel]. It is wickedness or evil that includes ill-will and all actions that come from it [TNTC].
2. It refers to the personal trait or attitude of ill-will or malice [Alf, EGT, IVP, NIBC, NIC, NTC, TG, WBC; all versions except REB, TEV].

**and all deceit[a] and hypocrisies[b] and envies[c] and all[d] slanders,[e]**

LEXICON—a. δόλος (LN 88.154) (BAGD p. 203): 'deceit' [BAGD, BNTC, LN, NIC, WBC; NIV, NLT, REB], 'guile' [KJV, NRSV], 'lying' [TEV], 'everything deceitful' [NAB]. The phrase 'having put away all deceit' is translated 'stop trying to fool people' [CEV].
b. ὑπόκρισις (LN 88.227) (BAGD p. 845): 'hypocrisy' [BAGD, LN; NAB, NIV, NJB, NLT, REB, TEV, TNT], 'hypocrisies' [WBC; KJV], 'insincerity' [NIC], 'pretenses' [BNTC; NAB]. The phrase 'having put away hypocrisies' is translated 'start being sincere' [CEV].
c. φθόνος (LN 88.160) (BAGD p. 857): 'envies' [KJV], 'envy' [BAGD, LN, NIC; NIV, NJB], 'jealousy' [BAGD, LN; NLT, REB, TEV, TNT], 'jealousies' [BNTC, WBC; NAB]. The phrase 'having put away jealousies' is translated 'don't be jealous' [CEV].
d. πᾶς (LN 59.23) (BAGD 1.a.β. p. 631): 'all' [BAGD, BNTC, LN; KJV, NJB, NRSV, TNT], 'every' [BAGD, LN], 'of every kind' [BAGD, WBC], 'every type of' [NIC], 'of any kind' [NAB, REB], not explicit [CEV, NLT, TEV].
e. καταλαλιά (LN 33.387) (BAGD p. 412): 'slanders' [WBC], 'slander' [BAGD, LN, NIC; NIV, NRSV], 'evil speech' [BAGD], 'recriminations'

[BNTC], 'evil speakings' [KJV], 'disparaging remarks' [NAB], 'carping criticism' [NJB], 'backstabbing' [NLT], 'malicious talk' [REB], 'insulting language' [TEV], 'abusive language' [TNT].

QUESTION—How is the word πᾶς 'all' used in this verse?
1. It is all-encompassing, referring to every possible kind and allowing no exceptions [NCBC, NTC, TG].
2. Used with the first two singular nouns, it indicates the generalized nature of those vices, whereas used with the last word (a plural), it refers inclusively to slanders against all people, whether believers or non-believers [WBC].
3. Used with the second word δόλος 'guile', it indicates that guile and all the other vices named are a different class of sins which are more likely to threaten believers than the first category, the κακία 'wickedness' of the pagan world [Sel].

QUESTION—What is the reason for the use of the plural with the last three vices?
It is an idiomatic plural intended to stress the separate acts [Alf, NTC]. The use of the plural means 'every kind' or 'every expression of' [ICC, IVP]. The plural fills the same function as πᾶς 'all', to refer to every expression of the vice [WBC].

QUESTION—In what way are these five vices related?
These vices have in common the fact that all represent actions or attitudes which are in opposition to love [BNTC, ICC, IVP, NCBC, NTC, TNTC, WBC] and which destroy fellowship [NIBC, NIC, TG, TH].
1. This is a listing of separate vices [NIC, NTC].
2. Κακία 'malice' is defined by the four that follow [ICC].
3. The first two, κακία 'malice' and δόλος 'deceit', are general vices of which the last three are specific expressions [BNTC, IVP].
4. Κακία 'malice' and δόλος 'deceit' are parallel, and ὑπόκρισις 'hypocrisy' and φθόνος 'envy' are aspects of δόλος [Alf].
5. Κακία, the desire to harm another person, is described more specifically in the three words guile, hypocrisy, and envy that follow, and expresses itself in acts of καταλαλιά 'backbiting' [EGT].
6. Malice leads to jealousy which is expressed in backbiting; deceit is almost synonymous with hypocrisy [WBC].

**2:2** as[a] newborn[b] babes[c] long[d] for pure[e] spiritual[f] milk,

LEXICON—a. ὡς (LN 64.12): 'as' [LN, WBC; KJV, NAB, NLT, TNT], 'like' [LN, NIC; CEV, NIV, NJB, NRSV, REB, TEV], 'as you are' [BNTC].
b. ἀρτιγέννητος (LN **23.48**) (BAGD p. 110): 'newborn' [BAGD, BNTC, NIC, WBC; all versions except NLT], 'newly born' [LN], not explicit [NLT].
c. βρέφος (LN 9.45) (BAGD 2. p. 147): 'babe' [BNTC; KJV], 'baby' [BAGD, LN, NIC, WBC; all versions except KJV, NRSV, REB], 'infant' [BAGD, LN; NRSV, REB].

d. aorist act. impera. of ἐπιποθέω (LN 25.18) (BAGD p. 297): 'to long for' [BAGD, LN, WBC; NJB, NRSV], 'to desire' [BAGD, NIC; KJV], 'to crave' [BNTC; NIV, NLT, REB], 'to be thirsty' [CEV, TEV], 'to be eager for' [NAB, TNT]. The imperative is translated 'be like' [CEV, TEV], 'your longing should be for' [NJB], 'you must crave' [NLT], 'you should be craving' [REB], 'you should be eager' [TNT].

e. ἄδολος (LN **79.98**) (BAGD p. 18): 'pure' [**LN**, NIC, WBC; CEV, NAB, NIV, NLT, NRSV, REB, TEV, TNT], 'unadulterated' [BAGD, LN; NJB], 'sincere' [KJV], 'that is free from deceit' [BNTC].

f. λογικός (LN **73.5**) (BAGD p. 476): 'spiritual' [BAGD, NIC, WBC; all versions except KJV, NAB], 'of the spirit' [NAB], 'of the word' [BNTC; KJV], 'genuine' [LN], 'true, unadulterated' [**LN**].

QUESTION—What relationship is indicated by ὡς 'as'?

1. It is used to introduce a comparison indicating that believers should hunger for spiritual nourishment in the same manner as babies hunger for milk [NTC, TH, TNTC; CEV, NAB, NJB, NLT, TEV, TNT].
2. It is used to introduce a metaphor which is assumed as a spiritual reality. That is, like the newborn babes you are, crave spiritual nourishment [BNTC, EGT, ICC, NCBC, NTC, WBC; REB].

QUESTION—What is implied by the word ἀρτιγέννητος 'newborn'?

1. It indicates that at least some of the readers were recent converts [BNTC].
2. It is used metaphorically in that believers are always babes or children, and does not imply immaturity on their part [Alf, ICC, NCBC, NIC, Sel, TNTC], nor that the readers were recent converts [EGT, NCBC, NTC, TNTC]. It is a call to dependence on God [NIC].

QUESTION—What is the point of comparison being made by the metaphor βρέφη 'babes'?

1. The point of comparison between the believer and a baby is the craving for nourishment [BNTC, IVP, NCBC, NTC, TG, TH, TNTC, WBC; CEV, NAB, NJB, NLT, REB, TEV, TNT].
2. The point of comparison between the believer and a baby is innocence [EGT, Sel] or childlikeness [ICC].

QUESTION—What is meant by the adjective ἄδολος 'pure'?

It means that it is free from fraud or deceit [BNTC, EGT, ICC, IVP, NCBC, NTC, TNTC]. It means that it is given with no ulterior motives, only the motive of nourishment [Alf]. It means that it is trustworthy and not watered down [NIC], it is not contaminated by foreign elements that don't belong [Sel, TG]. Milk that is ἄδολος 'pure' guards against the vices, especially δόλος 'deceit' [WBC].

QUESTION—What is meant by λογικός 'spiritual'?

1. It means 'spiritual' [Alf, IVP, NIBC, NIC, NTC, TG, TNTC, WBC; all versions except KJV].

  1.1 It is used to signal a metaphor, that he is referring not to the physical realm but to the spiritual realm [Alf, BAGD, TNTC, WBC], which is the same sense in which it is used in Romans 12:1 [NCBC, TNTC]. It

means 'spiritual' and is used in anticipation of and in conjunction with πνευμάτικος 'spiritual' in 2:5 [NIC, Sel].
    1.2 It means 'spiritual' in the sense that the gospel message or the word of God provides spiritual nourishment [IVP, NIBC, NIC, NTC, TG].
  2. It means 'of the word', referring to λόγος, which is the word of God [BNTC, EGT, ICC; KJV].
QUESTION—What is the 'milk' that is being referred to?
  1. It is the life of God himself that comes through the proclaimed word [WBC]. It is Christ [EGT]. It is the Lord himself received through teaching about him [IVP, NCBC].
  2. It is the word [ICC; KJV].
    2.1 It is the gospel message [Alf, BNTC, TG], or the nourishment given by the grace of God through the gospel message [Sel]. It is the teaching about Jesus [NIC].
    2.2 It is the written word of God [NTC, TNTC]. It is nourishment given by the Scripture [NIBC].

**so-that[a] by[b] it you-may-grow[c] into[d] salvation,[e]**

TEXT—The words εἰς σωτηρίαν 'into salvation' do not occur in some manuscripts. GNT does not mention this omission. They are omitted only by KJV.

LEXICON—a. ἵνα (LN 89.59): 'so that' [BNTC, LN, NIC; NIV, NRSV, REB, TEV], 'that' [KJV], 'in order to' [LN]. This word is translated in conjunction with the following two words as 'by which to grow up' [WBC], 'that will help you grow' [CEV], 'which will help you to grow' [NJB], 'to make you grow' [NAB] 'so that you can grow' [NLT], 'on which you will thrive' [TNT].
  b. ἐν with dative (LN 90.10): 'by' [BNTC, LN, NIC, WBC; NIV, NRSV, TEV], 'thereby' [KJV], 'on' [REB, TNT], 'with' [LN], not explicit [CEV, NAB, NJB, NLT].
  c. aorist pass. subj. of αὐξάνω (LN 59.62) (BAGD 2. p. 121): 'to grow' [BAGD, LN; CEV, KJV, NAB, NLT, NRSV], 'to grow up' [BNTC, NIC, WBC; NIV, NJB, TEV], 'to thrive' [REB, TNT].
  d. εἰς with accusative (LN 90.23) (BAGD 4.e. p. 229): 'into' [BAGD; NLT, NRSV], 'to' [BNTC, NIC, WBC; NJB], 'unto' [NAB], 'in' [LN; NIV], 'concerning, with respect to' [LN], 'and come to' [TNT], not explicit [CEV, REB, TEV].
  e. σωτηρία (LN 21.15) (BAGD 2. p. 801): 'salvation' [BAGD, BNTC, LN, NIC, WBC; NAB, NJB, NRSV, TNT], 'your salvation' [NIV], 'the fullness of your salvation' [NLT]. This noun is also translated as a verb phrase: 'and be saved' [CEV, REB, TEV]. See this word at 1:5 and 1:9.

QUESTION—What relationship is indicated by ἵνα 'so that'?
  It indicates the purpose of receiving the pure spiritual milk, which is growth [Alf, BNTC, NIC, WBC; all versions].

# 1 PETER 2:2

QUESTION—What relationship is indicated by ἐν αὐτῷ 'by it'?
  It is the instrument or means by which spiritual growth occurs [BNTC, NIC, WBC; all versions].

QUESTION—What is meant by the subjunctive verb αὐξηθῆτε 'that you may grow'?
  It means to thrive spiritually [Sel; REB, TNT]. It is an ongoing process [NIBC]. It indicates progress toward the goal of complete deliverance from sin and increasing in love [IVP]. It is the natural outcome of spiritual nourishment [Alf]. It is a continuation of the metaphor of birth, nurture, and growth toward the final goal of eschatological salvation [WBC].

QUESTION—What is the function of the phrase εἰς σωτηρίαν 'into salvation'?
  It marks a switch from metaphor back to eschatology, because growth is not toward maturity but toward final salvation or deliverance [WBC].

QUESTION—What is the salvation spoken of here?
  1. It refers to spiritual maturity which is a result of the growth process [TG]. It is the development of the soul in all that God wants for believers, a process that goes on now and in the next world [NIBC].
  2. It is an eschatological salvation, the final vindication of God's people which is the 'outcome' of faith mentioned in 1:9 [WBC]. It is ultimate and final deliverance from sin and its results, along with full growth in love [IVP]. It is eschatological glory and blessedness [BNTC]. It is the reward to be received at the end when Christ is revealed [NIC]. It means ultimate Christian maturity and having all the blessings of redemption [TNTC]. It is final eschatological salvation when Jesus is revealed [NCBC]. It is rescue from destruction along with positive blessedness [Alf]. The meaning is parallel to how the same word is used in 1:5 [Alf, NTC, TNTC].

**2:3** if/since[a] you-have-tasted[b] that[c] the Lord (is) good.[d]

LEXICON—a. εἰ (LN 89.30, 89.65): 'if' [LN (89.65); NJB], 'if indeed' [NRSV], 'if so be' [KJV], 'since' [LN (89.30), NIC], 'because' [LN (89.30)], 'seeing' [BNTC], 'now that' [WBC; NAB, NIV, NLT], 'surely' [REB], not explicit [CEV, TEV, TNT].

  b. aorist mid. indic. of γεύομαι (LN 90.78) (BAGD 2. p. 157): 'to taste' [BNTC, NIC, WBC; KJV, NAB, NIV, NJB, NRSV, REB], 'to have a taste' [NLT], 'to experience' [LN], 'to come to know something' [BAGD], 'to find out' [CEV], 'to find out for yourselves' [TEV], 'to find by experience' [TNT].

  c. ὅτι (LN 90.21): 'that' [BNTC, LN, WBC; all versions except CEV, NLT, TEV], 'the fact that' [LN], 'how (kind)' [CEV, TEV], not explicit [NIC; NLT].

  d. χρηστός (LN 88.68) (BAGD 1.b.β. p. 886): 'good' [BNTC, WBC; CEV, NAB, NIV, NJB, NRSV, REB], 'kind' [BAGD, LN], 'gracious' [LN; KJV], 'loving' [BAGD], 'kind' [TEV, TNT], 'benevolent' [BAGD]. This adjective is also translated as a noun: 'kindness' [NLT].

QUESTION—What relationship is indicated by εἰ 'if/since'?
It introduces a presupposition as an assumed fact. That is, since you have, in fact, tasted that the Lord is good, then do this [Alf, BNTC, IVP, NIBC, NIC, NTC, Sel, TH, TNTC, WBC; all versions except KJV, NJB, NRSV].

QUESTION—What is meant by ἐγεύσασθε 'you have tasted'?
1. It means to learn by experience [IVP, NTC, TG, TH, WBC], and the initial experience is motivation to continue to take needed spiritual nourishment [Alf, NTC]. It is having experienced the Lord Himself [NCBC]. It means to come to know by experience, especially through Scripture [TNTC]. It refers to the initial step of adherence to Christ [Sel].
2. It means to experience the Lord, particularly in the Eucharist [BNTC, NIC].

QUESTION—What relationship is indicated by ὅτι 'that'?
It marks indirect discourse 'that the Lord is good' which is a quote from Psalm 34:8 [Alf, WBC]. The fact that this is a scriptural quote is made explicit by the words 'as Scripture says' [TEV, TNT].

QUESTION—What is meant by χρηστός 'good'?
1. It means 'kind' or 'good' in a general sense [IVP, TG, TNTC]. It refers to the goodness of redemption [NIC]. It means to be kind or gracious [NTC, WBC]. It refers to an easy and gentle relationship in the tenderness of the love of God [NIBC].
2. It means 'good' in the sense of things tasted, in keeping with the figure of speech [Alf, BNTC, ICC, Sel, TH]. It is a pun or play on words, since χρηστός would be pronounced almost identically with Χριστός 'Christ' [EGT, NIBC, TH, WBC].

QUESTION—Who is the Lord in this passage?
It is Jesus Christ [Alf, BNTC, ICC, IVP, NIC, NTC, Sel, TG, TH, TNTC, WBC].

**DISCOURSE UNIT: 2:4–12** [NIV, NLT]. The topic is the living stone and a chosen people [NIV], living stones for God's house [NLT].

**DISCOURSE UNIT: 2:4–10** [IVP, NTC, Sel, TH; NJB]. The topic is the spiritual house and the chosen people [IVP], the second doctrinal section [Sel], election [NTC], the Christian community as the new people of God [TH], the new priesthood [NJB].

**DISCOURSE UNIT: 2:4–5** [Sel, WBC]. The topic is the church as God's true temple [Sel], coming to Christ in worship [WBC].

**2:4** To whom coming[a] a living[b] stone[c] by[d] men having-been-rejected[e]
LEXICON—a. pres. mid. participle of προσέρχομαι (LN 15.77) (BAGD 2.a. p. 713): 'to come to' [BNTC, LN, NIC, WBC; all versions except NJB], 'to approach' [BAGD, LN], 'to set oneself close to' [NJB].
b. pres. act. participle of ζάω (LN 23.88) (BAGD 4.b. p. 337): 'to live' [BAGD, BNTC, LN, NIC, WBC; all versions]. See this word at 1:3 and 1:23.

   c. λίθος (LN 2.24) (BAGD 2. p. 474): 'stone' [BAGD, BNTC, LN, NIC, WBC; all versions except NLT], 'cornerstone of God's temple' [NLT].
   d. ὑπό (LN 90.1): 'by' [BNTC, LN, NIC, WBC; all versions except CEV, KJV], 'of' [KJV], not explicit [CEV].
   e. perf. pass. participle of ἀποδοκιμάζω (LN 30.117) (BAGD 1. p. 90): 'rejected' [BAGD, BNTC, LN, NIC, WBC; all versions except KJV], 'rejected as worthless' [TEV], 'disallowed' [KJV], 'declared useless, regarded as unworthy' [BAGD].

QUESTION—What relationship is indicated by the use of the present participle προσερχόμενοι 'coming'?

   Whether or not this present participle will be taken as imperatival in force or as a statement of fact will depend in part on whether the main verb in 2:5, οἰκοδομέω 'to be built up', is taken as an imperative or as indicative.
   1. It is participial in force, stating a fact [Alf, BNTC, ICC, NCBC, NIC, NTC, Sel, TNTC, WBC; KJV, NIV]: as you come to a living stone, you are built up.
   2. It is imperatival in force [TG, TH; CEV, NAB, NJB, NLT, NRSV, REB, TEV, TNT]: come to a living stone.

QUESTION—What is the 'coming' referred to?

   1. It refers to new believers coming to Christ through the spread of the gospel and the growth of the church in Asia Minor [WBC]. It refers to conversion [NIC, Sel].
   2. It refers to approaching for worship or priestly service [NCBC, NIBC, NTC, TH]. It refers to approaching the Lord by faith for communion with him [Alf]. 'Coming to him' is an ongoing process [Alf, NTC, TNTC, WBC].
   3. It refers to conversion as well as to coming to him continually for worship [TNTC]. It refers to the readers as being recent converts now approaching for worship or priestly service [NIBC].

QUESTION—What is meant by the metaphor λίθος 'stone'?

   A λίθος 'stone' is a stone that is cut or dressed for building purposes [IVP, NCBC, Sel, TH] or a precious stone [Sel]. The imagery of the stone was used by Christ of Himself and comes from three OT passages: the rejected cornerstone of Psalm 118:22, the cornerstone of confidence of Isaiah 28:16, and the stumbling stone of Isaiah 8:14 [WBC]. The stone is a reminder of God's judgment as well as the foundation for the faith of believers [NTC].

QUESTION—What is meant by the participle ζῶντα 'living' used attributively with λίθος 'stone'?

   It signals a metaphorical use of 'stone' [Alf, ICC, NCBC, Sel, TNTC, WBC]. 'Living' means 'spiritual' as opposed to material or literal [Sel]. It means that which is spiritual, divine, eternal [ICC]. It is used to contrast the superiority of Christ to the old covenant with its temple of nonliving stones [TNTC]. It signals a contrast between the church and a pagan temple of nonliving material serving a nonliving religion [Sel]. It is used by Peter to contrast the emptiness of pagan religion and its lifeless idols with the living hope, the living God, and the living stone of the Christian faith [WBC]. 'Living' means that Christ is not only risen and alive, but is also the life-giver [BNTC, NCBC, Sel, TH].

QUESTION—Who are the 'men' spoken of in this passage?

They are unbelieving people [NTC], people in general [TNTC, WBC], the Jews who rejected Christ and all who reject the gospel [NCBC], most people outside the church [IVP], pagan enemies of Jews and Christians alike in pagan society [WBC].

**but[a] with[b] God chosen,[c] precious,[d]**

LEXICON—a. δέ (LN 89.136): 'but' [BNTC, LN, NIC, WBC; all versions except NRSV], 'yet' [NRSV], 'on the other hand' [LN]. This enclitic conjunction is part of the μὲν... δέ construction indicating contrastive elements. Μέν is untranslatable but the contrast of μὲν... δέ is represented by such constructions as 'indeed... but' [BNTC, NIC; KJV, TNT], 'but... nonetheless' [NAB], or 'though... yet' [NRSV]. See this construction at 1:20.

b. παρά (LN 90.20) (BAGD II.2.b. p. 610): 'with' [LN], 'in the sight of' [BAGD], 'in God's sight' [BNTC, WBC; NRSV, TNT], 'in God's eyes' [NIC; NAB], 'to' [NLT], '(chosen) by' [NIV, NJB, REB, TEV], '(chosen) of' [KJV], not explicit [CEV]. CEV takes 'God' as the subject of a verb phrase and the following two adjectives as verbs: 'God has chosen and highly honored'.

c. ἐκλεκτός (LN 30.93) (BAGD 2. p. 242): 'chosen' [BNTC, LN; CEV, KJV, NIV, NJB, NRSV, REB, TEV], 'choice' [BAGD, WBC; TNT], 'select' [NIC], 'approved' [NAB], 'to chose' [NLT]. See this word at 1:1.

d. ἔντιμος (LN **65.2**) (BAGD 2. p. 269): 'precious' [BAGD, LN, NIC, WBC; KJV, NAB, NIV, NJB, NLT, NRSV], 'valuable' [BAGD, **LN**; TEV, TNT], 'honored' [BNTC], 'highly honored' [CEV], 'of great worth' [REB].

QUESTION—What relationship is indicated by μὲν... δέ '... but'?

Prominence is given to the second of the two elements in the 'rejected by men/chosen by God' contrast [NIBC, NTC, WBC]. Believers can be encouraged by the fact that God has the last word in such concerns [NIBC].

**2:5 yourselves also[a] as[b] living stones are-being-built-up[c]**

LEXICON—a. καί (LN 89.93): 'and, and also' [LN]. Καὶ αὐτοί 'yourselves also' is translated 'you yourselves' [BNTC, WBC], 'you also yourselves' [NIC], 'ye also' [KJV], 'you too' [NAB, NJB], 'you also' [NIV, REB], 'and now... you' [CEV, NLT], 'yourselves' [NRSV, TEV], not explicit [TNT].

b. ὡς (LN 64.12): 'as' [BNTC, LN; KJV, NAB, NLT, REB, TEV, TNT], 'like' [LN, NIC, WBC; NIV, NRSV], not explicit [CEV, NJB].

c. pres. pass. indic. of οἰκοδομέω (LN 45.1) (BAGD 2. p. 558): 'to be built up' [BAGD, BNTC; KJV], 'to be built into' [NIC, WBC; NIV, NLT], 'to be used to build' [CEV], 'to be built' [LN; NAB]. Because the passive indicative and passive imperative forms are the same, this verb is also translated as a passive imperative: 'let yourselves be built' [NRSV], 'you must be built up' [REB], 'let yourselves be used in building' [TEV], 'be built up' [TNT]. The imperative is also made implicit in a verb phrase of purpose 'so that you may be living stones' [NJB].

QUESTION—Should the verb οἰκοδομεῖσθε 'to be built up' be taken as a passive indicative or as a passive imperative?

    1. It is indicative [BNTC, EGT, IVP, NCBC, NIBC, NIC, NTC, Sel, TNTC, WBC; CEV, KJV, NAB, NIV, NLT]: you are being built up.

    2. It is imperative [Alf, ICC; NJB, NRSV, REB, TEV, TNT]: let yourselves be built up.

QUESTION—What is meant by the metaphor λίθοι ζῶντες 'living stones'?

It indicates that the believers as living stones derive their life from Christ the living stone [Alf, NCBC, NTC, Sel]; they share the nature of Christ [TH]; they share Christ's triumph over death and disaster [BNTC]. It means they have become precious to God also, as Christ is [TNTC]. It indicates a likeness to Christ [IVP, NIBC], being chosen by God [IVP] and having a unique place in the divine master-plan [NIBC].

## a spiritual[a] house[b] for[c] a holy priesthood[d]

TEXT—The word εἰς 'for' does not occur in some manuscripts. Its omission is not mentioned in GNT. It is omitted only by KJV.

LEXICON—a. πνευματικός (LN 79.3) (BAGD 2.a.β. p. 679): 'spiritual' [BAGD, BNTC, LN, NIC, WBC; all versions except NAB], 'of spirit' [NAB].

    b. οἶκος (LN 7.2) (BAGD 1.b.α. p. 560): 'house' [BAGD, BNTC, LN, NIC, WBC; CEV, KJV, NIV, NJB, NRSV, TNT], 'temple' [LN; NLT, REB, TEV], 'edifice' [NAB].

    c. εἰς with accusative (LN 89.57): 'for' [WBC], 'for the purpose of' [LN], 'in order to' [LN], 'so as to form' [BNTC], 'to be' [NIC; NIV, NRSV], 'as' [NJB], 'into' [NAB, NLT, TNT], 'to form' [REB], not explicit [CEV, KJV, TEV].

    d. ἱεράτευμα (LN **53.86**) (BAGD p. 371): 'priesthood' [BAGD, BNTC, LN, NIC, WBC; all versions except CEV, NLT, TEV], 'priests' [CEV, NLT, TEV].

QUESTION—What relationship is indicated by οἶκος πνευματικός 'a spiritual house'?

It is a predicate nominative [WBC]. It can be either a predicate nominative or the subject of the following clause, but grammatically cannot be the object of οἰκοδομεῖσθε 'being built up' [NCBC].

QUESTION—What is meant by the term οἶκος πνευματικός 'a spiritual house'?

Οἶκος could be either 'household/family' or 'house/temple'. Taken either way, it shifts the focus from the individual 'stones' to the corporate 'house' [BNTC, ICC, NTC, WBC].

1. It describes believers as a house of God, or temple [EGT, IVP, NCBC, NIBC, NIC, TG, TH, TNTC], as a place of God's presence [IVP] and for the offering of spiritual worship [BNTC, IVP, WBC]. It is 'spiritual' in contrast to a material temple [Alf, BNTC, NIBC, NIC]. It is 'spiritual' in that it is built, influenced or indwelt by the holy spirit [Alf, NCBC, NIC, TH, TNTC].
2. It describes believers as a household of God, a community of priests [NTC].

QUESTION—What relationship is indicated by εἰς 'for'?

Εἰς indicates the priestly purpose or function of the spiritual house [BNTC, NIC, WBC; NAB, NIV, NJB, NRSV, REB, TEV, TNT]. It transitions to the infinitive of purpose that follows [Sel].

QUESTION—What is meant by the term 'holy priesthood'?

It defines the vocation of the church [Sel, TH] or the function of the church [WBC]. The priesthood is holy by virtue of its consecration to God [BNTC, NIC]. It is holy by contrast with idolatrous and immoral pagan priests [Sel].

**to offer[a] spiritual[b] sacrifices[c] acceptable[d] to God through[e] Jesus Christ.**

LEXICON—a. aorist act. infin. of ἀναφέρω (LN 53.17) (BAGD 2. p. 63): 'to offer' [BNTC, LN, NIC; all versions except KJV], 'to offer up' [BAGD, LN, WBC; KJV].

b. πνευματικός (LN 79.3) (BAGD 2.a.β p. 679): 'spiritual' [BAGD, BNTC, LN, NIC, WBC; all versions except CEV], not explicit [CEV].

c. θυσία (LN 53.20) (BAGD 2.b. p. 366): 'sacrifice' [BAGD, BNTC, LN, NIC, WBC; all versions].

d. εὐπρόσδεκτος (LN 25.86) (BAGD 1. p. 324): 'acceptable' [BAGD, BNTC, NIC, WBC; all versions except CEV, NLT], 'very acceptable' [LN], 'quite pleasing' [LN], 'that please' [CEV, NLT].

e. διά with genitive object (LN 90.4): 'through' [BNTC, LN, NIC, WBC; all versions except KJV, NLT], 'by' [LN; KJV], 'because of' [NLT].

QUESTION—What is meant by πνευματικός 'spiritual'?

It indicates a contrast with material sacrifices [BNTC, NCBC, NIC, Sel, TH, WBC]. It means inspired, influenced, or empowered by the Holy Spirit [BNTC, NIC, TH, TNTC].

QUESTION—What are the 'spiritual sacrifices'?

Spiritual sacrifices are such things as worship [NTC, TG, TH, TNTC, WBC], praise [ICC, IVP, NIBC, NIC], service or good deeds [NIC, TH, TNTC, WBC], the offering of oneself [IVP, NIBC, TNTC], social conduct [IVP, TH, WBC], and even material sacrifice such as giving [ICC, NIBC, NIC, TH, TNTC]. The idea of 'spiritual sacrifice' probably included the Eucharist [BNTC], or the worship associated with the Eucharist [NIC].

QUESTION—What does 'through Jesus Christ' refer to?

1. It refers to the offering of the spiritual sacrifices. They are offered through Jesus Christ [Alf, EGT, IVP, NIBC, NTC, TG, TNTC; TEV].

2. It refers to the acceptability of the sacrifices. That is, they are acceptable through Jesus Christ [ICC, NIC, Sel; KJV, NJB, NLT].
3. It refers to both, that is, the offering and the acceptability are through Jesus Christ [BNTC, WBC].

**DISCOURSE UNIT: 2:6–8** [Sel, WBC]. The topic is the church's relation to Christ [Sel], argument from Scripture [WBC].

**2:6** For[a] it-stands[b] in Scripture,[c]

LEXICON—a. διότι (LN 89.26): 'for' [BNTC, NIC, WBC; NAB, NIV, NRSV, REB, TEV, TNT], 'wherefore' [KJV], 'as' [NJB, NLT], 'because of, on account of' [LN], 'not explicit' [CEV]. See this word at 1:16 and 1:24.
   b. pres. act. indic. of περιέχω (LN 90.27) (BAGD 2.b. p. 647): 'to stand' [BAGD, NIC; NRSV], 'to have' [LN; NAB], 'to contain' [BAGD, LN], 'to be contained' [KJV], 'to be set down' [BNTC], 'to say' [WBC; NIV, NJB, TEV, TNT], 'to express' [NLT], 'to find' [REB].
   c. γραφή (LN 33.53) (BAGD 2.b.β. p. 166): 'scripture' [BAGD, BNTC, LN, NIC; all versions except CEV, NLT], 'scriptures' [CEV, NLT], 'writing' [WBC].

QUESTION—What relationship is indicated by διότι 'for'?
   It indicates the grounds for previous statements by quoting Scripture [Alf, ICC, IVP, NIBC, NIC, TH, TNTC]. It gives grounds for both previous statements and for those ideas which follow [BNTC, NCBC]. It is a formula to introduce a quotation of Scripture as in 1:16 and 1:24 [WBC].

**See[a] I-place[b] in Zion a stone, a cornerstone[c] chosen,[d] precious,[e]**

LEXICON—a. ἰδού (LN 91.13): 'see' [BNTC; NAB, NIV, NRSV, TNT], 'behold' [NIC, WBC; KJV], 'look' [LN; CEV], 'listen' [LN], 'now' [NJB], not explicit [NLT, REB, TEV].
   b. pres. act. indic. of τίθημι (LN 85.32) (BAGD I.1.a.α. p. 815): 'to place' [BAGD, LN; CEV, NLT, TEV, TNT], 'to put' [BAGD, LN], 'to lay' [BAGD, NIC, WBC; KJV, NAB, NIV, NJB, NRSV, REB], 'to appoint' [BNTC].
   c. ἀκρογωνιαῖος (LN 7.44) (BAGD p. 33): 'cornerstone' [BAGD, BNTC, LN, NIC, WBC; all versions].
   d. ἐκλεκτός (LN 30.93) (BAGD 2. p. 242): 'chosen' [BAGD; NIV, NJB, NLT, NRSV, REB], 'choice' [BAGD, BNTC, WBC; CEV, TNT], 'select' [NIC], 'elect' [KJV], 'approved' [NAB]. This adjective is also translated as a verb: 'to choose' [TEV]. See this word at 1:1 and 2:4.
   e. ἔντιμος (LN 65.2) (BAGD 2. p. 269): 'valuable' [BAGD], 'precious' [BAGD, NIC, WBC; CEV, KJV, NAB, NIV, NJB, NRSV], 'honored' [BNTC], 'of great worth' [REB], 'of great value' [TNT], 'valuable' [TEV], not explicit [NLT]. See this word at 2:4.

QUESTION—What is meant by 'Zion'?

It is Jerusalem [TG]. Zion is a synonym for Jerusalem or may refer to its inhabitants, and by extension, in this passage, to the church as the new place of God's presence, his new spiritual temple [NCBC, TH, TNTC].

QUESTION—What is the function of the ἀκρογωνιαῖος 'cornerstone'?

This stone is the visible stone at the corner that governs the design of the structure [Sel]. It hold the structure together and controls the design of the building, and in this passage signifies that believers have unity and interrelationship through the Lord [NIBC]. It is the corner that binds the two wings of the church together [EGT]. It is the great stone at the corner [NCBC]; it is the first stone laid as the corner of the foundation [TNTC]. It anchors the corner of the building [IVP]. It is the foundation stone on which the rest of the structure is built [NIC]. It could be either the cornerstone or the foundation stone [TG, WBC].

QUESTION—Who is the cornerstone?

The cornerstone is Christ [IVP, NTC, Sel, TG, TH, TNTC, WBC]. The cornerstone is either Jehovah or the messiah king [ICC].

**and the one believing[a] in[b] him/it never[c] shall-be-put-to-shame.[d]**

LEXICON—a. pres. act. participle of πιστεύω (LN **31.85**) (BAGD 2.a.γ. p. 661): 'to believe in' [BAGD, **LN**, WBC; KJV, NLT, NRSV, TEV, TNT], 'to trust' [BAGD, LN, NIC; NIV], 'to have faith in' [BNTC, LN; CEV, REB], 'to put faith in' [NAB], 'to rely on' [NJB].

b. ἐπί with the dative (BAGD II.1.b.γ. p. 287): 'in' [BAGD, BNTC, NIC, WBC; all versions except KJV, NJB], 'on' [BAGD; KJV, NJB].

c. οὐ μή with subjunctive (LN 69.5) (BAGD D.1.a. p. 517): 'never' [BAGD, NIC, WBC; NIV, NLT, TEV], 'by no means' [LN], 'certainly not' [BAGD, LN], 'not' [BNTC; KJV, NAB, NRSV, REB, TNT]. The negative is also expressed by negating the subject: 'no one (will be)' [CEV, NJB]. This double negative indicates an emphatic negation [LN].

d. aorist pass. subj. καταισχύνω (LN 25.194) (BAGD 3.b. p. 411): 'to be put to shame' [BAGD, BNTC, LN, NIC, WBC; NIV, NRSV, REB, TNT], 'to be disappointed' [BAGD; CEV, NLT, TEV], 'to be humiliated' [LN], 'to be brought to disgrace' [NJB], 'to be confounded' [KJV], 'to be shaken' [NAB].

QUESTION—Is αὐτῷ 'him/it' masculine or neuter?

1. It is the dative of the masculine pronoun αὐτός 'him' [NIC, TH, TNTC, WBC; CEV, KJV, NIV, NLT, NRSV, TEV, TNT]: whoever believes in him shall not be ashamed.
2. It is the dative of the neuter pronoun αὐτό 'it' [BNTC; NAB, NJB, REB]: whoever relies on it shall not be ashamed.

**2:7** Therefore[a] the honor[b] (is) to-you the-believing-ones,[c]

LEXICON—a. οὖν (LN 89.50) (BAGD 1.a. p. 593): 'therefore' [BAGD, BNTC, LN, NIC; KJV], 'now' [NIV], 'then' [LN; NRSV], 'so' [LN; REB], 'yes' [NLT], not explicit [WBC; CEV, NAB, NJB, TEV, TNT].

b. τιμή (LN 87.4) (BAGD 2.b. p. 817): 'honor' [BAGD, BNTC, LN, WBC; NJB]. This is also translated as an adjective describing the stone: 'precious' [NIC; CEV, KJV, NIV, NLT, NRSV], 'of value' [NAB], 'of great value' [TEV, TNT], 'to have great worth' [REB]. See this word at 1:7.

c. pres. act. participle of πιστεύω (LN 31.102) (BAGD 2.b. p. 661): 'to believe' [WBC; KJV, NIV, NLT, NRSV, TEV, TNT], 'to be a believer' [LN; NJB], 'to believe in' [BAGD], 'to have faith' [BNTC; NAB, REB], 'to trust' [BAGD, NIC], 'to be a follower of the Lord' [CEV].

QUESTION—What relationship is indicated by οὖν 'therefore'?

1. It links the conclusion in this sentence with the quote that immediately precedes it. Since those who believe will not be ashamed, therefore they will have honor [Alf, Sel, TNTC, WBC].
2. It expresses a logical conclusion in this sentence about the fact that God has appointed a precious stone, and those who believe will not be disappointed, so therefore those who believe find him to be precious [NIC; KJV].
3. It expresses emphasis regarding the preciousness of the stone to those who believe [NIV, NLT, NRSV, REB, TNT].

QUESTION—Is τιμή to be taken as a nominative 'honor' or as a predicate adjective 'precious' describing Christ the cornerstone?

1. It is an adjective, 'precious'. That is, Christ the cornerstone is precious to you who believe, but not to those who don't believe [NIC; CEV, KJV, NAB, NIV, NLT, NRSV, REB, TEV, TNT]. In this view τιμή would be seen as having the meaning of 'precious value' or 'preciousness' derived from the use of the adjective ἔντιμος 'precious' which describes the stone in the previous verse. The tradition of translating τιμή as 'precious' stems from Luther, Calvin, Bengal and Erasmus [Alf, ICC], and because of their influence has come into most English translations through Tyndale [ICC].
2. It is a nominative, 'honor'. That is, honor goes to you who believe, but not to those who don't believe [Alf, BAGD, BNTC, EGT, ICC, IVP, NIBC, NTC, Sel, TNTC, WBC; NJB].
   2.1 Τιμή is part of an explanatory note on the Scripture passage just quoted, with τιμή 'honor' stating in positive terms what 'shall not be ashamed' expresses negatively. Since those who believe will not be ashamed, therefore honor will be to those who believe [Alf, BNTC, EGT, ICC, IVP, Sel, TNTC, WBC].
   2.2 Τιμή 'honor' draws upon ἔντιμον 'precious' or 'honored' above, since the honor that God bestows on Christ the cornerstone is also bestowed upon those who honor Christ [Alf, BNTC, EGT, ICC, IVP, NTC, TNTC].

2.3 Τιμή is contrastive with the dishonor given to unbelievers as discussed in the following verses [Alf, ICC, NIBC].

QUESTION—What would be the τιμή 'honor' granted to the believers?
It is the privileges enumerated in 2:9 [WBC]. It is the honor granted by God to Christ and which is imparted to Christians through their relation to him [EGT, IVP, NTC, Sel]. It is their privileged status now [BNTC] and their hope of final vindication on the last day [BNTC, IVP]. It is the honor of being bought by the blood of Christ and being members and heirs in God's family [NIBC]. It is the fact that God honors believers and brings shame and dishonor to unbelievers [TNTC]. It is honor by union with the stone and the fact that they will not be ashamed [Alf].

**but[a] to-the-unbelieving-ones[b] the stone which the ones-building rejected,[c]**
LEXICON—a. δέ (LN 89.124): 'but' [BNTC, LN, NIC, WBC; all versions except NAB], 'rather' [NAB], 'on the other hand' [LN].
  b. pres. act. participle of ἀπιστέω (LN **31.105**) (BAGD 1.b. p. 85): 'not believing, to not be a believer' [LN], 'to disbelieve' [BAGD], 'unbelievers' [**LN**, WBC; NJB], 'those who do not believe' [NIV, NRSV, TEV, TNT], 'those who lack faith' [BNTC], 'those without faith' [NAB], 'those who have no faith' [REB], 'those who do not commit themselves' [NIC], 'those who refuse to follow him' [CEV], 'them which be disobedient' [KJV], 'those who reject him' [NLT].
  c. aorist act. indic. of ἀποδοκιμάζω (LN 30.117) (BAGD 1. p. 90): 'to reject' [BAGD, BNTC, LN, NIC, WBC; NAB, NIV, NJB, NLT, NRSV, REB, TNT], 'to reject as worthless' [TEV], 'to declare useless' [BAGD], 'to toss aside' [CEV], 'to disallow' [KJV].

QUESTION—What relationship is indicated by δέ 'but'?
It is contrastive [BNTC, NIC, WBC; all versions].

**this-one became[a] (the) head[b] of-(the)-corner**
LEXICON—a. aorist pass. (deponent = act.) indic. of γίνομαι (LN 13.48) (BAGD I.4.1. p. 159): 'to become' [BAGD, LN, NIC, WBC; NAB, NIV, NJB, NLT, NRSV, REB, TNT], 'to be made' [BNTC; KJV], 'to turn out to be' [CEV, TEV]. This aorist is translated by the perfect tense: 'has been made' [BNTC], 'has become' [NIC, WBC; NIV, NLT, NRSV, REB, TNT].
  b. κεφαλή (LN 7.44) (BAGD 2.b. p. 430): 'head' [BAGD, BNTC; KJV, NRSV], 'foundation' [WBC]. The phrase κεφαλὴν γωνίας 'head of the corner' is translated 'cornerstone' [BAGD, LN, NIC; NAB, NJB, NLT, REB, TNT], 'the capstone' [NIV], 'the most important stone' [**LN**], 'the most important stone of all' [CEV, TEV].

**2:8 and a stone for-stumbling-over[a] and a rock[b] for-falling-over;[c]**
LEXICON—a. πρόσκομμα (LN 15.229) (BAGD 1.a. p. 716): 'stumbling' [BAGD, WBC; KJV, NJB], 'stumbling stone' [LN], 'obstacle' [NAB]. This noun is also expressed in a verb phrase 'they stumbled' [CEV], 'to

trip men up' [BNTC], 'that makes people stumble' [NIC; NLT], 'that causes men to stumble' [NIV], 'that makes them stumble' [NRSV], 'to make men stumble' [TNT], 'that will make people stumble' [TEV], 'to trip over' [REB].
  b. πέτρα (LN 2.21) (BAGD 2. p. 654): 'rock' [BAGD, BNTC, LN, NIC, WBC; all versions except CEV, NAB], not explicit [CEV, NAB].
  c. σκάνδαλον (LN 6.25) (BAGD 2. p. 753): 'trap' [BAGD, LN], 'that makes them fall' [NIC; NIV, NRSV], 'that will make them fall' [NLT, TEV], 'to trip over' [WBC], 'to trip people up' [NJB], 'to trip them up' [TNT], 'to stumble over' [BNTC], 'to stumble against' [REB], 'stumbling' [NAB], 'of offense' [KJV]. This noun is also expressed in a verb phrase: 'they fell' [CEV].
QUESTION—What relationship is indicated by the first καί 'and'?
  It introduces the rest of this line as another OT quote separate and distinct from what immediately preceded it [Alf, BNTC, ICC, NTC, TG, TH, TNTC; all versions except CEV, KJV, NJB].
QUESTION—What distinction is there between 'rock' and 'stone'?
  The πέτρα 'rock' is like that out of which a tomb is hewn [BAGD]. It is bedrock or rocky crags as opposed to λίθος 'stone', which would be a smaller piece [LN, TH].

**they stumble[a] disobeying/disbelieving[b] the word, to which they also were-appointed.[c]**
  LEXICON—a. pres. act. indic. of προσκόπτω (LN 15.228, 25.182) (BAGD 2.a. p. 716): 'stumble' [LN (15.228), NIC, WBC; all versions except REB], 'to trip up' [BNTC], 'to trip' [REB], 'take offense at' [BAGD, LN (25.182)].
  b. pres. act. participle of ἀπειθέω (LN 36.23, 31.107) (BAGD 1., 3. p. 82): 'to disobey' [BAGD, BNTC, LN (36.23), WBC; CEV, KJV, NIV, NLT, NRSV, TNT], 'to disbelieve' [BAGD, NIC; NAB, NJB, TEV] 'to refuse to believe' [LN (31.107); REB], 'to reject the Christian message' [LN (31.107)].
  c. aorist pass. indic. of τίθημι (LN 37.96) (BAGD I.2.b. p. 816): 'to appoint' [BAGD, BNTC, LN, WBC; KJV], 'to destine' [BAGD, NIC; NIV, NRSV], 'to belong to one's destiny' [NAB], 'to be the fate for someone' [NJB], 'to be the fate appointed for someone' [REB], 'to meet the fate planned for one' [NLT], 'to be God's will for someone' [TEV], 'to be the appointed lot for someone' [TNT], 'to doom' [CEV]. See this word at 2:6.
QUESTION—What is meant by προσκόπτουσιν 'stumble'?
  1. It is taking offense at the gospel and rejecting it [TNTC] or rejecting Christ [Sel].
  2. It is the ruin, disaster, and judgment that come as a consequence of rejecting the message [Alf, BNTC, ICC, IVP, NIBC, NTC, TNTC, WBC].
QUESTION—What is meant by ἀπειθοῦντες 'disobeying'?

1. It means disobedience [Alf, BNTC, EGT, ICC, IVP, NTC, TH, WBC; CEV, KJV, NIV, NLT, NRSV, TNT]. It is to rebel [NIBC, TNTC], to reject the message [IVP], to refuse belief [Sel; REB].
2. It means disbelief [NIC; NAB, NJB, TEV].

QUESTION—What is meant by τῷ λόγῳ 'the word'?
1. It is the gospel message [BNTC, IVP, NIBC, NIC, Sel, TG, TH, TNTC, WBC].
2. It is the Word of God [NTC].
3. It is the word of prophecy that makes Christ the cornerstone [ICC].

QUESTION—Which verb takes τῷ λόγῳ 'the word' as its object?
1. It is the object of 'stumble' [EGT, IVP; KJV]: they stumble at the word.
2. It is the object of 'disobey' [Alf, BNTC, NIBC, NIC, NTC, TNTC, WBC; CEV, NAB, NIV, NJB, NLT, NRSV, REB, TEV, TNT]: they disobey the word.
3. It is the object of both verbs [EGT, ICC, Sel]: they stumble at the word, being disobedient to it.

QUESTION—To what were they appointed?
1. They were appointed to stumbling as a consequence of disobedience [BNTC, IVP, NCBC, NIBC, NIC, NTC, WBC; NJB, NLT, REB].
2. They were appointed both to unbelief and to stumbling [Alf, EGT, Sel, TNTC].

QUESTION—Who is the agent of the passive verb ἐτέθησαν 'appointed'?
God is the agent of the verb [Alf, BNTC, EGT, ICC, NCBC, NIBC, NIC, NTC, Sel, TH, TNTC, WBC; TEV]. The use of the passive is a typical Jewish practice in order to avoid mention of the sacred name of God [NCBC, NTC]. There is a correlation between the use of the verb τίθημι 'appoint' in this verse and its use in 2:6 where the stone is 'placed' or 'appointed' to its role, God being the one who appoints both the stone and the stumbling that it provokes [EGT, Sel, TNTC, WBC].

**DISCOURSE UNIT: 2:9–10** [Sel, WBC]. The topic is the church as the new Israel [Sel], an identity affirmed [WBC].

**2:9 But[a] you (are) a chosen[b] race,[c] a royal[d] priesthood,[e]**

LEXICON—a. δέ (LN 89.124): 'but' [LN, NIC; all versions except NAB, NLT], 'however' [BNTC, WBC; NAB], 'on the other hand' [LN]. The phrase 'but you' is translated 'but you are not like that' [NLT].
  b. ἐκλεκτός (LN **30.93**) (BAGD 1.b. p. 242): 'chosen' [BAGD, BNTC, LN, NIC, WBC; all versions].
  c. γένος (LN 10.1) (BAGD 3. p. 156): 'race' [BNTC, LN, WBC; NAB, NJB, NRSV, REB, TEV, TNT], 'people' [BAGD, NIC; CEV, NIV, NLT], 'generation' [KJV], 'nation' [BAGD, LN].
  d. βασίλειος (LN **37.69**) (BAGD p. 136): 'royal' [BAGD, **LN**, NIC; all versions except NJB, NLT, TEV], 'kingly' [LN]. This word is also translated as a noun: 'the king's (priests)' [WBC; TEV], 'a royal house' [BNTC], 'a kingdom' [NJB, NLT].

e. ἱεράτευμα (LN 53.86) (BAGD p. 371): 'priesthood' [BAGD, BNTC, LN, NIC, WBC; all versions except CEV, NJB, NLT], 'a group of priests' [CEV], 'priests' [NJB, NLT]. See this word at 2:5.

QUESTION—What relationship is indicated by ὑμεῖς δέ 'but you'?

The adversative δέ indicates contrast between believers and unbelievers [BNTC, NCBC, NIC, TG, TNTC, WBC; all versions]. Ὑμεῖς δέ makes the contrast emphatic [Alf, BNTC, NIC, NTC]. It contrasts the lot of unbelievers with the prospects of believers [NIBC]. It contrasts the readers with unbelievers in terms originally assigned to Israel [IVP]. It introduces the statuses or titles of honor to the church that explain what is the 'honor' to the believers mentioned in 2:7 [ICC, WBC].

QUESTION—What is the relationship between the words βασίλειον 'royal' and ἱεράτευμα 'priesthood'?

The phrase βασίλειον ἱεράτευμα is a quotation from the LXX of Exodus 19:6, which translates two Hebrew words meaning 'a kingdom of priests'.

1. They are two nouns [BNTC, NCBC, Sel; NJB, NLT].
   1.1 They are nouns in apposition. That is, the believers are 'a group of kings, a priesthood' [NCBC]. Βασίλειον means a palace or king's household as it is used in Luke 7:25, that is, the believers are 'a king's household, a priesthood' [BNTC, Sel], corresponding to 'a spiritual house ... holy priesthood' in 2:5 [BNTC].
   1.2 Βασίλειον is 'a kingdom' and ἱεράτευμα is used attributively to modify kingdom, as in the Hebrew of Exodus 19:6. That is, the believers are a kingdom of priests [NJB, NLT].
2. Βασίλειον is an adjective, meaning 'royal' and modifies 'priesthood'. That is, the believers are a royal priesthood [Alf, EGT, IVP, NIBC, NIC, NTC, TG, TH, WBC; all versions except NJB, NLT].
   2.1 Βασίλειον denotes the fact that the priests are royal, in that they serve a king as priests [NIBC, NIC, NTC, TG, TH, WBC; TEV].
   2.2 Βασίλειον denotes the fact that the priests themselves are kingly or regal [Alf, EGT].

**a holy[a] nation,[b] a people[c] for[d] possession,[e]**

LEXICON—a. ἅγιος (LN 88.24) (BAGD 1.a.α.. p. 9): 'holy' [BAGD, BNTC, LN, NIC, WBC; all versions except REB], 'dedicated to God' [BAGD], 'dedicated' [REB]. See this word at 1:15.

b. ἔθνος (LN 11.55): 'nation' [BNTC, LN, NIC, WBC; all versions], 'people' [LN].

c. λαός (LN 11.55) (BAGD 3.b. p. 467): 'people' [BAGD, BNTC, LN, NIC, WBC; all versions except NLT], 'nation' [LN], not explicit [NLT].

d. εἰς (LN 89.57): 'for' [BNTC; REB], 'destined for' [WBC], 'he claims for' [NAB], 'to be' [NJB], 'for the purpose of, in order to' [LN], not explicit [CEV, KJV, NIV, NLT, NRSV, TNT].

e. περιποίησις (LN 57.62) (BAGD 3. p. 650): 'possession' [BAGD, LN], 'God's possession' [BNTC], 'God's own' [NIC; NRSV, TEV], 'belonging to God' [NIV], 'belonging to him' [TNT], 'a personal possession' [NJB], 'his very own possession' [NLT], 'claimed by God for his own' [REB], 'special' [CEV], 'peculiar' [KJV], 'he claims for his own' [NAB], 'destined for vindication' [WBC].

**so-that[a] you-may-proclaim[b] the glorious deeds/praises[c]**
LEXICON—a. ὅπως (LN 89.59) (BAGD 2.a.α. p. 576): 'so that' [LN], 'in order to, for the purpose of' [LN], 'in order that' [BAGD, NIC], 'that' [BNTC], 'to' [WBC; NAB, NJB, REB], 'chosen to' [TEV], 'that you may' [NIV, NRSV, TNT], 'now you must' [CEV], 'that ye should' [KJV], 'this is so you can' [NLT].
b. aorist act. subj. of ἐξαγγέλλω (LN **33.204**) (BAGD p. 271): 'to proclaim' [BAGD, **BNTC, LN**; NAB, NRSV, REB, TEV], 'to announce' [LN, NIC], 'to declare' [NIV, TNT], 'to sound' [WBC], 'to tell' [CEV], 'show forth' [KJV], 'to show others' [NLT], 'to sing' [NJB].
c. ἀρετή (LN **76.14**) (BAGD 2., 3. p. 106): 'glorious deeds' [NIC; REB, TNT], 'mighty acts' [NRSV], 'mighty deeds' [BNTC], 'wonderful deeds' [**LN**], 'glorious works' [NAB], 'wonderful things he has done' [CEV], 'wonderful acts' [TEV], 'goodness' [NLT], 'praises' [BAGD, WBC; KJV, NIV, NJB].
QUESTION—What relationship is indicated by ὅπως 'so that'?
It indicates the purpose of God in choosing the believers [BNTC, IVP, NIBC, TH]. It indicates the purpose or task of God's people [IVP, NTC, TG, WBC]. It indicates the purpose of the church's special status as belonging to God [Alf, NIC]. It introduces the clause of purpose that explains all the titles of the church given in the first part of the sentence [NCBC]. It introduces a clause of purpose that is the pivotal point of this epistle, where it turns from dealing with the church's internal relationships to its relation with the outside world [EGT].
QUESTION—Does ἐξαγγείλητε 'proclaim' refer to worship or to preaching?
1. It means to proclaim to other people [Alf, EGT, ICC, NCBC, NTC, Sel, TG, TH]. The proclaiming or declaring is to be by word as well as by conduct [ICC, NCBC, NTC, TH].
2. It refers both to public proclamation as well as worship [BNTC, NIC].
3. It refers primarily to worship, but also includes testimony to others [NIBC, WBC].
QUESTION—What is meant by ἀρετάς 'glorious deeds/praises'?
The phrase 'proclaim the glorious deeds/praises' is taken from the LXX of Isaiah 42:12 and 43:21 where ἀρετάς, the plural form of ἀρετή 'excellence' or 'virtue' [BAGD (1. p. 106), LN (88.11)], is used to translate the Hebrew singular noun t^ehillah, 'praise' [EGT, WBC]. In secular Greek literature, the plural of ἀρετή was sometimes used to describe the miracles or mighty acts done by a god [BAGD, BNTC, ICC, NIBC, NIC, TH].

1. It means the wonderful, mighty, or praiseworthy deeds that God has done [BAGD, BNTC, IVP, LN, NCBC, NIBC, NIC, TG; CEV, NAB, NRSV, REB, TEV, TNT].
2. It means the praises of God [BAGD, NTC; KJV, NIV, NJB]. It means the praises for his glorious deeds [WBC].
3. It means the excellencies or praiseworthy qualities of God himself [ICC; NLT]. It means the excellencies or praiseworthy qualities of God and of the things he has done [Alf, TNTC].

**of-the-one having-called[a] you out-of[b] darkness[c] into[d] his marvelous[e] light;[f]**

LEXICON—a. aorist act. participle of καλέω (LN 33.307) (BAGD 2. p. 399): 'to call' [BAGD, BNTC, LN, NIC, WBC; all versions except CEV], 'to bring' [CEV]. See this word at 1:15.

b. ἐκ with genitive object (LN 84.4) (BAGD 1.a. p. 234): 'out of' [BAGD, BNTC, LN, NIC, WBC; all versions except NAB], 'from' [LN; NAB]

c. σκότος (LN 88.125) (BAGD 2.b. p. 758): 'darkness' [BAGD, BNTC, LN, NIC, WBC; all versions].

d. εἰς (LN 13.62): 'into' [BNTC, NIC, WBC; all versions], 'to' [LN].

e. θαυμαστός (LN 25.215) (BAGD 2. p. 352): 'marvelous' [BAGD, BNTC, LN, NIC, WBC; CEV, KJV, NAB, NRSV, REB, TEV], 'wonderful' [BAGD, LN; NIV, NJB, NLT, TNT].

f. φῶς (LN 14.36) (BAGD 3.a. p. 872): 'light' [BAGD, BNTC, LN, NIC, WBC; all versions].

QUESTION—What is the 'light' that is referred to here?

It represents God's presence [Alf, NIBC, NIC, Sel]. It refers to living in the messianic kingdom [BNTC, NIBC], to living in the kingdom of God's son [NTC]. It refers to the glory to be revealed in the last day when Jesus comes [WBC]. Coming into the light refers to conversion from heathenism to Christian faith [EGT, NCBC, NIBC, NIC, Sel], or to the light of God's revelation in Christ in contrast with ignorance and sin [IVP]. Light represents salvation and life [TG], or knowing God and belonging to him [TH].

**2:10** **who once[a] (were) no people[b] but now[c] (are) (the) people of God, the ones having-not-received-mercy[d] but now having-received-mercy.[e]**

LEXICON—a. ποτέ (LN 67.9): 'once' [BNTC, NIC, WBC; CEV, NAB, NIV, NJB, NLT, NRSV, REB, TNT], 'in time past' [KJV], 'at one time' [TEV], 'at some time' [LN].

b. λαός (LN 11.55) (BAGD 3.b. p. 467): 'people' [BNTC, NIC, WBC; all versions], 'nation' [LN]. Taken with the negative οὐκ, this is translated 'no people' [BNTC, WBC; NAB], 'not a people' [NIC; KJV, NIV, NLT, NRSV], 'not a people at all' [REB, TNT], 'nobody' [CEV], 'a non-people' [NJB], 'not God's people' [TEV]. This singular noun refers to a socio-political community [LN].

c. νῦν (LN 67.38) (BAGD 1.c. p. 545): 'now' [BAGD, BNTC, LN, NIC, WBC; all versions].

d. perf. pass. participle of ἐλεέω (LN 88.76) (BAGD p. 249): 'to receive mercy' [BAGD, BNTC, LN, NIC, WBC; NIV, NLT, NRSV], 'to obtain mercy' [KJV], 'to know (God's) mercy' [TEV], 'to be pitied' [BAGD; CEV, NJB]. Taken with the negative οὐ, this is translated 'to be destitute of mercy' [WBC], 'no one had pity on you' [CEV], 'there was no mercy for you' [NAB], 'to be outside of his pity' [NJB], 'to be outside of his mercy' [REB, TNT].

e. aorist. pass. participle of ἐλεέω (LN 88.76) (BAGD p. 249): 'to receive mercy' [BAGD, BNTC, LN, NIC, WBC; NIV, NLT, NRSV, TEV, TNT], 'to obtain mercy' [KJV], 'to find mercy' [NAB], 'to receive pity' [NJB], 'to be pitied' [BAGD], 'to be outside (his mercy) no longer' [REB], 'God has treated you with kindness' [CEV].

QUESTION—What is implied by the phrase λαὸς θεοῦ 'people of God'?

The Gentile believers have received a title and status that previously belonged only to Israel [BNTC]. It means that believers are heirs of the privileged status of Israel as illustrated by the titles of dignity in 2:9 regarding election, priesthood, and worship, and being a holy nation [NCBC, NTC, TNTC, WBC]. It means that Gentile believers are accepted now whereas they were rejected before [NIC]. It means that now, through belonging to a community, believers have a sense of identity which they previously lacked [Sel]. It means to be different from other people, being loved by God and called to holiness [IVP].

QUESTION—What is the mercy that is now shown to the believers?

It is that they have become God's people [WBC]. It is the forgiveness of sins [NTC]. It is God's care and concern [NIC]. It is God's tender care and love [TG], his pity, compassion, and concern [TH].

QUESTION—What relationship is indicated by the use of the perfect and aorist passive participles of ἐλεέω 'to have mercy'?

The perfect tense indicates an ongoing past state or condition of having received no mercy [NTC]. The aorist refers to a single occurrence in past time at conversion of being shown mercy [Alf, NTC, TH]. The use of the word 'now' with the aorist indicates that it is a present state resulting from the past event of conversion, which would be represented in English by the perfect tense [TH].

**DISCOURSE UNIT: 2:11–4:11** [NIC, WBC]. The topic is the responsibilities of the people of God [WBC], relating to societal institutions [NIC].

**DISCOURSE UNIT: 2:11–3:22** [TH; REB]. The topic is Christian behavior [TH], the Christian household [REB].

**DISCOURSE UNIT: 2:11–3:12** [IVP, NTC, Sel, TG]. The topic is social conduct [IVP], the second hortatory section [Sel], submission [NTC], practical aspects of Christian living [TG].

**DISCOURSE UNIT: 2:11–17** [CEV, NRSV, TEV]. The topic is live as God's servants should [CEV], live as servants of God [NRSV], slaves of God [TEV].

**DISCOURSE UNIT: 2:11–12** [IVP, NIC, Sel, TH, TNTC, WBC; NAB, NJB]. The topic is strangers in the world [IVP], integrity of life [Sel], the mission of God's people in the world [WBC], general principles [TNTC], exhortation to an ethical lifestyle [NIC]; good example [NAB], the obligations of Christians towards unbelievers [NJB].

**2:11** Beloved,[a] I-urge[b] (you) as[c] aliens[d] and exiles[e] to-abstain-from[f]

TEXT—Instead of ἀπέχεσθαι 'to abstain' (pres. inf.), some manuscripts have ἀπέχεσθε 'abstain' (pres. impera.). GNT does not mention this alternative. Only WBC and KJV translate it as an imperative.

LEXICON—a. ἀγαπητός (LN 25.45) (BAGD 2. p. 6): 'beloved' [BAGD, LN, NIC, WBC; NAB, NRSV], 'dear friends' [BNTC; CEV, NIV, REB, TNT], 'my friends' [TEV], 'my dear friends' [NJB], 'dearly beloved' [KJV], 'dear brothers and sisters' [NLT].

b. pres. act. indic. of παρακαλῶ (παρακαλέω) (LN 33.168) (BAGD 2. p. 617): 'to urge' [BAGD, NIC; NAB, NIV, NJB, NRSV, TNT], 'to appeal' [BAGD, BNTC, LN, WBC; REB, TEV], 'to exhort' [BAGD], 'to beg' [CEV], 'to beseech' [KJV], 'to warn' [NLT].

c. ὡς (LN 64.12) (BAGD III.1.a. p. 898): 'as' [BAGD, BNTC, LN, NIC, WBC; all versions except CEV, NAB, NLT], 'you are' [CEV, NAB, NLT].

d. παρεπίδημος (LN 11.77) (BAGD p. 625): 'alien' [BAGD, BNTC, LN, NIC, WBC; NIV, NRSV, REB], 'exile' [BAGD; TNT] 'stranger' [BAGD, LN; KJV, NAB, NJB, TEV], 'foreigners' [CEV, NLT]. The idea that believers do not belong to this world is expressed explicitly where this word is conflated with the next noun, πάροικος 'exiles', or paired with πάροικος with an additional explanatory phrase: 'exiles only passing through this world' [TNT], 'strangers and refugees in this world' [TEV], 'foreigners and aliens here' [NLT], 'aliens and strangers in this world' [NIV]. See this word at 1:1.

e. πάροικος (LN 11.77) (BAGD 2. p. 629): 'exiles' [NRSV], 'in exile' [NAB], 'in a foreign land' [REB], 'stranger' [BAGD, LN, WBC; CEV], 'strangers in the world' [NIV], 'refugees in this world' [TEV], 'passing through this world' [TNT], 'temporary sojourners' [BNTC], 'sojourners' [NIC], 'nomads' [NJB], 'alien' [BAGD, LN; NLT], 'pilgrims' [KJV].

f. pres. mid. infin. of ἀπέχω (LN 13.158) (BAGD 3. p. 85): 'to abstain' [BAGD, BNTC, NIC; KJV, NIV, NRSV], 'to avoid' [LN; REB], 'to renounce' [WBC] 'to not surrender to' [CEV] 'to not indulge' [NAB], 'to keep oneself free from' [NJB], 'to keep away from' [NLT], 'to not give in to' [TEV], 'to have nothing to do with'.

QUESTION—What is the function of the vocative ἀγαπητοί 'beloved' in this context?

It is a device used to signal a shift to a new section [IVP, NCBC, NIC, TH] or the introduction of traditional teaching [Sel]. It is a way to open a hortatory section with a meaningful term of endearment [Alf]. It appeals to the bonds of mutual love as a basis for exhortation [EGT, NIBC] or to God's love as that which prompts response [NTC]. God's love which chose them out of the world, and which grants them the titles of honor referred to in 2:9, also makes them strangers in the world [WBC].

QUESTION—Whose love is referred to in the term 'beloved'?
1. It refers to Peter's love for the believers [EGT, TNTC; CEV, NIV, NJB, NLT, REB, TEV, TNT].
2. It refers to Peter's love for them, but also God's love for them as well [BNTC, NIBC, NTC, WBC]. It also refers to the fact that they loved one another [BNTC].

QUESTION—How is the verb παρακαλῶ 'I exhort' used in this passage?
It is a common formula used among Christians as a stylistic device to introduce hortatory material about lifestyle or ethical behavior [NCBC, NIBC, NIC, WBC]. It marks the transition to a practical application of what has already been said [BNTC]. Use of the first person 'I exhort' constitutes a more personal appeal than would an imperative command [NTC].

QUESTION—What relationship is indicated by ὡς 'as'?
It introduces the grounds for the appeal to abstain from fleshly lust, which is that the readers don't belong to this world [Alf, EGT, Sel, TH, TNTC, WBC].

QUESTION—How is the phrase πάροικος καὶ παρεπίδημος 'aliens and exiles' used in this passage?
The two terms are complementary and similar in meaning [NCBC]. They are used more or less synonymously [IVP, Sel, TNTC]. The focus is not so much on where they are exiles from, which is heaven, but among whom they are exiles, the heathen [ICC]. The terms are probably drawn from the identical wording found in the LXX of Genesis 23:4 or Psalm 39:12 [BNTC, NIBC, NIC, Sel, WBC]. The focus is on transience and lack of a citizen's rights [IVP]. The focus is on detachment from this world [Sel]. The focus is on the fact that they belong elsewhere and this is not home [BNTC, NIBC, NIC], so consequently their allegiance should be elsewhere [BNTC]. The focus is on not adapting to pagan cultural values which are foreign to God's people [NCBC]. It extends the analogy of being the new Israel [WBC].

**fleshly[a] desires[b] which wage-war[c] against[d] the soul;[e]**
LEXICON—a. σαρκικός (LN 41.42) (BAGD 3. p. 743): 'fleshly' [BAGD, NIC; KJV], 'of the flesh' [BNTC; NRSV], 'carnal' [NAB], 'bodily' [REB, TEV], 'sinful' [NIV], 'evil' [NLT], 'of the earthly nature' [TNT], 'worldly' [LN], 'natural' [WBC], not explicit [CEV]. This word is translated in conjunction with the following noun as 'disordered natural inclinations' [NJB].
b. ἐπιθυμία (LN 25.20) (BAGD 3. p. 293): 'desire' [BAGD, LN; CEV, NAB, NIV, NRSV, REB, TNT], 'evil desires' [LN; NLT], 'lust' [LN; KJV], 'passion' [TEV], 'natural inclination' [NJB]. See this word at 1:14.

c. pres. mid. indic. of στρατεύω (LN 55.4) (BAGD 2. p. 770): 'to wage war' [BNTC; NAB, NRSV, TNT], 'to war' [KJV, NIV], 'to be at war' [WBC; TEV], 'to make war' [NIC; REB], 'to battle, to engage in war' [LN], 'to fight' [LN; CEV, NLT], 'to attack' [NJB].

d. κατά with accusative (LN **90.31**) (BAGD I.2.b.α. p. 405): 'against' [BAGD, BNTC, LN, NIC; CEV, KJV, NIV, NLT, NRSV, TEV, TNT], 'with' [WBC], 'on' [NAB, REB], not explicit [NJB].

e. ψυχή (LN 26.4) (BAGD 1.c. p. 893): 'soul' [BAGD, BNTC, NIC, WBC; all versions except CEV], 'life' [BAGD], 'inner self' [LN], 'you' [CEV].

QUESTION—How is the term σαρκικός 'fleshly' used in this context?

It refers to the lower nature with its impulses [Sel]. It is the sinful nature [TNTC]. It is the seat of desire [Alf, ICC]. The flesh represents physical frailty and moral weakness [NCBC], or human weakness and passions apart from God [NIBC]. It represents the lower nature that is weak and subject to temptation, physical or otherwise [IVP]. It is the physical nature [TH]. It is that which is in contrast to the soul [ICC] or in opposition to the soul [NCBC]. The flesh represents the earthly life as the temporary home of the soul [EGT].

1. 'Fleshly' refers to the pull toward sins of the body such as sexual immorality [BNTC]. It refers to that which is physical in motivation such as self-preservation or physical security [WBC].
2. It refers not to sexual sins in particular, but to human self-centeredness as addressed in the subsequent passages [NIC]. It encompasses all sins of mind and body [NCBC].

QUESTION—What is the nature of the ἐπιθυμία 'desires' which must be abstained from?

1. The ἐπιθυμία 'desires', while not sinful in and of themselves, are those which must be bridled lest they take over the soul [NIC, WBC]. It is the drive to comfort, gratify, or protect the self [WBC].
2. Επιθυμία is sinful desire [NTC, Sel, TNTC]. It is lust [Alf, EGT]. It is wrongful appetites connected to the body and which lead to immorality [BNTC].

QUESTION—What relationship is indicated by ὅστις (αἵτινες, plural) 'which'?

This plural relative pronoun serves to indicate a reason for the foregoing statement such as could be expressed by 'for' or 'because' [Alf, BNTC, EGT, ICC, NTC, WBC]. It lumps all the desires into a class 'all of which', and makes an assertion about them [Alf].

QUESTION—What is meant by ψυχή 'soul' in this context?

It means the individual person or self [NIC, TH]. It is the true self, that which makes one a spiritual being [Sel]. In this passage it is that which stands in opposition to flesh [NCBC]. It is the spiritual or higher aspect of a person [ICC, TG, TNTC], the personal immortal aspect [Alf]. It is that which can be saved [Alf, ICC, IVP, WBC], wherein faith lives [ICC, IVP], wherein the divine life of Christ dwells [BNTC], which is alive toward God [IVP], which accepts God's word and is cared for by God [WBC]. It is that part of man in which sinful desires originate [NTC] and which can be influenced from below to its ruin [Alf].

QUESTION—What is the nature of the 'war' waged against the soul?

The use of the present tense indicates the continual and on-going nature of the conflict [TNTC]. 'Wage war' indicates more than just a fight; it is an engagement with a view to destruction [NTC]. Selfish desires hinder salvation and are incompatible with the spiritual sacrifices that we are to offer [Sel]. It is the inner rebellion of natural impulses that seek to comfort, protect, and gratify the self [WBC]. Self-centered, unbridled desires fight to take over the self [NIC]. Entertaining such desires make a person's spiritual life weak and ineffective [TNTC]. The former desires of the lower nature can divert faith and even destroy the person's life [IVP]. The desires such as drunkenness, immorality, and idolatry may give physical satisfaction but will destroy the soul [NTC]. Wrongful appetites and fleshly passions that lead to immorality destroy the divine life that Christ gives [BNTC].

**2:12** having<sup>a</sup> your conduct<sup>b</sup> good<sup>c</sup> among<sup>d</sup> the Gentiles,<sup>e</sup>

LEXICON—a. pres. act. participle of ἔχω (LN 90.65): 'to have' [LN; KJV]. The phrase 'having your conduct good' is translated 'see that your conduct is good' [BNTC], 'make sure your conduct is good' [WBC], 'let others see you behaving properly' [CEV], 'conduct yourselves blamelessly' [NAB], 'conduct yourselves honorably' [NRSV], 'always behave honorably' [NJB], 'live such good lives' [NIV], 'you should live such good lives' [TNT], 'living a good manner of life' [NIC], 'be careful how you live' [NLT], 'let your conduct be so good' [REB], 'your conduct should be so good' [TEV].

b. ἀναστροφή (LN 41.3) (BAGD p. 61): 'conduct' [BAGD, BNTC, LN, WBC; REB, TEV], 'behavior' [LN], 'conversation' [KJV], 'manner of life' [NIC], 'life' [NIV, TNT]. This noun is also translated as a verb: 'to conduct oneself' [NAB, NRSV], 'to live' [NIV, NLT, TNT]. See this word at 1:15.

c. καλός (LN 88.4) (BAGD 2.b. p. 400): 'good' [BAGD, BNTC, LN, NIC, WBC; NIV, REB, TEV, TNT], 'morally good' [BAGD], 'praiseworthy' [BAGD, LN], 'honest' [KJV]. This adjective is also translated as an adverb: 'blamelessly' [NAB], 'properly' [CEV], 'honorably' [NJB, NRSV]; as a verb: 'be careful (how you live)' [NLT].

d. ἐν with dative object (LN 83.9): 'among' [BNTC, LN, NIC, WBC; all versions except CEV, TNT], 'amongst' [TNT], not explicit [CEV].

e. ἔθνη (plural of ἔθνος) (LN 11.37): 'gentiles' [WBC; KJV, NJB, NRSV], 'heathen' [LN; TEV, TNT], 'nations' [NIC], 'pagans' [BNTC, LN; NAB, NIV], 'others' [CEV], 'unbelieving neighbors' [NLT], 'unbelievers' [REB].

QUESTION—What relationship is indicated by the present participle ἔχοντες 'having'?

It is used imperatively [BNTC, NTC, Sel, WBC]. It carries the main focus of the commands in this section, more so than ἀπέχω 'abstain' [WBC]. It is used to give vividness to the description that follows and functions to separate the participle from the influence of the verb παρακαλέω 'I urge', with the result that it depicts the condition that it recommends as though it were already true [Alf].

**so-that,[a] wherein[b] they-speak-against[c] you as[d] evildoers[e]**

LEXICON—a. ἵνα (LN 89.59) 'so that' [BNTC, LN, NIC, WBC; NJB, NRSV], 'that' [KJV, NIV, REB, TEV, TNT], not explicit [CEV, NAB, NLT].

b. ἐν ᾧ (preposition ἐν with relative pronoun ὅ in the dative case) (LN 67.139) (BAGD I.2.a. p. 583): 'in that, in which' [BAGD], 'while' [LN], 'whereas' [KJV], 'though' [NAB, NIV, NRSV], 'although' [REB], 'even while' [TNT], 'in cases where' [BNTC], 'in a case where' [WBC], 'with respect to the very things' [NIC], 'the things which' [NJB], 'even if' [NLT], 'when' [TEV], not explicit [CEV].

c. pres. act. indic. of καταλαλέω (LN 33.387) (BAGD p. 412): 'to speak against' [BAGD; KJV], 'to speak evil of' [BAGD], 'to slander' [BAGD, NIC; NAB], 'to vilify' [BNTC], 'to accuse' [WBC; CEV, NIV, NLT, TEV, TNT], 'to denounce' [NJB], 'to malign' [NRSV, REB].

d. ὡς (LN 64.12): 'as' [BNTC, LN, NIC; KJV, NAB, NJB, NRSV, REB]. The phrase 'they speak against you as evildoers' is translated 'to accuse someone of doing wrong' [WBC; CEV, NIV, NLT], 'to accuse someone of being evildoers' [TEV, TNT].

e. κακοποιός (LN **88.114**) (BAGD p. 397): 'evildoer' [BAGD, LN, NIC; KJV, NRSV, TEV, TNT], 'wrongdoer' [BNTC; REB], 'criminal' [BAGD; NJB], 'troublemaker' [NAB], 'doing wrong' [WBC; CEV, NIV, NLT].

QUESTION—What relationship is indicated by ἵνα 'so that'?

1. It indicates that the purpose of the good deeds is that those who observe them might come to glorify God [TH, WBC] or that they might be converted [BNTC, EGT, ICC, IVP, NIBC, Sel, WBC].
2. It indicates that the purpose of abstaining from lusts and having excellent behavior will be that those who observe might glorify God [Alf] or that they might be converted [TNTC].
3. It indicates that the purpose of the good deeds is that others will see them [NIC].

QUESTION—What relationship is indicated by ἐν ᾧ 'wherein'?

1. It is used as a temporal conjunction or to posit a hypothetical case in the sense of 'if ever or whenever they slander you' [WBC; NLT, TEV, TNT].
2. It is used concessively in the sense of 'although they slander you' [KJV, NAB, NIV, NRSV, REB, TNT].

3. It is a used as a relative pronoun in the sense of 'in the matter in which they slander you' [Alf, BAGD, BNTC, EGT, ICC, NIC, Sel; NJB].

**by[a] observing[b] your good[c] deeds[d] they-may-glorify[e] God in (the) day of-visitation.[f]**

LEXICON—a. ἐκ with genitive object (LN 89.25) (BAGD 3.g.β. p. 235): 'by' [BAGD; KJV, NAB], 'because of' [LN], 'through' [BNTC], 'from' [WBC], not explicit [NIC; CEV, NIV, NJB, NLT, NRSV, REB, TEV, TNT].

b. pres. act. participle of ἐποπτεύω (LN 24.45) (BAGD p. 305): 'to observe' [BAGD, LN, NIC, WBC; NAB], 'to watch' [LN], 'to see' [LN; CEV, NIV, NJB, NLT, NRSV], 'to behold' [KJV], 'to take note of' [BNTC], 'to note' [TNT], 'to reflect' [REB], 'to recognize' [TEV].

c. καλός (LN 88.4) (BAGD 2.b. p. 400): 'good' [BAGD, BNTC, LN, NIC, WBC; all versions except NJB, NLT, NRSV], 'praiseworthy' [BAGD, LN], 'moral' [NJB], 'honorable' [NLT, NRSV].

d. ἔργον (LN 42.11): 'deed' [LN, NIC; NIV, NRSV, REB, TEV, TNT], 'act' [LN], 'action' [BNTC], 'work' [WBC; KJV, NAB], 'things you do' [CEV], 'lives you lead' [NJB], 'behavior' [NLT]. See this word at 1:17.

e. aorist act. subj. of δοξάζω (LN 87.24): 'to glorify' [BNTC, LN, WBC; KJV, NIV, NRSV], 'to give glory to' [NIC; NAB, REB, TNT], 'to honor' [CEV], 'to give honor to' [NLT], 'to give thanks to' [NJB], 'to praise' [TEV].

f. ἐπισκοπή (LN 34.51) (BAGD 1., 2. p. 299): 'visitation' [BAGD, BNTC, LN, NIC, WBC; KJV, NAB], 'judgment' [CEV], 'reckoning' [NJB], 'of his coming' [TEV]. The phrase 'day of visitation' is translated 'when he comes to judge' [NRSV, TNT], 'when he comes in judgment' [REB], 'when he comes to judge the world' [NLT], 'the day he visits us' [NIV].

QUESTION—What relationship is indicated by ἐκ 'by'?

It indicates the means by which they glorify God, which is the good works [BAGD, BNTC, TNTC; KJV, NAB].

QUESTION—What is meant by ἐποπτεύοντες 'observing'?

The use of the present participle indicates the passage of time in which reflection may also be given to what is seen [BNTC, Sel]. It means to observe with scrutiny [NTC] or to long-term reflective observation [NIC]. It refers to being a spectator and becoming informed by what is seen [Alf]. It means to observe and come to a conclusion from what is learned [NCBC] and to have conviction or a change of mind as a consequence [EGT, TG, TH, WBC]. It is used in the same sense as Jesus' statement in Matthew 5:16 where people will glorify God based on what they see in believers [BNTC, EGT, ICC, IVP, NCBC, Sel, TH, WBC].

QUESTION—What is the nature of the 'good deeds' Peter is referring to?

It refers to that which is not only good in itself, but is seen as such even by non-Christians [ICC, IVP, NCBC, NIC, NTC, Sel, TH, WBC]. The adjective καλός refers to the quality of attractiveness in the behavior [BNTC, NIBC].

QUESTION—What does δοξάσωσιν 'glorify God' refer to in this passage?
1. It refers to the praise or worship given by those who are converted because of what they saw [BNTC, ICC, IVP, NTC, Sel, TNTC, WBC].
2. Following the sense of 'glorify God' as it is used in Joshua 7:19, it refers to unbelievers being forced to acknowledge what is right prior to their being judged [NIC].

QUESTION—What is meant by ἡμέρα ἐπισκοπῆς 'day of visitation'?
The definite article is absent in this phrase, so it could be referring either to 'a day of visitation' or to 'the day of visitation' [TNTC]. The biblical concept of a 'day of visitation' could mean either a visitation for judgment or a visitation for God's blessing and mercy [Alf, BNTC, EGT, ICC, IVP, NCBC, NIBC, NIC, NTC, Sel, TH, TNTC, WBC].
1. It refers to a day of visitation for blessing and mercy prior to the last day, in which unbelievers will be converted [Alf, BNTC, EGT, IVP, NTC, Sel, TH, TNTC].
2. It refers to the last day.
2.1 It refers to the day of judgment [ICC, NCBC, NIC, TG].
2.2 It refers to the final day, in which unbelievers' eyes will be opened so that they will repent and be converted, and God will be glorified thereby [NIBC, WBC].

**DISCOURSE UNIT: 2:13–3:12** [WBC]. The topic is respect: the key to living in the world.

**DISCOURSE UNIT: 2:13–25** [NIV]. The topic is submission to rulers and masters.

**DISCOURSE UNIT: 2:13–17** [IVP, NIC, Sel, TH, TNTC, WBC; NAB, NJB, NLT]. The topic is the ruling authorities [IVP], the duty of Christians regarding civil power [Sel], respect for everyone [WBC], living as citizens in subjection for the Lord's sake [TNTC], propriety in relation to the state [NIC], for the citizen [NAB], the obligations of unbelievers toward civil authority [NJB], respecting people in authority [NLT].

**2:13** Be-subject-to[a] every human[b] authority/creature[c] for-the-sake-of[d] the Lord

LEXICON—a. aorist pass. impera. of ὑποτάσσω (LN 36.18): 'to be subject to' [BNTC], 'to submit (oneself) to' [LN, NIC; KJV, NIV], 'to obey' [LN; CEV, REB, TEV, TNT], 'to be obedient to' [NAB], 'to defer' [WBC], 'to accept the authority of' [NJB, NLT, NRSV].
b. ἀνθρώπινος (LN 9.6) (BAGD 3. p. 68): 'human' [BAGD, BNTC, LN, NIC, WBC; all versions except KJV, NIV, NLT], 'of man' [KJV], 'among men' [NIV], not explicit [NLT].
c. κτίσις (LN **42.39, 37.43**) (BAGD 2. p. 456): 'authority' [BAGD, LN (37.43); CEV, NLT, REB, TEV, TNT], 'authority instituted' [NIV], 'authority of (every human) institution' [NJB, NRSV], 'institution'

[BAGD, LN (42.39); NAB], 'ordinance' [KJV], 'creature' [BNTC, WBC], 'created (human) being' [NIC].

d. διά with the accusative object (LN 90.38): 'for the sake of' [BNTC, LN, WBC; all versions except CEV, NAB], 'on account of' [NIC], 'because of' [NAB]. This word is also translated as a verb phrase: 'the Lord wants you to' [CEV].

QUESTION—How is the term ἀνθρώπινος 'human' used in this passage?
1. It refers to creatures that are human, that is, human beings [BNTC, NIC, WBC].
2. It refers to that which is established and operated by and among humans, in this case the social institution of civil government [Alf, EGT, ICC, NTC, Sel, TNTC; CEV, KJV, NAB, NIV, NJB, NRSV, REB, TEV, TNT].
3. It refers to what God has ordained for the benefit of humans, in this case the civil authority [NCBC].

QUESTION—What is meant by κτίσις 'authority/creature'?
1. It refers to that which has been established or instituted among men, including civil government [Alf, EGT, ICC, NCBC, NIBC, NTC, Sel, TG, TH, TNTC; all versions].
2. It means 'creation' or 'creature' and refers to people, who have been created by God [BNTC, NIC, WBC].

QUESTION—Who is 'the Lord' in this passage?
1. It is God [BNTC, NTC].
2. It is Christ [Alf, ICC, NIC, Sel, TH, WBC].

QUESTION—What relationship is indicated by διά 'for the sake of'?
It means to be in subjection for the sake of the Lord, motivated by the fact that he was subject to rulers and commanded his followers to do the same [Alf, ICC, NIC, TNTC]. It means to be in subjection to the authorities because the Lord has established them [NIBC, TNTC] or to human creatures out of regard for him as creator [BNTC]. It means to be in subjection for the sake of the Lord, motivated to be a positive example so that the gospel not be brought to disrepute [NIC, WBC]. It projects the motive for obedience past human beings to the Lord [NIC, Sel].

**whether to-(the)-emperor[a] as[b] being-in-authority[c]**

LEXICON—a. βασιλεύς (LN 37.67) (BAGD 1. p. 136): 'emperor' [BNTC, WBC; CEV, NAB, NJB, NRSV, REB, TEV, TNT], 'king' [BAGD, LN, NIC; KJV, NIV, NLT].

b. ὡς (LN 89.37) (BAGD III.1.a. p. 898): 'as' [BNTC, NIC; all versions except CEV, TEV], 'because' [BAGD, WBC], 'on the grounds that' [BAGD], not explicit [CEV, TEV]. This relational word indicates the characteristic quality of a person [BAGD]. It indicates grounds or reason [LN, WBC].

c. pres. act. participle of ὑπερέχω (LN **37.17**) (BAGD 2.a. p. 841): 'to be in authority over' [BAGD], 'to control' [LN]. This participle is translated as a predicate adjective: 'supreme' [KJV, NRSV, REB, TNT], 'sovereign' [BNTC, WBC; NAB]; as a predicate nominative: 'supreme authority' [NIC; NIV, NJB, TEV], 'head of state' [NLT]; as a verb phrase: 'who rules over everyone' [CEV], 'who is the one who controls' [LN].

**2:14** or to-rulers[a] as being-sent[b] by/through[c] him

LEXICON—a. ἡγεμών (LN 37.83) (BAGD 2. p. 343): 'governor' [BAGD, BNTC, LN, NIC; all versions except NLT], 'magistrate' [WBC], 'official' [NLT].
  b. pres. pass. participle of πέμπω (LN 15.66) (BAGD 1. p. 642): 'to be sent' [BNTC, LN, NIC, WBC; CEV, KJV, NIV, NRSV, TNT], 'to be appointed' [BAGD; NLT, TEV], 'to be commissioned' [BAGD; NAB, NJB]. This participle is also translated as a substantive: 'deputy' [REB].
  c. διά with genitive (LN 90.4): 'by' [LN, NIC, WBC; all versions except NAB, NLT, REB], 'under (his) commission' [BNTC], not explicit [NAB, NLT, REB].

QUESTION—What relationship is indicated by δι' αὐτοῦ 'by/through him'?
  1. It means that the governors are sent by the emperor [Alf, BNTC, ICC, NIC, NTC, Sel, TG, TH, WBC; all versions].
  2. It means that the governors are sent by God through the emperor [EGT, TNTC]. It means that the emperor is the mediate source and God the ultimate source of the authority by which governors rule [NCBC].

**for[a] punishment[b] of-evildoers[c] and[d] praise[e] of-good-doers[f]**

LEXICON—a. εἰς (LN 89.57): 'for' [BNTC; KJV, NAB, REB], 'for the purpose of' [LN], 'in order to' [LN]. This preposition is expressed in conjunction with the following noun as an infinitive showing purpose, 'to (punish)' [NIC, WBC; CEV, NIV, NJB, NLT, NRSV, TEV, TNT].
  b. ἐκδίκησις (LN **38.8**) (BAGD p. 238): 'punishment' [BAGD, BNTC, LN; KJV, NAB, REB]. This noun is also translated as a verb: 'to punish' [**LN,** NIC, WBC; CEV, NIV, NJB, NLT, NRSV, TEV, TNT].
  c. κακοποιός (LN 88.114) (BAGD p. 397): 'evildoer' [BAGD, LN; KJV, TEV, TNT], 'wrongdoer' [BNTC, LN, WBC], 'those who do wrong' [NIV, NRSV, REB], 'all who do wrong' [NLT], 'those doing evil' [NIC], 'criminals' [BAGD; CEV, NAB, NJB]. See this word at 2:12.
  d. δέ (LN 89.94): 'and' [BNTC, LN, NIC, WBC; all versions].
  e. ἔπαινος (LN 33.354) (BAGD 1.a.α. p. 281): 'praise' [BAGD, LN; KJV], 'commendation' [BNTC; REB], 'recognition' [NAB]. This noun is also translated as a verb: 'to commend' [NIC, WBC; NIV], 'to praise' [CEV, NJB, NRSV, TEV, TNT], 'to honor' [NLT]. See this word at 1:7.
  f. ἀγαθοποιός (LN **88.8**) (BAGD p. 2): 'one who does good' [LN], 'those who do right' [BNTC; NIV, NLT, NRSV, REB], 'those doing good' [NIC], 'those who do good' [**LN;** NJB, TEV, TNT], 'those who do good deeds' [WBC], 'them that do well' [KJV], 'the upright' [NAB], 'good citizens' [CEV], 'doing good' [BAGD].

**2:15** For<sup>a</sup> thus<sup>b</sup> is the will<sup>c</sup> of God, (by) doing-good<sup>d</sup> to-silence<sup>e</sup> the ignorance<sup>f</sup> of foolish<sup>g</sup> people,

LEXICON—a. ὅτι (LN 89.33): 'for' [BNTC, LN, NIC, WBC; KJV, NIV, NRSV, REB, TEV, TNT], 'because' [LN], not explicit [CEV, NAB, NJB, NLT].
  b. οὕτως (LN 61.9, 61.10) (BAGD 2. p. 598): 'thus' [BAGD, LN (61.9)], 'so' [BAGD, LN (61.9); KJV], 'in this way' [LN (61.9)], 'in this manner' [BAGD], 'as follows' [BAGD, LN (61.10)], not explicit [CEV, TEV, TNT]. This adverb is also expressed as a pronoun, referring to God's will: 'this' [NIC], 'it' [NIV, NJB, NLT, NRSV, REB], 'such' [BNTC], 'such obedience' [NAB]. It is also translated as a verb phrase with an implied verb stated explicitly to indicate how God's will is done: '(God's will) is accomplished by' [WBC].
  c. θέλημα (LN 25.2) (BAGD 1.c.γ. p. 354): 'will' [BAGD, BNTC, NIC, WBC; all versions except CEV, TEV, TNT], 'wish, desire' [LN]. This noun is also translated as a verb: 'to want' [CEV, TEV, TNT].
  d. pres. act. participle of ἀγαθοποιέω (LN 88.3) (BAGD 2. p. 2): 'to do good' [BAGD, LN, NIC, WBC; NIV, TNT], 'to do what is right' [BAGD], 'to do right' [BNTC; CEV, NRSV, REB], 'to do well' [KJV]. This participle is also translated as a noun phrase: 'good behavior' [NAB], 'good deeds' [NJB], 'good lives' [NLT], 'good things you do' [TEV].
  e. pres. act. infin. of φιμόω (LN 33.123) (BAGD p. 861): 'to silence' [BAGD, LN, NIC; all versions except KJV], 'to put to silence' [BNTC, WBC; KJV].
  f. ἀγνωσία (LN **28.16, 32.8**) (BAGD p. 12): 'ignorance' [BAGD, BNTC, LN (28.16), WBC; KJV, NRSV, REB, TNT], 'ignorant charges' [NIC], 'ignorant talk' [NAB, NIV, NJB, TEV], 'ignorant people' [CEV], 'what is not understood' [LN (32.8)]. The phrase 'the ignorance of foolish people' is translated as two nouns 'ignorance and stupidity' [REB] or as a verb phrase 'those who make foolish accusations against you' [NLT].
  g. ἄφρων (LN **32.52**) (BAGD p. 127): 'foolish' [BAGD, BNTC, LN, NIC, WBC; all versions except CEV, NJB, REB], 'ignorant' [BAGD], 'stupid' [CEV]. The phrase ἀφρόνων ἀνθρώπων 'foolish people' is translated 'fools' [NJB], 'stupidity' [REB].

QUESTION—What relationship is indicated by ὅτι 'because'?
  1. It indicates the reason for the moral function of civil government, which is that it is the will of God [Sel].
  2. It indicates the reason or ground for what has just been said in 2:13–14, which is that one may fulfill the will of God by silencing slander [Alf, BNTC, NIC, TNTC, WBC].

QUESTION—What relationship is indicated by οὕτως 'thus'?
  1. It is retrospective, referring to what was just said.
    1.1 The will of God is that you be subject to human institutions [BNTC; NAB].

1.2 The will of God is expressed through the function of civil government in punishing wrong and praising good [Sel]. Οὕτως indicates a conclusion which is that since God's will is expressed through civil government which praises well-doers, therefore you will be able to silence slander [EGT].
2. It is prospective, referring to what follows.
2.1 The will of God is to silence the ignorance of foolish people, which is accomplished by doing good [Alf, NIBC, TNTC, WBC; CEV, NIV, NJB, NLT, NRSV, REB, TEV, TNT].
2.2 The will of God is that one should do good, which would also include the obedience to civil authority and the good deeds mentioned previously [NIC].

QUESTION—How is ἀγνωσία 'ignorance' used in this context?

It is a metonymy; what is being silenced is the talk which proceeds from ignorance or the talk which is characterized by uninformed statements [Alf, BNTC, EGT, ICC, NIBC, NIC, NTC, TG, TH, TNTC, WBC; NAB, NIV, NJB, NLT, TEV].

QUESTION—What is implied by the term 'ignorance of foolish people'?

It is arrogant unbelief and opposition to all that is right and true [BNTC]. It is ignorance as a habit or way of life [Alf], which involves leaving God out of one's thinking [NIBC]. It is being inexcusably ignorant because of disobedience and closing of the mind [NTC]. It indicates a lack of understanding or insight that comes from looking at things outwardly [EGT]. It is being opposed to God, ignorant by flaw of character [NCBC]. It describes those who deliberately disregard the truth [TG], who oppose God, truth and right [TH], or who are estranged from God [NIC].

**2:16** as[a] free (people) and not having[b] freedom as a cloak[c] of-evil[d] but as slaves[e] of-God.

LEXICON—a. ὡς (LN 64.12): 'as' [BNTC, LN, NIC, WBC; KJV, NAB, NIV, NRSV, REB, TEV], 'like' [NJB], not explicit [CEV, NLT, TNT].
b. pres. act. participle of ἔχω (LN 57.1): 'to have' [LN], 'to use' [BNTC, NIC; all versions except NLT, REB], not explicit [NLT]. The phrase 'having as a cloak' is translated 'to make excuse' [WBC], 'to provide excuse' [REB]. See this verb at 2:12.
c. ἐπικάλυμμα (LN **28.56**) (BAGD p. 294): 'cloak' [KJV, NAB, REB, TNT], 'cover' [BAGD, NIC; NJB], 'covering' [BNTC], 'pretext' [LN; NRSV], 'veil' [BAGD], 'excuse' [WBC; CEV, NLT], 'cover-up' [NIV], 'a means of covering up' [**LN**]. This noun is also translated as a verb: 'to cover up' [TEV].
d. κακία (LN 88.105) (BAGD 1.a. p. 397): 'evil' [LN, NIC; NIV, NRSV, TEV], 'wickedness' [BAGD, BNTC, LN; NJB, TNT], 'vice' [BAGD; NAB], 'wrongdoing' [REB], 'maliciousness' [KJV]. This noun is also translated as a verb: 'to cause trouble' [WBC], 'to do evil' [NLT], 'to do wrong' [CEV]. See this word at 2:1.

e. δοῦλος (LN 87.76) (BAGD 4. p. 206): 'slave' [BAGD, LN, NIC, WBC; NJB, NLT, REB, TEV], 'servant' [BNTC; CEV, KJV, NAB, NIV, NRSV, TNT].

QUESTION—What relationship is indicated by ὡς 'as' in the phrase 'as free people'?
1. It refers to and expands on what has been said previously.
  1.1 It conjoins this clause to ὑποτάγητε 'submit' of 2:13, that is, submit as free people [EGT, ICC, IVP, Sel, TH].
  1.2 It refers to ἀγαθοποιοῦντας 'doing good' of 2:15, that is, doing good as free people [Alf, EGT]. It expresses an actual quality that believers have, that is, doing good as the free people you are [Alf].
  1.3 It refers to the will of God of 2:15.
    1.3.1 It is used to assure the believers that they are able to live in obedience to God's will as free people [TNTC].
    1.3.2 It is used to assure the believers that the will of God is that they be free and that they use their freedom as God's servants [TNT].
2. It modifies an implied imperative verb within the same sentence.
  2.1 It modifies an implied imperative 'to live' or 'to behave', and functions to introduce a command to live or behave as free people who do not use freedom as a cloak for evil [BNTC, NIC, TG, TH; NAB, NIV, NJB, NRSV, REB, TEV].
  2.2 It modifies an implied imperative 'to be' and functions to introduce a command to be free people who do not use freedom as a cloak for evil [NTC].
3. It is used to state the actual fact that the believers are free as a grounds for exhortation about how they should live [CEV, NLT].
4. It conjoins this clause with the four imperatives that follow in 2:17, and expresses an actual quality that believers have. That is, do these four things because you are free people and servants of God [WBC].

QUESTION—What does μὴ ὡς 'not as' refer to?
1. It refers to the cloak, 'not as a cloak or excuse' [TNTC; CEV, KJV, NAB, NIV, NJB, NLT, NRSV, TNT].
2. It refers to the participle ἔχοντες 'not as having' [Alf, WBC; REB]
3. It refers to the implied agent of the participle ἔχοντες 'not as those having or using freedom' [ICC, NIC].

QUESTION—What is the function of the present participle ἔχοντες 'having'?
1. It qualifies an implied imperative verb regarding how to live or behave as free people [BNTC, NIC; REB]: live this way, but not using your freedom for . . .
2. It qualifies an implied indicative verb by defining the purpose of freedom [NLT, TNT]: you are free, but your freedom is for the purpose of serving God.
3. It qualifies the four imperatives of the following verse [WBC]: do those four things without misusing freedom like this.

94 1 PETER 2:16

4. It functions imperatively [CEV, NAB, NIV, NJB, NRSV, TEV]: don't use your freedom this way.

QUESTION—What is the freedom spoken of here?

It is a change of master [IVP, Sel]. It is the freedom to do what is right [IVP]. It is a freedom from the power of sin [Alf, BNTC, NIBC, NIC, Sel, TG, TNTC]. It is freedom from living by the natural impulses which they formerly had in pagan ignorance [WBC]. It is freedom from the law [Alf, BNTC, NIC]. It is a freedom to do good and be submissive [EGT], to live life in a spiritual dimension [NIBC], to be God's children, people, and priests [Alf]. It is freedom from guilt and from having to earn merit [TNTC].

QUESTION—What is meant by the metaphor of a 'cloak'?

1. It refers to covering over evil deeds [NIBC, TG, TH, TNTC] or hiding evil intent [Alf].
2. It refers to a pretext or excuse for doing evil [IVP, NCBC, NIC, TG, TH, WBC], for rejecting moral restraint [ICC] or for serving oneself [NTC].

QUESTION—What is the κακία 'evil' spoken of here?

It is to react with harshness to critics or slanderers, to be antisocial or to fail to fulfill legitimate responsibilities [WBC]. It is malice [EGT]; it is actions that are in conflict with the law [NCBC]; it is lack of good citizenship [TH], or disobedience to God or to authorities [IVP].

**2:17** Honor[a] all (people), love[b] the brotherhood,[c] fear[d] God, honor[e] the emperor.

LEXICON—a. aorist. act. impera. of τιμάω (LN 87.8) (BAGD 2. p. 817): 'to honor' [BAGD, LN, NIC; KJV, NRSV, TNT], 'to do honor to' [BNTC], 'to give due honor to' [REB], 'to respect' [LN; CEV, TEV], 'to have respect for' [NJB], 'to show respect for' [WBC; NLT], 'to show proper respect to' [NIV], 'to esteem the person of' [NAB].

b. pres. act. impera. of ἀγαπάω (LN 25.43, 25.44): 'to love' [BNTC, LN (25.43), NIC; all versions except CEV, NAB, NJB], 'to show love' [LN (25.44), WBC], 'to show special love' [CEV], 'to foster love' [NAB], 'to have love for' [NJB].

c. ἀδελφότης (LN **11.22**) (BAGD 1. p. 16): 'brotherhood' [BAGD, BNTC, LN, WBC; KJV, TNT], 'fellow believers' [LN; NJB, TEV], 'fellow Christians' [NIC; REB], 'God's people' [CEV], 'the brothers' [NAB], 'the brethren' [**LN**], 'the brotherhood of believers' [NIV], 'Christian brothers and sisters' [NLT], 'the family of believers' [NRSV].

d. pres. mid. impera. of φοβέω (LN 87.14) (BAGD 2.a. p. 863): 'to fear' [BAGD, BNTC, LN; KJV, NIV, NJB, NLT, NRSV], 'to show great reverence or respect for' [LN], 'to reverence' [NIC; REB, TNT], 'to show reverence toward' [WBC], 'to foster reverence for' [NAB], 'to have reverence for' [TEV], 'to honor' [CEV].

e. pres. act. impera. of τιμάω (LN 87.8) (BAGD 2. p. 817): 'to honor' [BAGD, LN, NIC; KJV, NIV, NJB, NRSV, REB, TNT], 'to respect' [LN;

CEV, TEV], 'to show respect for' [WBC; NLT], 'to foster respect for' [NAB].

QUESTION—Who is the 'all' that is the object of 'honor'?
1. It refers to all people, all human beings [Alf, BNTC, EGT, ICC, IVP, NCBC, NIBC, NIC, NTC, Sel, TG, TH, TNTC, WBC; KJV, NAB, TNT].
2. It refers to the brotherhood, God, and the emperor [NIV, REB].

QUESTION—What is the significance of the aorist imperative τιμήσατε 'honor' followed by three present imperatives, 'love, fear, honor'?
1. There is no distinction of meaning intended between aorist and present imperatives [BNTC, ICC, NIC].
2. The first imperative sums up the other three, which amplify it [NIV, REB].
3. The first imperative is a general statement, and would tend to indicate to do something if and when the case arises that requires it. The present imperatives denote habitual thinking and practice and also form a transition to the next paragraph where he becomes more specific [Alf].
4. The aorist is used for the first verb to avoid ambiguity [EGT]. Since the three present imperatives could be confused as present indicatives, the first imperative in the aorist tense serves to clarify that the three that follow are also imperatives [WBC].
5. The initial imperative in the aorist means to take this attitude once and for all, and the present imperatives that follow indicate ongoing obligation to continue to do those things [NIBC]. The aorist imperative followed by present imperatives indicates a moment of decision followed by permanent action, that is, let this be your motto from now on to do these things [Sel]. The aorist imperative serves as an effective or programmatic aorist, that is, begin doing these things and then keep on doing them [WBC].
6. The initial aorist carries no special meaning, whereas the three present imperatives indicate a continuing necessity [TNTC].
7. The initial aorist is constative, indicating action in its entirety, whereas the three present imperatives indicate the continuing nature of the action [NTC].

QUESTION—What is the relationship of the four verbs in this verse?
1. The verbs move from the general to the limited, with actions relating to all people, believers, God, and the emperor [Sel].
2. The first gives a general statement followed by three verbs that outline specific duties and which form a transition to the next section [Alf].
3. The verbs are in two balanced sets of pairs, indicating general duties to all people and all believers, and then specific duties to God and the emperor [NTC, TH].
4. The verbs are in two balanced sets of pairs in a chiastic arrangement, wherein the second and third have more weight or richer content than the first and fourth [BNTC, NIC].

5. The second and third verbs have more weight or richer content than the first and fourth, but the third, which is to fear God, is paramount [TNTC].
6. The verbs are a single series linked together, and the verb τιμάω at the beginning and end of the series forms a unit or group which relates back to the exhortation to submission in 2:13 [WBC].

QUESTION—What attitude toward the emperor is indicated by the choice and arrangement of verbs in this passage?

The emperor is to be honored but God alone is to be feared [BNTC, IVP, NCBC, NIBC, NIC, TH, TNTC, WBC]. The fear of God and the love of the brotherhood set limits on how the emperor is to be honored [NTC].

**DISCOURSE UNIT: 2:18–25** [NIC, TH, TNTC, WBC; CEV, NAB, NJB, NLT, NRSV, TEV]. The topic is deference of slaves to masters [WBC], living as servants subject to your masters [TNTC], propriety of slaves in relation to masters [NIC], the example of Christ's suffering [CEV, TEV], the obligations of Christian towards masters [NJB], slaves [NAB, NLT].

**DISCOURSE UNIT: 2:18–20** [IVP]. The topic is slaves and their masters.

**2:18** Household-servants[a] submitting[b] with all respect/fear[c] to-(your) masters,

LEXICON—a. οἰκέτης (LN 46.5) (BAGD p. 557): 'household servant' [LN], 'house servant' [BNTC, LN], 'servant' [WBC; CEV, KJV, REB, TEV, TNT], 'slave' [BAGD; NIV, NJB, NLT, NRSV], 'household slave' [NIC; NAB], 'house slave' [BAGD].

b. pres. mid. participle of ὑποτάσσομαι (ὑποτάσσω) (LN 36.18) (BAGD 1.b.β. p. 848): 'to submit to' [LN, NIC; NIV, REB, TEV, TNT], 'to obey' [BAGD, LN; CEV, NAB, NJB], 'to subject oneself' [BAGD], 'to be subject to' [BNTC; KJV], 'to defer to' [WBC], 'to accept the authority of' [NRSV], 'to accept the authority of and do whatever they tell you' [NLT]. See this word at 2:13.

c. φόβος (LN 53.59) (BAGD 2.b.β. p. 864): 'respect' [BAGD; NIV, TNT], 'due respect' [REB], 'reverence' [LN], 'deep reverence' [WBC], 'due reverence' [NIC], 'deference' [NAB, NRSV], 'fear' [BNTC; KJV], not explicit [NLT]. The phrase 'with all respect/fear' is translated as an adverb: 'respectfully' [NJB]; as a verb phrase: 'always show respect to them' [CEV], 'show them complete respect' [TEV].

QUESTION—What relationship is indicated by the participle ὑποτασσόμενοι 'submitting'?

It is used as an imperative [BNTC, EGT, ICC, NIBC, Sel, TH, TNTC, WBC; all versions]. It resumes the thought of one of the previous imperatives [EGT, ICC]. It is an extension of the same imperative verb in 2:13 [NIC]. It extends the thought of 'honor all' by 'being in subjection' [Alf].

QUESTION—What is the nature of the servitude of the οἰκέτης 'household servant', and in what way does this differ from δοῦλος 'slave' in 2:16?
  The two terms are almost synonymous [TNTC, WBC]. Οἰκέτης 'household servant' is somewhat milder than δοῦλος 'slave' [Alf, EGT, NIBC]. The οἰκέτης 'household servant' represented a class of people without rights, but which comprised the bulk of teachers, doctors, and many professionals [BNTC, NCBC, TH, TNTC]. It was the most common form of employment in that society [TNTC]. Peter is addressing the slave as a member of a social unit, the household [Sel]. Since he has used the term δοῦλος 'slave' in 2:16 for all believers, he now switches to οἰκέτης 'household servant' to distinguish those who were actually slaves and to whom he is now addressing specific instructions [NIC, WBC]. The use of οἰκέτης 'household servant' suggests a parallel between slaves and all believers as God's household [EGT].
QUESTION—What is meant by ἐν παντὶ φόβῳ 'with all respect/fear' and toward whom is the respect/fear directed?
  1. It is the respect for or fear of God [BNTC, EGT, ICC, IVP, NCBC, NIC, Sel, WBC]. The fear of God is the motivation for submission to masters [IVP, NIC]. The phrase διὰ συνείδησιν θεοῦ 'because of consciousness of God' in 2:19 directs the focus toward God, not the master [ICC, NCBC]. Παντί 'all' intensifies the reference so that παντὶ φόβῳ 'with all respect/fear' functions as διὰ τὸν κύριον 'for the sake of the Lord' in 2:13 and διὰ συνείδησιν θεοῦ in the next verse [WBC]. It is the fear of God as indicated syntactically by its placement before 'masters' and as also indicated by the fact that Peter uses 'fear' only with reference to God and not man in the six other uses of φόβος in this epistle [NIC].
  2. It is respect for the master [Alf, TG; CEV, NAB, NJB, NRSV, REB, TEV]. It means to give all due respect to the master and thereby fear God [NTC]. It is the strong motivation to avoid displeasing the master [TNTC].

**not only to the good[a] and gentle[b] (ones) but also to the harsh[c] (ones).**
LEXICON—a. ἀγαθός (LN 88.1) (BAGD 1.b.α. p. 3): 'good' [LN, NIC; KJV, NAB, NIV, TNT], 'benevolent' [BAGD], 'kind' [BAGD, BNTC; CEV, NJB, NLT, NRSV, REB, TEV], 'just' [WBC].
  b. ἐπιεικής (LN 88.63) (BAGD p. 292): 'gentle' [BAGD, LN; KJV, NRSV], 'gracious' [LN], 'forbearing' [LN; REB], 'kind' [BAGD, NIC], 'considerate' [BNTC; NIV, TEV, TNT], 'reasonable' [NAB, NJB, NLT], 'thoughtful' [CEV], 'fair' [BNTC].
  c. σκολιός (LN 88.268) (BAGD 2. p. 756): 'harsh' [BNTC; NAB, NIV, NLT, NRSV, TEV], 'crooked, unscrupulous, dishonest' [BAGD, LN], 'unjust' [NIC; REB], 'cruel' [WBC; CEV], 'froward' [KJV], 'difficult to please' [NJB], 'perverse' [TNT].

# 1 PETER 2:19

**2:19** For<sup>a</sup> this (is) commendable,<sup>b</sup> if<sup>c</sup> because<sup>d</sup> of consciousness<sup>e</sup> of-God

LEXICON—a. γάρ (LN 89.23): 'for' [BNTC, LN, NIC, WBC; KJV, NIV, NLT, NRSV, TNT], 'because' [LN], 'you see' [NJB], not explicit [CEV, NAB, REB, TEV].

    b. χάρις (LN 25.89) (BAGD 2.b. p. 877): 'commendable' [NIV], 'that which brings favor' [BAGD, NIC], 'credit' [BAGD], 'grace' [WBC], 'a fine thing' [BNTC], 'thankworthy' [KJV]. The clause 'this is commendable' is translated 'it is grace' [WBC], 'it wins God's favor' [NIC], 'God will bless you' [CEV, TEV], 'this is the work of grace' [NAB], 'there is merit' [NJB], 'God is pleased with you' [NLT], 'it is a credit to you' [NRSV], 'it is a sign of grace' [REB], 'this is a mark of God's approval' [TNT].

    c. εἰ (LN 89.65): 'if' [BNTC, LN, NIC; all versions except NAB, NLT], 'when' [WBC; NAB, NLT].

    d. διά with accusative object (LN 89.26): 'because of' [BNTC, LN], 'because' [NIV, REB, TEV], 'on account of' [LN, NIC], 'out of' [WBC], 'for' [CEV, KJV], 'through' [NAB], 'in' [NJB], 'for the sake of' [NLT], not explicit [NRSV, TNT].

    e. συνείδησις (LN **28.4**) (BAGD 1. p. 786): 'consciousness of' [BAGD, BNTC], 'to be conscious of' [LN; NIV, TEV], 'conscious commitment to' [WBC], 'conscience' [NIC; KJV, NLT], 'awareness' [NAB, NJB], 'to be aware' [NRSV, TNT], 'in (his) thoughts' [REB], not explicit [CEV]. The phrase συνείδησιν θεοῦ 'consciousness of God' is translated 'a conscious commitment to God' [WBC], 'being loyal to him' [CEV], 'consciousness of God' [BNTC], 'conscious of God' [NIV], 'awareness of God's presence' [NAB], 'aware of God's presence' [TNT], 'being aware of God' [NRSV], 'awareness of God' [NJB], 'your conscience' [NLT], 'conscience toward God' [KJV], 'conscience before him' [NIC], 'because God is in his thoughts' [REB], 'conscious of his will' [TEV].

QUESTION—What relationship is indicated by γάρ 'for'?

Γάρ indicates the grounds of the previous specific statement about submission, by explaining it in terms of a general principle [TNTC].

QUESTION—What is meant by χάρις 'commendable'?

It refers to a good action that merits approval or praise [TH] or which is thankworthy and which wins favor or gains recognition from God [Alf, NIC]. Χάρις can be either a gracious act or, as in this case, the response to a gracious act [NIBC, Sel]. It is used in the same sense as it is used in Luke 6:32ff. as an act that counts with God, merits 'credit' with him, or evokes his approval [Alf, EGT, ICC, IVP, NCBC, NIC, NTC, Sel, WBC]. It is explained by the parallel term κλέος 'credit' in 2:20 [BNTC, ICC, IVP, NCBC].

QUESTION—What logical relation is introduced by εἰ 'if'?

    1. It introduces the clause that is the antecedent to τοῦτο 'this'.

        1.1 It states the condition for what would be commendable [Alf, BNTC, EGT, ICC, IVP, NCBC, NIBC, NIC, NTC, Sel, TH, TNTC, WBC;

KJV, NIV, NJB, NLT, NRSV, TEV]: if because of consciousness of God or of his will one endures unjust suffering, this results in the approval of God.
1.2 It states what would be the evidence of God's grace at work in a person [NAB, REB]: if someone patiently endures unjust suffering because of his awareness of God, it is a sign of God's grace at work in him.
1.3 It states what would be the evidence of God's approval of a person [TNT]: if someone patiently endures unjust suffering because of awareness of God's presence, it is a sign of God's approval.
2. It introduces the possibility that one might be mistreated because of conscience or of loyalty to God [CEV]: blessing comes from submission, not from endurance of unjust suffering, and the suffering comes because of loyalty to God.

QUESTION—What is meant by συνείδησις θεοῦ 'consciousness of God'?
1. The genitive θεοῦ is an objective genitive, so συνείδησις θεοῦ would be 'consciousness' or 'awareness' of God [Alf, BNTC, EGT, ICC, NCBC, NTC, TNTC, WBC; NAB, NIV, NJB, NRSV, REB, TEV, TNT]: he is conscious of God.
2. The word συνείδησις means 'conscience' in this passage [IVP, NIBC, NIC, Sel; KJV, NLT].
  2.1 The genitive θεοῦ means that the conscience is oriented toward and sensitive to God [IVP; KJV]. Conscience is used here as an equivalent for a faith that determines one's actions, so that θεοῦ becomes the object of that conscience or faith [IVP].
  2.2 The genitive θεοῦ is a reference to place or sphere similar to 'resurrection of life', 'resurrection of judgment', 'baptism of repentance', or 'body of sin' in other NT passages. The word θεοῦ 'of God' means 'for God's sake' [Sel].
  2.3 The genitive θεοῦ describes the character of the conscience as a conscience shaped by the knowledge of God [NIC] or a knowledge of God's will that is shared with other Christians [NIBC].

**someone[a] endures[b] affliction[c] suffering [d] unjustly.[e]**
LEXICON—a. τις (LN 92.12): 'someone' [LN, WBC; REB], 'they' [NIC], 'a man' [BNTC; KJV, NAB, NIV, TNT], 'you' [CEV, NJB, NLT, NRSV, TEV].
  b. pres. act. indic. ὑποφέρω (LN 25.175) (BAGD p. 848): 'to endure' [BAGD, LN; KJV, NAB, NLT, NRSV, REB, TEV], 'to put up with' [BNTC, LN, WBC; NJB], 'to bear up under' [BAGD, NIC; NIV], 'to bear' [TNT], not explicit [CEV].
  c. λύπη (LN 25.273) (BAGD p. 482): 'affliction' [BAGD, WBC], 'grief' [BAGD; KJV], 'pain' [BNTC, NIC; NIV, NJB, NRSV, REB, TEV], 'hardship' [NAB], 'troubles' [TNT], not explicit [CEV, NLT].

d. pres. act. participle of πάσχω (LN 24.78) (BAGD 3.a.β. p. 634): 'to suffer' [BAGD, BNTC, LN, NIC, WBC; all versions except CEV, NJB, NLT], 'punishment' [NJB], 'treatment' [NLT], not explicit [CEV].

e. ἀδίκως (LN 88.20) (BAGD p. 18): 'unjustly' [BAGD, BNTC, LN, WBC; NRSV], 'unfairly' [CEV], 'wrongfully' [KJV], 'undeservedly' [BAGD]. This adverb is also translated as an adjective: 'undeserved' [NJB, REB, TEV, TNT], 'unfair' [NLT], 'unjust' [NIC; NIV]; as a noun: 'injustice' [NAB].

**2:20** **For what credit[a] (is there) if doing-wrong[b] and being-beaten[c] you-will-endure?[d]**

LEXICON—a. κλέος (LN **87.5**) (BAGD p. 434): 'credit' [BAGD, BNTC; all versions except CEV, KJV, NJB], 'glory' [BAGD, NIC; KJV, NJB], 'renown' [WBC], 'honor' [LN]. The rhetorical question 'for what credit (is there)?' is also translated as an indicative statement: 'you don't gain anything' [CEV].

b. pres. act. participle of ἁμαρτάνω (LN 88.289) (BAGD 1. p. 42): 'to do wrong' [BAGD, BNTC, NIC, WBC; CEV, NAB, NIV, NLT, NRSV, REB, TEV], 'to do something wrong' [NJB], 'to sin' [BAGD, LN], 'to deserve (a beating)' [TNT]. This participle is also translated as a noun: 'faults' [KJV].

c. pres. pass. participle of κολαφίζω (LN 19.7) (BAGD 1. p. 441): 'to be beaten' [BAGD, BNTC, WBC; NLT, NRSV], 'to get beaten' [NAB], 'to be beaten with the fist' [LN], 'to receive a beating' [NIC; NIV], 'to be punished' [CEV], 'to be buffeted' [KJV]. This participle is also translated as a noun: 'beating' [NJB, TEV, TNT].

d. fut. act. indic. of ὑπομένω (LN 25.175) (BAGD 2. p. 846): 'to endure' [LN; NIV, NRSV, REB, TEV, TNT], 'to endure patiently' [NIC, WBC], 'to take it patiently' [BNTC; KJV], 'to put up with' [BAGD, LN; NJB], 'to be patient' [NLT], not explicit [CEV, NAB].

QUESTION—What relationship is indicated by the use of the future tense ὑπομενεῖτε 'you will endure' with the two present participles?

The future indicative verb used with the present participles indicates a sequence in time in which the doing good and being beaten precede the enduring [NIBC, TH, WBC]. The same effect would be achieved if aorist participles were used with a present indicative [WBC]. The present participles indicate habitual action [Alf].

**But if doing-good[a] and suffering you-will-endure, this (is) commendable in-the-sight-of[b] God.**

LEXICON—a. pres. act. participle of ἀγαθοποιέω (LN 88.3) (BAGD 2. p. 2): 'to do good' [BAGD, LN, NIC, WBC; NIV, TNT], 'to do something good' [CEV], 'to do rightly' [BNTC], 'to do right' [NLT, NRSV, TEV], 'to do well' [KJV], 'to behave well' [REB], 'to do what is good' [NAB], 'to do your duty' [NJB]. See this word at 2:15.

b. παρά with dative object (LN 90.20) (BAGD II.2. p. 610): 'in the sight of' [BAGD, BNTC, LN, NIC; NJB, REB], 'in (God's) eyes' [NAB], 'before (God)' [WBC; NIV], 'with (God)' [KJV]. The phrase χάρις παρὰ θεῷ 'commendable in the sight of God' is translated 'God is pleased with you' [NLT], 'you have God's approval' [NRSV], 'this is a mark of God's approval' [TNT], 'God will bless you for it' [TEV].

QUESTION—What is the relationship between the two participles ἀγαθοποιοῦντες 'doing good' and πάσχοντες 'suffering'.

1. The suffering is undeserved in that the person does right but suffers despite the good he has done [BNTC, NIBC, NTC, Sel, TH, TNTC; TEV]. The godless environment is antagonistic to anything that exposes its low standards and the good that the slave does may be misconstrued by the master [NIBC].
2. The doing good is the cause of the suffering, that is, he suffers for the good he has done [Alf, ICC, IVP, NIC, TG, WBC; all versions except TEV]. This refers to a slave who has chosen to do what is good in the sight of God instead of please his master and is therefore punished [WBC].

**DISCOURSE UNIT: 2:21–25** [IVP]. The topic is the basis for Christian living.

**2:21** For[a] to this you-were-called,[b] because[c] Christ also suffered for[d] you

TEXT—Instead of ὑπὲρ ὑμῶν 'for you', some manuscripts have ὑπὲρ ἡμῶν 'for us'. GNT selects the reading 'for you' with an A rating, indicating that the text is certain. The reading 'for us' is taken only by KJV.

LEXICON—a. γάρ (LN 89.23): 'for' [BNTC, LN, NIC; KJV, NRSV], 'in fact' [NJB], 'after all' [CEV], not explicit [WBC; NAB, NIV, NLT, REB, TEV, TNT].
  b. aorist pass. indic. of καλέω (LN 33.312) (BAGD 2. p. 399): 'to be called' [BAGD, BNTC, LN, NIC, WBC; all versions except REB], 'to be chosen' [CEV]. This verb is also translated as a verb phrase: 'it is your vocation' [REB]. See this word at 1:15, 2:9.
  c. ὅτι (LN 89.33): 'because' [BNTC, LN, NIC; KJV, NIV, NJB, NRSV, REB], 'since' [LN; NAB], 'for' [LN, WBC; TEV, TNT], not explicit [CEV, NLT].
  d. ὑπέρ with genitive object (LN 90.36) (BAGD 1.a.ε. p. 838): 'for' [LN, WBC; all versions except REB], 'on behalf of' [BNTC, LN, NIC; REB].

QUESTION—What is the antecedent of εἰς τοῦτο 'to this', to which they are called?
  1. They are called to do good, even if it means suffering for it [WBC].
  2. They are called to suffering [NCBC, NTC; CEV, NLT].
  3. They are called to endure patiently when suffering for doing good [Alf, BNTC, EGT, ICC, IVP, NIBC, NIC, Sel, TG, TH, TNTC; NAB, NJB, TEV, TNT].

QUESTION—Whom is Peter addressing?
  1. He is still addressing slaves [NIBC, NIC, Sel, TH].

2. He is addressing all the believers [IVP, NTC, TG, TNTC, WBC].
QUESTION—Who has called them?
It is God who has called them [BNTC, EGT, IVP, NCBC, NIBC, NIC, NTC, TG, TH, TNTC, WBC; CEV, NLT, TEV].
QUESTION—What relationship is indicated by ὅτι 'because'?
It introduces the grounds for the assertion regarding what believers are called to [Alf, BNTC, IVP, NTC, TH, TNTC, WBC]. It introduces a liturgical citation or creedal statement which amplifies the point he makes about suffering [BNTC]. It introduces a digression on Christ's passion in connection with suffering for doing good [WBC]. It explains that Christians suffer because Christ did, and they share his life and lot [IVP, NTC, TH]. It explains that suffering was part of Christ's life and we are called to imitate him [TNTC].
QUESTION—What is the function of καί 'also'?
It indicates that Christ underwent suffering too, just as some believers had [BNTC, EGT, TG, WBC; NAB, REB, TEV, TNT].
QUESTION—What is the significance of his use of the verb 'suffered' instead of 'died'?
Suffering is a theme throughout this epistle, and this passage in particular focuses on the suffering servant of Isaiah 53 [IVP]. The focus is on Christ's life of suffering, especially the passion [TNTC]. The focus in this passage is suffering, and Christ's suffering included his death [BNTC]. Peter uses 'suffered' instead of 'died' because what is in focus is the exemplary role, not the redemptive role [WBC]. Peter focuses on suffering as an example to the slaves who suffer [NIBC]. He uses 'suffer' because that is how Jesus referred to his death and also to relate more closely to the readers' situation [NIC].
QUESTION—What relationship is indicated by ὑπὲρ ὑμῶν 'for you'?
1. It indicates that the benefit for the believer is the example Christ set [TNTC, WBC].
2. It indicates that the benefit for the believer is the redemption that results from Christ's suffering [BNTC, EGT, IVP, NIBC, NIC, Sel, TG].
3. It indicates that the benefit for the believer is the redemption that results from Christ's suffering and the example that he set [Alf, TH].
4. It indicates that Christ's suffering benefits the believer morally and spiritually but does not say how in this passage [ICC].

**to-you leaving[a] a pattern[b] so-that[c] you-should-follow[d] the steps[e] of-him,**
TEXT—Instead of ὑμῖν 'to-you', some manuscripts have ἡμῖν 'to-us'. GNT selects the reading 'to-you' with an A rating, indicating that the text is certain. The reading 'to-us' is taken only by KJV.
LEXICON—a. pres. act. participle of ὑπολιμπάνω (LN **13.91**) (BAGD p. 845): 'to leave' [BNTC, NIC, WBC; all versions except CEV, NLT], 'to leave behind' [BAGD, LN]. The phrase 'to leave an example' is translated 'to be an example' [NLT], 'to set an example' [CEV].

b. ὑπογραμμός (LN **58.59**) (BAGD p. 843): 'example' [LN, NIC, WBC; all versions], 'pattern' [BAGD, BNTC], 'model' [BAGD, LN].
c. ἵνα (LN **89.59**): 'so that' [LN, NIC; NRSV, TEV], 'that' [BNTC, LN, WBC; KJV, NIV, REB, TNT], not explicit [CEV]. This conjunction along with the subjunctive verb that follows is translated as an infinitive: 'for you to follow' [NJB], 'to have you follow' [NAB]; by the imperative verb: 'follow (in his steps)' [NLT].
d. aorist act. subj. of ἐπακολουθέω (LN **41.47**) (BAGD 1. p. 282): 'to follow' [BAGD, BNTC, LN, NIC, WBC; all versions].
e. ἴχνος (LN **41.47**) (BAGD p. 384): 'steps' [all versions except CEV, NAB], 'footstep' [BAGD, NIC, WBC; CEV, NAB], 'footprint' [BAGD], 'tracks' [BNTC, LN].

QUESTION—What is meant by the metaphor of a ὑπογραμμός 'pattern'?

A ὑπογραμμός is a copy-book pattern for a child to use for learning to write letters by tracing or copying them [Alf, BNTC, EGT, ICC, IVP, NCBC, NIC, NTC, Sel, TH, WBC], or the sketch of an artist or architect that someone else traces or fills in [Alf, ICC, IVP, Sel, TH]. The idea here is that Christ is the model in a moral sense [WBC], a pattern that believers are to copy until they are like him [ICC, TH]. The believer follows in the lines already traced out by the exemplar [NIBC], since Christ sets the example of the kind of life that pleases God [TNTC]. The model is the manner in which Jesus endured suffering [IVP].

QUESTION—What is meant by the metaphor of 'following in the steps'?

It means to follow closely behind in as exact a manner as possible [Alf, NIBC]. The reference to footsteps means to move in the same direction, not necessarily in all the details, but in terms of the uncomplaining acceptance of suffering [BNTC]. It means to follow the example of his attitude as he endured undeserved suffering [TG, TH]. It means to trace Christ's path in meekness, integrity, patience, and honesty [NTC]. It means to follow Christ's precedent, moving in the same direction with the same goal and with the same attitude toward whatever experiences may come [WBC]. It means to share the same destiny and entrust the results to him, since the trail of Christ entails suffering [NIC].

**2:22** **who did not commit[a] sin[b] and-not was-found[c] deceit[d] in his mouth,**

LEXICON—a. aorist act. indic. of ποιέω (LN 42.7) (BAGD I.1.c.γ. p. 682): 'to commit' [BAGD, BNTC, NIC, WBC; NIV, NRSV], 'to do' [BAGD, LN; KJV, NAB, NJB]. The phrase ἁμαρτία ποιέω 'to commit sin' is translated 'to sin' [CEV, NLT].
b. ἁμαρτία (LN 88.289) (BAGD 1. p. 43): 'sin' [BAGD, LN; KJV, NIV, NRSV, REB, TEV, TNT], 'wrong' [NAB, NJB].
c. aorist pass. indic. of εὑρίσκω (LN 27.27) (BAGD 1.b. p. 325): 'find' [BAGD, BNTC, LN, NIC, WBC; KJV, NAB, NIV, NRSV], not explicit [TEV]. The phrase 'deceit is found in one's mouth' is translated 'to tell a

lie' [CEV], 'to speak deceit' [NJB], 'to deceive' [NLT], 'to be guilty of falsehood' [REB], 'to utter a lie' [TNT].
- d. δόλος (LN 88.154) (BAGD p. 203): 'deceit' [BAGD, LN, NIC, WBC; NAB, NIV, NJB, NRSV], 'lie' [CEV, TEV, TNT], 'deception' [BNTC], 'guile' [KJV], 'falsehood' [REB], not explicit [NLT]. See this word at 2:1.

**2:23** **who being-reviled<sup>a</sup> was not reviling-back,<sup>b</sup> (while) suffering (was) not threatening,<sup>c</sup>**

LEXICON—a. pres. pass. participle of λοιδορέω (LN 33.393) (BAGD p. 479): 'to be reviled' [BAGD, BNTC; KJV], 'to be abused' [BAGD; CEV, NRSV, REB, TNT], 'to be insulted strongly' [LN], 'to be insulted' [NIC, WBC; NAB, NJB, NLT, TEV]. This passive verb is also translated as an active verb with an indefinite subject 'they': 'to hurl insults' [NIV].
- b. imperf. act. indic. of ἀντιλοιδορέω (LN **33.394**) (BAGD p. 75): 'to revile in return' [BAGD, BNTC], 'to revile again' [KJV], 'to insult in return' [LN, WBC], 'to insult back' [NIC], 'to answer back with an insult' [TEV], 'to return an insult' [NAB], 'to get even' [CEV], 'to retaliate' [NIV, NLT, REB], 'to retaliate with insults' [NJB], 'to return abuse' [NRSV, TNT].
- c. imperf. act. indic. of ἀπειλέω (LN **33.291**) (BAGD p. 83): 'to threaten' [BAGD, BNTC, LN, NIC, WBC; KJV, NRSV, TEV, TNT], 'to threaten to get even' [NLT], 'to make threats' [CEV, NIV, NJB], 'to utter threats' [REB], 'to counter with threats' [NAB].

**but<sup>a</sup> entrusted<sup>b</sup> to the one judging<sup>c</sup> righteously;<sup>d</sup>**

LEXICON—a. δέ (LN 89.124): 'but' [BNTC, LN, NIC, WBC; KJV, NJB, NRSV, REB, TEV, TNT], 'instead' [CEV, NAB, NIV], not explicit [NLT].
- b. imperf. act. indic. of παραδίδωμι (LN 57.77) (BAGD 2. p. 615): 'to entrust' [BNTC, NIC; NIV], 'to commend' [BAGD], 'to commit' [BAGD; KJV], 'to leave' [WBC], 'to have faith in God' [CEV], 'to put trust in' [NJB], 'to deliver' [NAB], 'to give over, to hand over' [LN].
- c. κρίνω pres. act. participle (LN 56.20) (BAGD 4.b.α. p. 452): 'to judge' [BAGD, BNTC, NIC, WBC; all versions except NJB, TEV], 'to act as judge' [LN]. The relative clause 'the one who judges justly' is translated 'the upright judge' [NJB], 'the righteous judge' [TEV].
- d. δικαίως (LN 88.15) (BAGD 1.a. p. 198): 'justly' [BAGD, BNTC, WBC; NAB, NIV, NRSV, REB], 'fairly' [CEV, NLT], 'righteously' [NIC; KJV, TNT], 'right, just' [LN]. This adverb is also translated as an adjective modifying the judge: 'upright' [NJB], 'righteous' [TEV].

QUESTION—What is implied by the tenses of the verb forms in this verse?
The imperfect tense of the verb παρεδίδου 'entrusting', indicates an action that was repeated [TH, TNTC]. The imperfect tense of ἀντελοιδόρει 'reviling back' and ἠπείλει 'threatening' indicate habitual action [Alf] or action that was repeated [TH]. The imperfect tense of 'reviling back' and

'threatening' combined with the negative οὐκ indicates a consistent refusal to do so [WBC]. The present tense of κρίνοντι 'judging' indicates one whose office it is to judge [Alf]. The present tense of 'judging' indicates one who always does this, both in the past as well as the present [TH].

QUESTION—What is the implied object of παρεδίδου 'he was entrusting'?
1. He was entrusting his cause to God for ultimate vindication [BNTC].
2. He was entrusting himself to God [ICC, NCBC, NIBC, NIC, Sel, TG]. He was entrusting himself and his cause to God [NTC]. He was entrusting his case and his destiny to God [IVP].
3. He was entrusting or consigning his enemies over to God, leaving their fate in God's hands [WBC]. He was entrusting those who reproached him to God, possibly for forgiveness rather than for judgment [Alf].
4. He was entrusting the entire situation to God, including himself, his enemies, and his followers [TNTC].

**2:24** who himself bore[a] our sins in his body on/to[b] the tree[c]

TEXT—Instead of ἡμῶν 'our', some manuscripts have ὑμῶν 'your'. GNT does not mention this alternative. Only NAB reads 'your'.

LEXICON—a. aorist act. indic. of ἀναφέρω (LN 15.206) (BAGD 2. p. 63): 'to bear' [BNTC, NIC; KJV, NIV, NJB, NRSV, TNT], 'to carry' [WBC; CEV, REB, TEV], 'to carry up' [LN], 'to carry away' [NLT], 'to bring' [LN; NAB].
b. ἐπί with accusative object (LN 83.46, 84.17): 'on' [BNTC, LN (83.46), NIC; all versions except NAB, TEV], 'to' [LN (84.17), WBC; NAB, TEV].
c. ξύλον (LN 6.28) (BAGD 2.c. p. 549): 'tree' [BNTC, NIC; KJV, NIV], 'cross' [BAGD, LN, WBC; CEV, NAB, NJB, NLT, NRSV], 'gibbet' [REB].

QUESTION—What is meant by ἀνήνεγκεν 'bore'?
1. It means 'to carry up' in the sense of carrying a sacrifice to offer on an altar. The cross would take the place of the altar of sacrifice as the complement of ἀναφέρω [Alf, ICC; NAB, TEV].
2. It means 'to bear' in the sense of accepting the guilt, blame, and punishment for sins vicariously [BNTC, IVP, NCBC, NIBC, NIC, NTC, Sel]. His taking the punishment on the cross carried the sins away from us [BNTC, IVP, WBC].
3. It has both connotations, that of carrying up a sacrifice and of bearing sins vicariously [EGT].

QUESTION—What relationship is indicated by ἐπί 'on/to'?
1. It means 'to' or 'toward'.
   1.1 It means 'to' or 'up to' in the sense of carrying a sacrifice to an altar [Alf, EGT, ICC].
   1.2 It means that he carried sins in his body to the cross [NAB, TEV] or that he carried sins in his body, which was nailed to the cross [CEV].

# 1 PETER 2:24

1.3 It means 'to' but not in the sense of the cross being the destination to which sins are carried, but rather that in going to the cross he carried sins away [WBC].
2. It means 'on' [BNTC, NIC, NTC, TH, TNTC; all versions except CEV, NAB, TEV].

QUESTION—What is the reason for Peter's shift to the first person plural 'our'?

It focuses on the experience Peter had in common with the believers to whom he is writing [WBC]. It is intended to show that the community of believers after the time of Jesus were also included in the extent of the sacrifice [NIC]. It broadens the application of the passage to all people everywhere [NIBC, TG].

QUESTION—What is the significance of ἐν τῷ σώματι αὐτοῦ 'in his body'?

It amplifies and interprets 'himself' [WBC]. It points to the vicarious nature in which he endured in himself the penalty of sins as a representative [BNTC, TNTC]. It roots the event in history [NCBC, NIC]. It focuses on the reality of his personal suffering [ICC, IVP].

QUESTION—Why does he use the word ξύλον 'tree, wood (or wood object)' instead of σταυρός 'cross'?

In secular Greek usage, ξύλον was used for a stake or gallows and comes into Christian use from that source [NCBC]. In ancient Jewish usage, ξύλον had associations with a stake or gallows, and becomes almost a technical term for the cross [WBC]. It brings out the association with the curse of being hung on a tree for criminal punishment in Deuteronomy 21:22–23 [ICC, NIBC, NIC, NTC, TNTC].

**so-that[a] to-sins having-died/ceased[b] we-might-live[c] to-righteousness,[d]**

LEXICON—a. ἵνα (LN 89.59): 'so that' [BNTC, LN, NIC, WBC; all versions except KJV, NLT, TNT], 'that' [KJV, TNT], 'so' [NLT].
  b. aorist mid. (deponent = act.) participle of ἀπογίνομαι (LN **68.40, 74.27**) (BAGD p. 89): 'to die' [BAGD, **LN** (74.27), NIC; NIV, NJB, TEV, TNT], 'to be dead' [KJV, NLT], 'to cease to live for' [REB], 'to cease' [**LN** (68.40)], 'to stop (sinning)' [**LN** (68.40); CEV], 'to part with' [WBC], 'to break with' [BNTC]. This verb is also translated as an adjective: 'dead (to sin)' [NAB], 'free (from sins)' [NRSV].
  c. aorist act. subj. of ζάω (LN 41.2) (BAGD 3.b. p. 337): 'to live' [BAGD, BNTC, LN, NIC, WBC; all versions]. The subjunctive mood is indicated by various devices such as 'would start living' [CEV], 'should live' [KJV], 'could live' [NAB], 'might live' [NIV, NJB, NRSV, TEV, TNT], 'might begin to live' [REB], 'can live' [NLT].
  d. δικαιοσύνη (LN 88.13) (BAGD 4. p. 197): 'righteousness' [BAGD, BNTC, LN, NIC; KJV, NIV, NRSV, REB, TEV, TNT], 'what is right' [WBC; NLT], 'uprightness' [NJB], 'right' [CEV], 'in accord with God's will' [NAB].

QUESTION—What relationship is indicated by ἵνα 'so that' used with the aorist participle ἀπογενόμενοι 'having-died/ceased' and the aorist subjunctive verb ζήσωμεν 'we might live'?
1. The conjunction ἵνα introduces a purpose, 'that we might live (to righteousness)' which would be based on and follow the fact of having died/ceased to sins. That is, Christ bore our sins so that you might live for righteousness, having died/ceased to sins [Alf, BNTC, EGT, ICC, NIBC, NIC, Sel, TNTC, WBC; KJV, NAB, NRSV].
2. The conjunction ἵνα introduces two purposes, that a believer die/cease to sins and live to righteousness [NCBC, NTC; CEV, NIV, NJB, NLT, REB, TEV, TNT].

QUESTION—What is meant by ἀπογενόμενοι 'having died/ceased'?
This verb occurs only here in the NT, and indicates separation from or having no part in something, and hence, by extension, is sometimes used to refer to the separation of death [BNTC, ICC, IVP, NIBC, WBC].
1. It is used here in the sense of 'to be separated from or to cease from' [BNTC, ICC, NCBC, NIBC, Sel, WBC; CEV, NRSV, REB].
2. It is used here in the sense of 'to die to' [Alf, EGT, IVP, NIC, NTC, TNTC; all versions except CEV, NRSV, REB].

QUESTION—Is there any significance in his use of the plural 'sins'?
1. The plural is used to make it concrete, not abstract, and refers specifically to the sins carried by Christ on the tree, which include the 'impulses' referred to in 1:14 and 2:11 [WBC]. It is translated in the plural by KJV, NIV, NJB, NRSV.
2. The plural 'sins' is used as an equivalent for 'sin' [BNTC, ICC, IVP, NIC, Sel; NAB, NLT, REB, TEV, TNT].

QUESTION—Is righteousness used here in the sense of imputed righteousness or of right living?
It is an actual, practical righteousness in this life, an ethical and moral change from previous living [BNTC, ICC, NIC, NTC, Sel, TG, TH, TNTC, WBC; CEV, NAB].

**by-the-wound[a] of-whom you-were-healed[b].**
LEXICON—a. μώλωψ (LN 20.29) (BAGD p. 531): 'wound' [BAGD, LN], 'wounding' [WBC], 'bruise' [BNTC]. This singular noun is also translated as a plural: 'wounds' [NIC; NAB, NIV, NLT, NRSV, REB, TEV, TNT], 'cuts and bruises' [CEV], 'stripes' [KJV], 'bruises' [NJB].
b. aorist pass. indic. of ἰάομαι (LN 13.66, 23.136) (BAGD 2. p. 368): 'to be healed' [BNTC, LN (23.136, 13.66), NIC, WBC; all versions], 'to be cured, to be made well' [LN (23.136)], 'to be renewed' [LN (13.66)].

QUESTION—What is the μώλωψ 'wound' of Christ?
The word 'wound' is a synecdoche representing his entire passion or suffering [BNTC, WBC]. The slaves among Peter's readers could especially identify with Christ's suffering as they often had bruises or welts on their

backs through beatings such as he endured [Alf, BNTC, EGT, NCBC, NTC, Sel, TH].

QUESTION—What is meant by the use of the verb ἰάθητε 'to be healed'?

It refers to the benefit brought by Christ's vicarious suffering [BNTC, ICC, NCBC, NIBC, NIC, TH, TNTC]. To be healed is to be forgiven and restored to fellowship with God [NTC]. It refers to the strength to overcome temptation and do what is good [IVP]. It refers to being given spiritual health or life [TG]. It means spiritual healing from sin and its effects [BNTC, NIBC, TNTC], although physical healing is not excluded [NIBC]. It refers to religious conversion [WBC].

**2:25** For you-were straying[a] like sheep, but now you-have-returned[b] to the shepherd[c] and guardian[d] of-your souls.

TEXT—Instead of ἦτε γὰρ ὡς πρόβατα πλανώμενοι 'you were straying like sheep', some manuscripts have ἦτε γὰρ ὡς πρόβατα πλανώμενα 'you were like straying sheep'. GNT selects the reading πλανώμενοι 'you were straying' with a B rating, indicating that the text is almost certain. The reading πλανώμενα 'straying sheep' is taken by NIC; KJV, NIV, TEV.

LEXICON—a. pres. pass. participle of πλανάω (LN 15.24) (BAGD 2.b. p. 665): 'to stray' [WBC; NAB, REB], 'to go astray' [BAGD; KJV, NIV, NJB, NRSV, TNT], 'to stray away' [NIC], 'to wander' [NLT], 'to wander astray' [BNTC], 'to wander away' [CEV], 'to wander about' [BAGD, LN], 'to lose one's way' [TEV].
  b. aorist pass. indic. of ἐπιστρέφω (LN **31.60**) (BAGD 2.b. p. 301): 'to return' [**LN**, NIC; CEV, KJV, NAB, NIV, NJB, NRSV], 'to turn' [BAGD], 'to turn to' [BNTC, LN, WBC; NLT], 'to turn towards' [REB], 'to be brought back' [TEV], 'to turn back' [TNT].
  c. ποιμήν (LN 44.4) (BAGD 2.b.β. p. 684): 'shepherd' [BAGD, BNTC, LN, NIC, WBC; all versions].
  d. ἐπίσκοπος (LN **35.43**) (BAGD 1. p. 299): 'guardian' [BNTC, LN, WBC; NAB, NJB, NLT, NRSV, REB, TNT], 'overseer' [BAGD, NIC; NIV], 'keeper' [**LN**; TEV], 'protector' [CEV], 'bishop' [KJV].

QUESTION—What relationship is indicated by γάρ 'for'?

It introduces another reference from Isaiah to sum up the change of life experienced at conversion [NIC]. It justifies the previous statement by another quote from Isaiah [Alf]. It links the metaphor of straying sheep with that of healing in the previous passage [WBC].

QUESTION—What relationship is indicated by the use of the passive voice of the aorist verb ἐπεστράφητε 'you have returned'?
  1. In this context the passive voice has the connotation of the middle voice, meaning 'you have turned' or 'you have returned' [Alf, BNTC, ICC, NIBC, NIC, NTC, TNTC, WBC; all versions except TEV].
  2. The passive voice is used as a true passive and indicates an implied agent who causes the turning or bringing back, 'you have been brought back' [TG, TH; TEV].

QUESTION—What relationship is indicated by the use of the aorist tense of ἐπεστράφητε 'you have returned' with νῦν 'now'?
The aorist tense as it is used here with νῦν 'now' is a functional equivalent for the English perfect tense [Alf, BNTC, NIC, Sel, TH, WBC; all versions].
QUESTION—Does the use of ἐπεστράφητε 'you have returned' imply that the readers had once known God and 'wandered away'?
In this context the verb means 'to turn toward' and does not imply a return in the sense of once having been in fellowship with God [BNTC, NCBC, TNTC, WBC; NLT, REB].
QUESTION—Who is the shepherd?
Christ is the shepherd [Alf, BNTC, ICC, IVP, NCBC, NIBC, NIC, NTC, Sel, TG, TH, TNTC, WBC].
QUESTION—What does the genitive construction 'of your souls' modify?
1. It modifies both 'shepherd' and 'guardian'. Jesus is the shepherd of your souls and the guardian of your souls [ICC, NCBC, NIBC, NIC, TG, TNTC].
2. It modifies 'guardian'. The phrase 'guardian of your souls' interprets and defines 'shepherd'. Jesus is the shepherd, the guardian of your souls [BNTC, IVP, TH, WBC; NAB, NLT].

**DISCOURSE UNIT: 3:1-7** [IVP, NIC, TH, TNTC; CEV, NAB, NIV, NJB, NRSV, TEV]. The topic is wives and their husbands [IVP], living as married persons [TNTC], propriety of spouses in relation to their unbelieving spouses [NIC], relationship between husbands and wives [TH], wives and husbands [CEV, NIV, NRSV, TEV], for wife and husband [NAB], in marriage [NJB].

**DISCOURSE UNIT: 3:1-6** [Sel, WBC; NLT]. The topic is the duty of Christian wives [Sel], deference of wives to husbands [WBC], wives [NLT].

**3:1** Likewise[a] wives,[b] submitting[c] to their-own[d] husbands,[e]
LEXICON—a. ὁμοίως (LN 64.1) (BAGD p. 568): 'likewise' [BAGD, LN; KJV], 'in the same way' [BAGD, BNTC; NIV, NJB, NLT, NRSV, REB, TEV], 'too' [WBC], 'also' [TNT], not explicit [CEV, NAB].
b. γυνή (LN 10.54): 'wife' [BNTC, LN, NIC, WBC; all versions except NAB, REB], 'woman' [REB], 'married woman' [NAB].
c. pres. mid. participle of ὑποτάσσομαι (ὑποτάσσω) (LN 36.18) (BAGD 1.b.β. p. 848): 'to submit to' [LN; REB], 'to submit oneself to' [TEV], 'to subject oneself' [BAGD], 'to be subject to' [BNTC, NIC], 'to be in subjection to' [KJV], 'to be submissive to' [NIV], 'to defer to' [WBC], 'to put (your husband) first' [CEV], 'to obey' [BAGD, LN; NAB], 'to be obedient to' [NJB], 'to accept the authority of' [NLT, NRSV]. See this word at 2:13 and 2:18.
d. ἴδιος (LN 57.4) (BAGD 2.b. p. 370): 'their own' [NIC], 'your own' [KJV], 'your' [BNTC, WBC; all versions except KJV], 'one's own' [BAGD, LN].

e. ἀνήρ (LN 10.53) (BAGD 1. p. 66): 'husband' [BAGD, BNTC, LN, NIC, WBC; all versions].

QUESTION—What relationship is indicated by ὁμοίως 'likewise'?
1. It refers back to the general theme of submission began in 2:13 [Alf, BNTC, IVP, NCBC, NIC, NTC, Sel, TNTC].
2. It indicates a comparison with the command for slaves to submit to their masters in 2:18 [ICC, TG, TNTC]. The comparison of a wife's submission to a slave's submission is not extended in every way that the slave would be subject to a master, but is similar in terms of doing it reverently for the Lord's sake, whether the husband is bad or good [TNTC].
3. The word is used as a connective adverb only, as in 3:7 [NIBC, WBC].

QUESTION—What is implied by the use of the word ἴδιος 'their own'?
Since γυναῖκες 'wives' could be 'women' and ἄνδρες 'husbands' could be 'men', the use of ἴδιος 'their own' clarifies that the reference is to the marriage relationship [WBC]. It makes it clear that the reference is to the marriage relationship, not the relationship between men and women in general within society at large [IVP, NCBC, NTC, Sel]. It places submission within the sphere of an institution, the family, which has a recognized head [Sel]. 'Your own' makes it clear that the wives are not subject to any stranger [ICC].

**so-that[a] even if any[b] disobeys/disbelieves[c] the word,[d]**

LEXICON—a. ἵνα (LN 89.59): 'so that' [BNTC, LN, NIC, WBC; NAB, NIV, NRSV, REB, TEV], 'that' [KJV], not explicit [CEV, NJB, NLT, TNT].
b. τινες (LN 92.12): 'any' [BNTC; KJV, TNT], 'anyone' [LN], 'any of them' [NAB, NIV, REB, TEV], 'some' [NJB], 'some of them' [NIC; NRSV], 'any among them' [WBC], not explicit [CEV, NLT].
c. pres. act. indic. of ἀπειθέω (LN 36.23, 31.107) (BAGD 1., 3. p. 82): 'to disobey' BAGD, [LN (36.23)], 'to be disobedient' [WBC], 'to not obey' [BNTC; KJV, NRSV], 'to refuse to believe, to reject the Christian message' [LN (31.107)], 'to disbelieve' [BAGD; REB], 'to not believe' [NIC; NAB, NIV, NJB, TEV, TNT], 'to oppose (the message)' [CEV], 'to refuse to accept' [NLT]. See this word at 2:8.
d. λόγος (LN 33.260) (BAGD 1.b.β. p. 478): 'word' [BAGD, BNTC, NIC, WBC; KJV, NIV, NJB, NRSV], 'the word of the gospel' [NAB], 'God's word' [TEV], 'message' [CEV, TNT], 'Christian message' [BAGD], 'the good news' [NLT], 'the gospel' [BAGD, LN; REB]. See this word at 1:23.

QUESTION—How is the word εἴ 'if' used in this context?
1. It posits that there may be unbelieving husbands, but does not assume it as the norm [Alf, EGT, TNTC, WBC]. Peter is speaking to all women, not just those whose husbands do not believe [Sel].
2. It introduces a conditional clause that assumes a case that really exists in which some women have husbands who do not believe [NTC].

# 1 PETER 3:1

3. It is presented as a possibility, but represents the actual fact that most of the Christian women had unbelieving husbands [BNTC, TG].
4. This entire section is addressed to women whose husbands did not believe [NIC].

**through[a] the conduct[b] of the wives without[c] a word[d] they-may/will-be-gained,[e]**

LEXICON—a. διά (LN 89.76): 'through' [LN; NAB], 'by' [BNTC, LN, NIC, WBC; all versions except NAB, TEV], not explicit [TEV].
- b. ἀναστροφή (LN 41.3) (BAGD p. 61): 'conduct' [BAGD, LN, WBC; NAB, NRSV, TEV], 'behavior' [BNTC, LN; NIV, REB], 'life-style' [NIC], 'what you do' [CEV], 'conversation' [KJV], 'the way they behave' [NJB], 'how you live' [TNT], 'your lives' [NLT]. See this word at 1:15, 1:18, and 2:12.
- c. ἄνευ (LN **89.120**) (BAGD 2. p. 65): 'without' [BAGD, BNTC, **LN**, NIC, WBC; KJV, NIV, NJB, NRSV, REB], 'apart from' [LN; NAB], not explicit [CEV, NLT, TEV, TNT]. Ἄνευ λόγου 'without a word' is variously expressed in verb phrases: 'no one will have to say anything' [CEV], 'your godly lives will speak better to them than any words' [NLT], 'it will not be necessary for you to say a word' [TEV], 'there will be no need for words' [TNT].
- d. λόγος (LN 33.99) (BAGD 1.a.α. p. 478): 'word' [BAGD, BNTC, NIC, WBC; all versions except CEV, NAB], 'speech' [LN], 'preaching' [NAB], not explicit [CEV]. This noun is singular and anarthrous (lacking an article), but is also translated as a plural: 'words' [NIV, NLT, TNT]; as having a definite article: 'the word' [KJV].
- e. fut. pass. indic. of κερδαίνω (LN 57.189) (BAGD 1.b. p. 429): 'to gain' [BAGD, LN], 'to win over' [BNTC, WBC; all versions except KJV], 'to win' [NIC; KJV].

QUESTION—How does the use of λογος 'word' in this clause compare with its use in the previous clause?
1. Both refer to the word of the gospel message [ICC; KJV, NAB].
2. The first use refers to the message of the gospel, and the second simply to speech in general [NCBC, NIC, NTC, Sel, TG, TH, TNTC; all versions except KJV, NAB]. This represents a rhetorical device called antanaclasis which is a play on words wherein the word is repeated with a different sense of meaning the second time [Alf, BNTC, EGT, WBC].

QUESTION—What meaning is implied by the use of the verb κερδηθήσονται 'they-may/will-be-gained' in the future indicative instead of in the aorist subjunctive, as would normally be expected with ἵνα 'so that'?
1. The future tense is used with ἵνα in place of the subjunctive, but with the same meaning as the subjunctive, indicating what is hoped for or what may happen [Alf, BNTC, ICC, NIC, Sel, TG, TNTC, WBC; all versions except CEV, NLT, TEV].

2. It is used as a future tense, indicating what will happen [CEV, NLT, TEV].

**3:2** having-observed<sup>a</sup> the pure<sup>b</sup> conduct of-you in reverence/fear.<sup>c</sup>

LEXICON—a. aorist. act. participle of ἐποπτεύω (LN 24.45) (BAGD p. 305): 'to observe' [BAGD, LN, NIC, WBC; NAB, REB, TNT], 'to watch' [LN; NLT], 'to see' [LN; CEV, NIV, NJB, NRSV, TEV], 'to behold' [KJV], 'to take note' [BNTC]. See this word at 2:12.

b. ἁγνός (LN **88.28**) (BAGD 2. p. 12): 'pure' [BAGD, BNTC, LN, WBC; CEV, NLT, TEV], 'holy' [BAGD], 'chaste' [REB]. This adjective is also translated as a noun: 'purity' [NIC; NAB, NIV, NJB, NRSV]; as an adverb: 'chastely' [TNT].

c. φόβος (LN 53.59) (BAGD 2.b.β. p. 864): 'reverence' [BAGD, LN, NIC; NIV, NJB, NRSV], 'respect' [BAGD], 'fear' [KJV]. The phrase 'in reverence' is translated as an adjective: 'reverent' [BNTC, WBC; NAB, TEV], 'respectful' [REB], 'godly' [NLT]; as an adverb: 'respectfully' [TNT]; as a verb phrase: 'you honor (God)' [CEV]. See this word at 1:17 and 2:18.

QUESTION—What is meant by ἁγνός 'pure' in this context?

It refers to being chaste, that is, morally and sexually pure [IVP, TNTC, WBC]. It refers to moral purity, virtue, or sincerity that arises out of reverence to God [ICC, NCBC, NIC, Sel]. It is purity in a wider sense, including moral and sexual purity but not limited to that [Alf, BNTC, EGT, TG, TH]. It is separation from the world [NIBC]. It is exemplary moral purity and holy behavior [NTC].

QUESTION—How is the term ἐν φόβῳ 'in reverence/fear' used in this context?

The term ἐν φόβῳ 'in fear' serves as an adjective since there is no adjectival form of φόβος for 'reverent' [WBC]. It is used as an adjective to modify the conduct or way of life [BNTC, WBC; NIV, NJB, NLT, NRSV, REB, TEV, TNT] or the purity of the life [NAB].

QUESTION—To whom is the reverence/fear directed?

1. It refers to respect for the husband [Alf, NTC, TG].
2. It refers to the fear of God [BNTC, ICC, IVP, NCBC, NIC, WBC; CEV, NLT].

**3:3** Of-whom the adornment<sup>a</sup> let-it-not-be<sup>b</sup> the outward<sup>c</sup> adornment

LEXICON—a. κόσμος (LN **6.188, 79.12**) (BAGD 1. p. 445): 'adornment' [BAGD, BNTC, LN (6.188), NIC, WBC; NIV, NJB, REB], 'adorning' [BAGD, LN (79.12); KJV], 'affectation' [NAB], 'beauty' [NLT, TNT], 'aids to make yourself beautiful' [TEV], not explicit [CEV]. This noun is also translated as a verb: 'to adorn' [NRSV].

b. pres. act. impera. of εἰμί (LN 13.1): 'to be'. The negative command ἔστω οὐχ 'let it not be' is translated 'let it not be' [BNTC, NIC; KJV], 'it should not be' [NJB], 'it should not consist of' [WBC], 'don't depend on' [CEV], 'it should not depend on' [TNT], 'it should not come from' [NIV],

'it should lie not in' [REB], 'is not for you' [NAB], 'don't be concerned about' [NLT], 'do not (adorn)' [NRSV], 'you should not use' [TEV].
c. ἔξωθεν (LN **83.21**) (BAGD 1.b.γ. p. 279): 'outward' [KJV, NIV, NLT, REB, TEV, TNT], 'external' [BAGD, BNTC, NIC, WBC], 'outside' [BAGD, LN], 'exterior' [NJB], not explicit [CEV, NAB]. This adjective is also translated as an adverb: 'outwardly' [NRSV].

**of-the-braiding[a] of-hair[b] and putting-on[c] of-gold[d] or wearing[e] of-garments[f]**
  LEXICON—a. ἐμπλοκή (LN **49.26**) (BAGD p. 256): 'braiding' [BAGD, BNTC, LN; NRSV, REB], 'braided' [NIC, WBC; NIV, NJB], 'plaiting' [KJV]. The expression ἐμπλοκῆς τριχῶν 'the braiding of hair' is translated 'fancy hairdos' [CEV], 'elaborate hairdress' [NAB], 'hairstyles' [TNT], 'fancy hairstyles' [NLT], 'the way you fix your hair' [TEV].
  b. θρίξ (LN **8.12**) (BAGD 2. p. 364): 'hair' [BAGD, BNTC, LN, NIC, WBC; KJV, NIV, NJB, NRSV, REB, TEV], 'hairdo' [CEV], 'hairdress' [NAB], 'hairstyles' [NLT, TNT].
  c. περίθεσις (LN **49.7**) (BAGD p. 647): 'putting on' [BAGD, LN, NIC], 'wearing' [BAGD, **BNTC, LN**; KJV, NAB, NIV, NRSV, REB], not explicit [CEV, NJB, NLT, TNT]. This noun is also translated as a verb: '(you) put on' [WBC; TEV].
  d. χρυσίον (LN **6.189**) (BAGD p. 888): 'gold jewelry' [BAGD, LN, NIC; CEV, NIV, NJB], 'golden jewelry' [NAB], 'gold ornaments' [BAGD, LN; NRSV, REB], 'gold trinkets' [BNTC], 'gold' [WBC; KJV], 'expensive jewelry' [NLT], 'jewelry' [TEV, TNT].
  e. ἔνδυσις (LN **49.11**) (BAGD 1. p. 263): 'wearing' [**LN**; NIV, NRSV], 'dressing' [LN, NIC], 'dressing up' [REB], 'putting on' [BAGD, BNTC; KJV], 'donning' [NAB], '(you) wear' [WBC; TEV], not explicit [CEV, NJB, NLT, TNT].
  f. ἱμάτιον (LN **6.162**) (BAGD 1. p. 376): 'garment' [BAGD], 'clothes' [NIC, WBC; TNT], 'clothing' [LN], 'expensive clothes' [CEV], 'beautiful clothes' [NLT], 'fine clothes' [NIV, REB], 'fine clothing' [NJB, NRSV], 'apparel' [KJV], 'gowns' [BNTC], 'rich robes' [NAB], 'dresses' [TEV]
QUESTION—What is the intent of this exhortation?
  1. Believing women should not adorn themselves outwardly by braiding hair, or by wearing gold ornaments or fine clothes [NRSV] or use outward aids to make themselves beautiful [TEV]. They should not use elaborate hairstyles, wear gold jewelry, or rich robes [NAB].
  2. The beauty of believing women should not consist of or depend on outward adornment [BNTC, NIC, WBC; all versions except NAB, NRSV, TEV]. The intent is to promote certain positive values, not to prohibit specific things [BNTC]. There is a shift of focus from ostentatious, elaborate or luxurious outward adornment to the inner self [IVP, NCBC, NIBC, NTC, Sel, TNTC, WBC]. It is a figurative prohibition, not a literal

one [NIBC]. He is not prohibiting the braiding of hair, but rather elaborate hairdos [TG, TH].

**3:4** but[a] the hidden[b] person[c] of-the heart[d] in the incorruptible[e] (adornment)

LEXICON—a. ἀλλά (LN 89.125): 'but' [BNTC, LN; KJV, NJB, REB], 'but rather' [NIC], 'rather' [WBC; NAB, NRSV], 'instead' [NIV, TEV], not explicit [CEV, NLT, TNT].
  b. κρυπτός (LN 26.1) (BAGD 1. p. 454): 'hidden' [BAGD, BNTC, LN, NIC, WBC; KJV, NAB], 'inner' [LN; NIV, NRSV, TEV, TNT], 'interior' [NJB], 'within' [NLT], 'inmost' [REB], not explicit [CEV]. The phrase ὁκρυπτός τῆς καρδίας ἄνθρωπος 'the hidden person of the heart' is translated 'that comes from within' [NLT], 'the inner springs of a person's nature' [TNT], 'in your heart' [CEV].
  c. ἄνθρωπος (LN 26.1) (BAGD 2.c.α. p. 68): 'person' [BNTC, LN, WBC], 'self' [NIV, NRSV, REB, TEV], 'man' [BAGD; KJV], 'character' [NAB], 'disposition' [NJB], not explicit [CEV, NLT, TNT]. 'Person of the heart' is also translated 'inner self' [LN, NIC; NIV, NRSV], 'true inner self' [TEV], 'inmost self' [REB].
  d. καρδία (LN 26.3) (BAGD 1.b.α. p. 403): 'heart' [BAGD, BNTC, LN, WBC; CEV, KJV, NAB, NJB], 'inner self' [LN], not explicit [NLT]. 'Hidden' and 'of the heart' are conflated and translated by an adjective: 'inner' [NIC; NIV, NRSV, TEV, TNT], 'inmost' [REB].
  e. ἄφθαρτος (LN 23.128) (BAGD p. 125): 'imperishable' [BAGD, BNTC, LN, NIC, WBC; NJB, REB], 'incorruptible' [BAGD], 'not corruptible' [KJV], 'unfading' [NAB, NIV, NLT], 'lasting' [NRSV], 'ageless' [TEV], 'immortal' [BAGD, LN]. This word is also translated by a verb phrase: 'this kind will last' [CEV], 'that spirit nothing can destroy' [TNT]. See this word at 1:4 and 1:23.

QUESTION—What does the adjective ἄφθαρτος 'incorruptible' modify?

There is no word in the Greek text corresponding to 'adornment', but if ἄφθαρτος is taken as being adjectival then a word must be supplied in English translation for it to modify. English versions employ words such as 'adornment' [NIC, WBC; NAB, NRSV], 'beauty' [CEV, NIV, NLT, TEV], 'quality' [BNTC; NJB, REB], 'ornament' [KJV], 'spirit' [TNT].
  1. It is used adjectivally and refers to the quality of a gentle and quiet spirit [BNTC, IVP, WBC], or the beauty or adornment of a gentle and quiet spirit [Alf, EGT, NIBC, NIC, TG, TH, TNTC; all versions].
  2. It is used as an abstract noun, 'the incorruptibility' [ICC, NCBC, Sel]. Even though used as a noun, the sense is 'incorruptible apparel' [ICC].

QUESTION—What is meant by καρδία 'heart' in this verse?

The 'person of the heart' is the inner nature or personality [BNTC, NCBC, NTC, TNTC]. 'Of the heart' is used appositively, meaning that 'the hidden person' is 'the heart', and refers to the mind, as opposed to the flesh [EGT]. It refers to what a person really is inside [NIC, Sel, TG, TH], who the person is at the deepest level [WBC]. It is not so much the invisible nature of the person, but the entire person as determined by the inner nature [IVP]. It is the regenerated inner self [Alf].

**of the gentle[a] and quiet[b] spirit,[c] which is of-great-worth[d] in-the-sight-of[e] God.**

LEXICON—a. πραΰς (LN 88.60) (BAGD p. 699): 'gentle' [BAGD, BNTC, LN, NIC; all versions except KJV], 'humble' [BAGD, WBC], 'meek' [BAGD, LN; KJV].

   b. ἡσύχιος (LN **88.104**) (BAGD p. 349): 'quiet' [BAGD, LN, WBC; all versions except NAB, NJB, TNT], 'calm' [NAB, TNT], 'peaceful' [**LN**, NIC; NJB], 'tranquil' [BNTC].

   c. πνεῦμα (LN 30.6) (BAGD 3.c. p. 675): 'spirit' [BNTC, NIC, WBC; all versions except CEV, NAB], 'disposition' [BAGD, LN; NAB], 'attitude' [LN], not explicit [CEV].

   d. πολυτελής (LN **65.3**) (BAGD p. 690): 'of great worth' [NIV], 'of high value' [REB], 'of the greatest value' [TEV], 'precious' [NAB], 'so precious' [NJB, NLT], 'very precious' [BNTC; NRSV, TNT], 'most lavish' [WBC], 'very special' [CEV], 'of great price' [KJV], 'expensive' [BAGD, LN], 'costly' [BAGD], 'very costly' [NIC].

   e. ἐνώπιον (LN 90.20) (BAGD 3. p. 270): 'in the sight of' [LN; KJV, NJB, REB], 'in (God's) sight' [BNTC, NIC, WBC; NIV, NRSV, TEV, TNT], 'in (God's) eyes' [NAB], 'before' [BAGD], 'in the judgment of' [BAGD, LN], 'to (God)' [NLT], '(God) considers it' [CEV].

QUESTION—What does the term 'spirit' refer to in this context?

   1. It is the inner disposition, the inner qualities of character [BNTC, ICC, NIC, NTC, Sel, TG, TH, TNTC, WBC; CEV, NAB].
   2. It refers to the spirit of God [NCBC].

QUESTION—What is of great worth in God's sight?

   1. It is the gentle and quiet spirit [Alf, BNTC, EGT, NTC, TNTC; TNT].
   2. It is the beauty or adornment that comes from a gentle and quiet spirit [NIBC, TG, TH; CEV, TEV].
   3. It is all that has been described in this verse, which amounts to true virtuous character [NCBC, NIC, WBC].

**3:5** **For thus[a] long-ago[b] also the holy[c] women the-ones hoping[d] in God would-adorn[e] themselves submitting[f] to their own husbands,**

LEXICON—a. οὕτως (LN 61.9, 61.10): 'thus' [LN (61.9)], 'in this way' [LN (61.9)], 'as follows' [LN (61.10)], 'that was how' [BNTC, WBC; NJB], 'this is how' [REB, TNT], 'in this way' [NIC; NAB, NRSV], 'that is the way' [NLT], 'this is the way' [NIV], 'after this manner' [KJV], not explicit [CEV, TEV]. The LN entry 61.9 refers to that which precedes, and entry 61.10 refers to that which follows. See this word at 2:15.

   b. ποτέ (LN 67.30): 'long ago' [WBC; CEV, NRSV], 'in the old days' [BNTC], 'of old' [NLT], 'in the old time' [KJV], 'of past ages' [NAB],

'in past days' [REB], 'of the past' [NIV, NJB, TEV], 'in bygone days' [TNT], 'once' [NIC], 'when' [LN].
c. ἅγιος (LN 53.46) (BAGD 1.b.α. p. 9): 'holy' [BAGD, BNTC, NIC, WBC; KJV, NAB, NIV, NJB, NLT, NRSV], 'devout' [LN], 'godly' [LN]. This word is also translated as a verb phrase: 'who worshipped God' [CEV]. See this word at 1:15–16 and 2:9.
d. pres. act. participle of ἐλπίζω (LN 25.59) (BAGD 3. p. 252): 'to hope' [BNTC, LN, WBC; NJB, NRSV], 'to put one's hope in' [BAGD; CEV, NIV, REB], 'to place one's hope in' [NIC; TEV], 'to look in hope to' [TNT], 'to trust' [KJV, NLT], 'to be reliant' [NAB].
e. imperf. act. indic. of κοσμέω (LN 79.12) (BAGD 2.b.α. p. 445): 'to adorn' [BAGD, LN; KJV, NAB, NRSV, TNT], 'to beautify' [LN], 'to make beautiful' [BAGD; CEV, NIV, NLT, TEV], 'to make attractive' [BAGD; REB], 'to dress attractively' [NJB].
f. pres. mid. participle of ὑποτάσσομαι (ὑποτάσσω) (LN 36.18) (BAGD 1.b.β. p. 848): 'to submit to' [LN; REB, TEV], 'to submit to the authority of' [TNT], 'to subject oneself' [BAGD], 'to be submissive to' [BNTC, NIC; NIV, NJB], 'to be in subjection to' [KJV], 'to accept the authority of' [NLT, NRSV], 'to obey' [BAGD, LN], 'to be obedient to' [NAB], 'to defer to' [WBC], 'to put (their husbands) first' [CEV]. See this word at 2:13, 2:18, and 3:1.

QUESTION—To what does οὕτως 'thus' refer?
1. The word οὕτως 'thus' refers to the statements of the previous verse [Alf, BNTC, IVP, NIC, NTC, TNTC; KJV, NAB, NIV, NJB, NLT]: the holy women adorned themselves with a humble and quiet spirit. They adorned themselves with the hidden person of the heart, having the quality of the humble and quiet spirit [WBC]. They adorned themselves with holiness [Sel].
2. The word οὕτως 'thus' refers to what follows immediately in this verse [TG, TH; CEV, TEV]: the holy women adorned themselves by submitting to their husbands.
3. The word οὕτως 'thus' refers to the whole context [NRSV]: the women adorned themselves with a gentle and quiet spirit by accepting the authority of their husbands.

QUESTION—What is meant by the designation ἅγιαι γυναῖκες 'holy women'?
It refers to the saintly women of the OT [IVP]. It refers to women who were called by God and inspired by the spirit of God [BNTC]. It refers to believing women who worshipped God and had a special relationship of consecration and dedication to him [TH]. It refers to the four matriarchs, Sarah, Rebecca, Rachel, and Leah, who were considered holy because of their faith in God and their deference to their husbands [WBC]. The holy women were heroines of the OT who placed their faith in God and who looked forward to redemption [NIC]. The holy women were believing women whose lives showed that they are God's people [NIBC]. They are called holy because they had a relationship with God in that they hoped in

him, cultivated virtuous character, and submitted to their husbands [NTC]. They were called holy because they belonged to God's chosen people [NCBC]. They were called holy because they were godly [TNTC].

**3:6** as Sarah obeyed[a] Abraham calling[b] him "lord,"[c] of-whom you-have-become[d] children[e]

LEXICON—a. aorist act. indic. of ὑπακούω (LN 36.15) (BAGD 1. p. 837): 'to obey' [BAGD, BNTC, LN, NIC, WBC; all versions except NAB, NJB], 'to be obedient to' [NJB], 'to be subject to' [BAGD; NAB].
- b. pres. act. participle of καλέω (LN 33.131) (BAGD 1.a.β. p. 399): 'to call' [BAGD, LN; all versions].
- c. κύριος (LN 57.12) (BAGD 1.b. p. 459): 'lord' [BAGD, BNTC, LN, NIC, WBC; KJV, NJB, NRSV], 'master' [BAGD, LN; all versions except KJV, NJB, NRSV].
- d. aorist pass. (deponent = act.) indic. of γίνομαι (LN 13.48): 'to become' [BNTC, LN, WBC; NRSV, REB, TNT], 'to be' [NIC; all versions except NRSV, REB, TNT]. Those versions that translate this verb as 'become' render it in the perfect tense 'you have become' and those that translate it as 'to be' do so in the present tense 'you are'.
- e. τέκνον (LN 10.28) (BAGD 2.d. p. 808): 'child' [BAGD, BNTC, WBC; CEV, NAB, NJB], 'daughter' [NIC; all versions except CEV, NAB, NJB].

QUESTION—What obedience is he referring to?

The verb ὑπήκουσεν 'obeyed' is a constative aorist which refers not to a specific event, but to an ongoing pattern of conduct in time past [TNTC]. This word refers to Sarah's whole course of obedience [Alf]. Her obedience was her submissive character [NIC]. Peter uses ὑπακούω 'obey' as a synonym for ὑποτάσσομαι 'to be subject' for stylistic reasons, and is referring to her subjection to Abraham, not to any specific incident [WBC].

QUESTION—What did it mean for Sarah to call Abraham κύριος 'lord'?

The Greek word κύριος represents a Hebrew word that refers to lords and masters in general [IVP].
1. This was a customary title of respect for a husband [NIBC, NTC].
1.1 This was a conventional title in the Orient, but it demonstrates Sarah's respect and obedience [BNTC, NIC]. It implies at least some degree of subjection [EGT].
1.2 This term was synonymous with 'husband' and had little if any other implied meaning [NCBC].
2. Sarah does not use the normal Hebrew term for husband, which would have been *Ba[]aλ*, and through her respectful way of addressing Abraham, she becomes a conspicuous OT example of godly submission [IVP]. In ancient literature the Hebrew word *[]aΔov* is not often used to refer to a husband and, for this reason, it catches Peter's attention as an unusual example of respect and deference by Sarah [WBC].

QUESTION—What does it mean to be or have become a child of Sarah?
1. It is an idiomatic expression in Hebrew and is used figuratively to refer to imitating Sarah's example or to exhibiting the same character that she exhibited [ICC, IVP, NIBC, Sel, TG, TH].
2. It refers to conversion.
2.1 All believers are spiritual children of Abraham and Sarah by virtue of their faith in Christ [Alf, TNTC, WBC]. Daughters of Sarah are joint heirs of the honor and promises that Abraham and Sarah received and members of Sarah's true spiritual family [TNTC]. It also implies a similar inward nature as expressed in conduct and ethics [WBC].
2.2 All believers are spiritual children of Abraham, and women, in particular, are children of Sarah by virtue of their faith [BNTC, NCBC, NIC]. Being a child of Sarah refers primarily to conversion but also implies following Sarah's example [BNTC].
2.3 Men are spiritual children of Abraham by virtue of their faith and women are children of Sarah [EGT, NTC].

**doing-good<sup>a</sup> and not fearing<sup>b</sup> any terror.<sup>c</sup>**

LEXICON—a. pres. act. participle of ἀγαθοποιέω (LN 88.3) (BAGD 2. p. 2): 'to do good' [BAGD, LN, WBC; REB, TEV, TNT], 'to do what is good' [NRSV], 'to do what is right' [BAGD, BNTC, NIC; NAB, NIV, NLT], 'to do right' [CEV], 'to do well' [KJV], 'to live a good life' [NJB]. See this word at 2:15, 20.
b. pres. mid. (deponent = act.) participle of φοβέομαι (φοβέω) (LN 25.252) (BAGD 1.b.γ. p. 863): 'to fear' [LN, NIC], 'to be afraid' [LN; KJV], 'to be terrified' [BNTC], 'to be frightened' [WBC; CEV], 'to be alarmed' [NAB]. The participial phrase 'not fearing any terror' is translated 'let nothing terrify you' [BNTC], 'let nothing frighten you' [WBC], 'don't let anything frighten you' [CEV], 'let no fears alarm you' [NAB], 'do not give way to fear' [NIV], 'live free from fear and worry' [NJB], 'without fear of what your husbands may do' [NLT], 'never let fears alarm you' [NRSV], 'showing no fear' [REB], 'not afraid of anything' [TEV], 'never let your calm be disturbed' [TNT].
c. πτόησις (LN **25.265**) (BAGD 2. p. 727): 'terror' [BAGD], 'fear' [BAGD], 'something alarming' [LN], 'intimidation' [NIC], 'amazement' [KJV]. 'Not fearing any terror' is translated 'don't let anything frighten you' [CEV], 'not afraid with any amazement' [KJV], 'let no fears alarm you' [NAB], 'do not give way to fear' [NIV], 'live free from fear and worry' [NJB], 'without fear of what your husbands might do' [NLT], 'never let fears alarm you' [NRSV], 'showing no fear' [REB], 'not afraid of anything' [TEV], 'never let your calm be disturbed' [TNT].

QUESTION—What is the function of the participles 'doing good' and 'not fearing'?
1. They are imperatival and form an exhortation based on the fact of having become Sarah's daughters at conversion [NCBC, NTC, WBC].

2. They are conditional.
2.1 They are conditions for becoming or continuing to be Sarah's daughters [Alf, ICC, NIBC, TG, TH, TNTC; all versions except REB]. These conditions represent a pattern of life over a period of time [TNTC]. Since being Sarah's daughter is a figurative term for being like Sarah, these conditions are a definition of what it means to be her daughter [TG, TH].
2.2 They are the conditions by which the women have already become Sarah's daughters [REB].
2.3 They are conditions for demonstrating that one truly is Sarah's daughter [BNTC, EGT, IVP, NIC].

QUESTION—What is the πτόησις 'terror' which they should not fear?
It refers to fear from external threats, especially persecution [Alf, BNTC], or to any difficult circumstances [TNTC]. It refers to intimidation or threats from an unbelieving husband [BNTC, IVP, NCBC, NIC, NTC, TG, TNTC, WBC; NLT]. It refers to threats from any unbeliever [NIBC]. It refers to any external cause of alarm whether from the husband, hostile pagan neighbors, or concerns for the needs of the family [ICC]. It refers to anxiety or fearful concerns [TH]. It refers to Sarah's falsehood which came from yielding to a sudden terror [EGT].

**DISCOURSE UNIT: 3:7** [Sel, WBC; NLT]. The topic is the duty of husbands [Sel], respect of husbands for wives [WBC], husbands [NLT].

**3:7** Husbands likewise,[a] living-together-with[b] (them) according-to knowledge[c]

LEXICON—a. ὁμοίως (LN 64.1) (BAGD p. 568): 'likewise' [BAGD, LN; KJV], 'in the same way' [BAGD, BNTC; NIV, NJB, NLT, NRSV, REB, TEV], 'too' [WBC; NAB], 'also' [TNT], not explicit [CEV]. This word is seen as a reference to a command already given and translated by the clause 'husbands should do this' [NIC].

b. pres. act. participle of συνοικέω (LN **41.9**) (BAGD p. 791): 'to live with' [BAGD, LN, NIC, WBC; NIV, TEV], 'to dwell with' [KJV], not explicit [BNTC; CEV, NLT]. The phrase 'living together with them' is translated 'in your marital relations' [BNTC], 'in your married life' [REB, TNT], 'in your life together' [NJB, NRSV], 'who share your lives' [NAB].

c. γνῶσις (LN 32.16) (BAGD 2. p. 163): 'knowledge' [BAGD; KJV], 'consideration' [NJB, NRSV], 'understanding' [BNTC; NLT, REB, TEV]. The phrase 'according to knowledge' is translated 'considerately' [NIC], 'you must know how' [WBC], 'be thoughtful' [CEV], 'be considerate' [NIV, TNT], 'show consideration for' [NAB].

QUESTION—What relationship is indicated by ὁμοίως 'likewise'?
1. It is a loose connective used as transition to the next topic [NIBC, NTC, Sel, TG, WBC]. It continues the discussion about obligations within marriage [IVP, TNTC].

2. It refers to and continues the thought begun in 2:17, 'honor all', this being the way husbands are to fulfill that exhortation [Alf, EGT, ICC].
3. It refers to and continues the thought of 2:13 regarding submission to every human creature, showing how husbands do that by accepting responsibilities of the marriage relationship [NIC] or exercising authority with deference [BNTC].

QUESTION—What is meant by the term συνοικοῦντες 'living together with (them)'?

It refers to the whole of married life in general [Alf, TNTC]. It refers to the total marriage relationship, including the sexual aspect [IVP, NIC, Sel, TH, WBC]. It refers generally to the day-to-day relationship, but specifically to the sexual relationship [BNTC, NIBC].

QUESTION—What is the 'knowledge' with which Christian men are supposed to live?

It refers to consideration and understanding [ICC, NCBC, NIC; all versions except KJV, TEV]. It refers to living in an intelligent and reasonable manner which would include consideration [Alf], or to personal insight and understanding that leads to consideration [NIC]. It refers to knowing and understanding what is appropriate in marriage [TH, TNTC, WBC], as well as having knowledge of God [WBC]. It means having a Christian point of view or understanding God's will concerning marriage [BNTC, NTC, Sel, TG]. It refers to knowing the wife in terms of her needs or wishes [NIBC, TNTC]. It refers to understanding that the wife is weaker [TEV].

**(to) the female[a] as to-a-weaker[b] vessel[c] showing[d] honor[e] as also (being) joint-heirs[f] of-(the)-grace[g] of-life**

LEXICON—a. γυναικεῖος (LN 9.36) (BAGD p. 168): 'female' [**BNTC, LN**], 'woman' [BAGD, LN, WBC; NAB], 'wife' [BAGD, NIC; all versions except NAB, NJB, NRSV]. This word is also translated both as 'wife' and 'woman': 'treat . . . wives with consideration . . . respecting a woman' [NJB], 'show consideration to your wives . . . paying honor to the woman' [NRSV].

b. ἀσθενής (LN **79.69**) (BAGD 1.b. p. 115): 'weak' [BAGD, LN], 'weaker' [BNTC, **LN**, WBC; all versions], 'vulnerable' [NIC]. The phrase 'weaker vessel' is translated 'she isn't as strong as you are' [CEV], 'she may be weaker than you are' [NLT], 'they are physically weaker' [REB].

c. σκεῦος (LN 8.6) (BAGD 2. p. 754): 'vessel' [BAGD, BNTC; KJV], 'body' [LN], 'sex' [NIC; NAB, NRSV, TEV, TNT], 'partner' [NIV, NJB], not explicit [CEV, NLT, REB].

d. pres. act. participle of ἀπονέμω (LN **90.54**) (BAGD p. 97): 'to show' [BAGD, LN, NIC, WBC], 'to pay' [BNTC; NRSV], 'to treat with' [CEV, NAB, NIV, REB, TEV, TNT], 'to give' [KJV, NLT], not explicit [NJB].

e. τιμή (LN 87.4) (BAGD 2.b. p. 817): 'honor' [BAGD, BNTC, LN, NIC; CEV, KJV, NLT, NRSV], 'respect' [WBC; NAB, NIV, REB, TEV,

TNT]. The phrase 'showing honor' is translated 'to respect' [NJB]. See this word at 1:7 and 2:7.
- f. συγκληρονόμος (LN 57.134) (BAGD p. 774): 'joint heir' [BNTC, NIC], 'fellow heir' [BAGD, LN], 'co-heir' [WBC], 'heirs together' [KJV], 'heirs just as much as you' [NAB], 'heirs with you' [NIV], 'also heirs' [NRSV], 'equally an heir' [NJB], 'equal partner' [NLT]. This noun is also translated as a verb: 'to share with' [CEV, TNT], 'to share together' [REB], 'to receive together with' [TEV].
- g. χάρις (LN 57.103) (BAGD 3.b. p. 878): 'grace' [BNTC, WBC; KJV], 'gift' [LN; CEV, NLT, REB, TEV], 'gracious gift' [BAGD, LN, NIC; NAB, NIV, NRSV], 'generous gift' [NJB], 'free gift' [TNT].

QUESTION—What is the function of the two participles συνοικοῦντες 'dwelling together with' and ἀπονέμοντες 'showing (honor)'?

They function as imperatives [BNTC, ICC, NIC, NTC, Sel, TG, TH, TNTC, WBC; all versions].

QUESTION—Of what is τῷ γυναικείῳ 'the female' the object?
1. It is the object of ἀπονέμοντες 'showing (honor)' [BNTC, EGT, ICC, NIC, NTC; NAB, REB].
2. It is the object of συνοικοῦντες 'living together with' [Alf, Sel; TEV].
3. It functions as the object of both verbs [TNTC, WBC; CEV, NIV, NJB, NLT].

QUESTION—Is γυναικεῖος 'female' used as an adjective or as a substantive?
1. It is an adjective having a neuter particle and which functions as an abstract noun 'woman', 'wife', or 'the female' [Alf, BNTC, Sel, TNTC, WBC; KJV, NAB, NJB, NRSV, REB].
2. It is used as an adjective to modify 'vessel' [ICC].

QUESTION—In what way is she weaker?

She is weaker physically [Alf, BNTC, EGT, ICC, IVP, NIBC, NIC, NTC, Sel, TG, TH, TNTC, WBC; CEV, REB]. She is weaker in terms of social status [TG, TH]. She is weaker in that she is subject to the authority of her husband and is emotionally more sensitive [TNTC]. She is less capable of bearing heavy responsibility outside the home, such as major business dealings or war [Sel]. She is weaker in terms of having fewer legal rights [ICC].

QUESTION—What is meant by the analogy of the σκεῦος 'vessel'?
1. The σκεῦος is a thing, vessel, or tool, and can be used of women or men [NCBC]. A σκεῦος is an instrument, meaning that men and women are God's instruments in procreation of the human race [Alf]. It can mean chattel or furnishings, and in this context means that both husband and wife are part of the furnishings in God's household [ICC]. They are creations of God for his use and purposes [TNTC].
2. It is a metaphor for the human body [BNTC, Sel, WBC]. It refers to the body and therefore the whole personality, and by extension it refers to the female gender in this context [Sel].

>     3. It is a metaphor meaning person [NIBC]. In this context it means 'somebody', that is, a person [WBC], and by extension is used to refer to a gender [NIC, TH]. It refers to a marriage partner [NTC].
>
> QUESTION—What relationship is indicated by ὡς...ὡς 'as (to)...as (also)'?
>
>     1. It indicates the grounds for the exhortation to husbands.
>         1.1 The exhortation is based on the fact that the wife is a joint heir of the grace of life [NIC; NRSV, TEV, TNT].
>         1.2 The exhortation is based on the fact that the wife is weaker and that she is a joint heir of the grace of life [BNTC, NTC, Sel, TG, WBC; CEV, REB].
>     2. It emphasizes the manner in which honor is bestowed [TNTC]. It qualifies the command [ICC].

**so-that**[a] **your prayers not be-hindered.**[b]

LEXICON—a. εἰς (LN 89.57): 'so that' [BNTC; NIV, NRSV, TEV], 'for the purpose of, in order to' [LN], 'in order that' [NIC], 'that' [KJV], 'that way' [WBC], 'then' [CEV, REB, TNT], not explicit [NJB]. This word is also translated as introducing a conditional clause: 'if you do so, nothing will keep your prayers from being answered' [NAB], 'if you don't, your prayers will not be heard' [NLT].

b. pres. pass. infin. of ἐγκόπτω (LN 13.147) (BAGD p. 216): 'to be hindered' [BAGD, BNTC, LN, NIC, WBC; KJV, TNT], 'to be thwarted' [BAGD] 'to be impeded' [REB]. The phrase 'your prayers not be hindered' is translated 'nothing will stand in the way of your prayers' [CEV], 'nothing will keep your prayers from being answered' [NAB], 'nothing will hinder your prayers' [NIV], 'so that nothing may hinder your prayers' [NRSV], 'this will prevent anything from coming in the way of your prayers' [NJB], 'nothing will interfere with your prayers' [TEV], 'your prayers will not be heard' [NLT].

QUESTION—What is meant by χάριτος ζωῆς '(the) grace of life'?

>     1. It is the gracious gift of eternal life [Alf, BNTC, ICC, IVP, NCBC, NIBC, NIC, TG, TH, TNTC, WBC; NLT]. 'Grace' and 'life' are appositional: 'the grace that is life' [BNTC, WBC].
>     2. It is grace for daily living [NIBC, NTC].

QUESTION—Whose prayers would be hindered if this condition were not fulfilled?

>     1. The prayers of the husband would be hindered [EGT, ICC, NIC, TG, TNTC].
>     2. The prayers of the couple would be hindered [Alf, BNTC, IVP, NIBC, NTC, WBC].

**DISCOURSE UNIT: 3:8–4:19** [TNTC]. The topic is returning blessing for evil.

# 1 PETER 3:8

**DISCOURSE UNIT: 3:8–22** [NIC; CEV, NIV, NRSV, TEV]. The topic is a summary call to virtue and suffering [NIC], suffering for doing right [CEV, NRSV, TEV], suffering for doing good [NIV].

**DISCOURSE UNIT: 3:8–12** [IVP, Sel, TH, WBC; NAB, NJB, NLT]. The topic is general instructions [IVP], ethical qualities required of Christians [Sel], respect for everyone [WBC], relationship of Christians with one another [TH], in Christian charity [NAB], love the brothers [NJB], all Christians [NLT].

**3:8** Now the end[a] all-of-you (be) of-one-mind,[b] sympathetic,[c] loving-(the)-brothers,[d] compassionate,[e] humble,[f]

LEXICON—a. τέλος (LN **61.17**) (BAGD 1.d.α p. 812): 'end' [BAGD]. The phrase τὸ δὲ τέλος 'now the end' is translated 'finally' [BAGD, BNTC, LN, NIC, WBC; all versions except NAB, TEV], 'in summary, then' [NAB], 'to conclude' [TEV].
  b. ὁμόφρων (LN **30.21**) (BAGD p. 569): 'of one mind' [WBC; KJV, NLT, TNT], 'like-minded' [BAGD, LN; NAB], 'of the same mind' [BNTC], 'united in spirit' [NIC], 'united in thought' [REB]. This adjective is also translated as a verb: 'to agree' [CEV], 'to live in harmony with one another' [NIV], 'to agree among yourselves' [NJB], 'to have unity of spirit' [NRSV], 'to have the same attitude' [TEV].
  c. συμπαθής (LN **25.58**) (BAGD p. 779): 'sympathetic' [BAGD, LN, NIC, WBC; NAB, NIV, NJB, TNT], 'full of sympathy' [BNTC; NLT], 'united in feeling' [REB]. Those that supply 'to have' as the implied imperative verb instead of 'to be' translate this adjective as 'having compassion' [KJV], 'have concern for each other' [CEV], 'have sympathy' [NRSV], 'have the same feelings' [TEV].
  d. φιλάδελφος (LN **25.35**) (BAGD p. 858): 'loving one's brother' [BAGD], 'loving one another as brothers' [LN], 'full of brotherly affection' [WBC; REB], 'full of love of your brothers' [BNTC], 'love for each other' [CEV], 'love for one another' [NRSV]. This adjective is also translated as a participial phrase: 'loving toward one another' [NAB], 'loving one another' [NLT], 'loving your brothers and sisters' [NIC]; as an imperative clause: 'love as brethren' [KJV], 'love as brothers' [NIV], 'love the brothers' [NJB], 'love one another as brothers' [TEV].
  e. εὔσπλαγχνος (LN 25.51) (BAGD p. 326): 'compassionate' [BAGD, BNTC, LN, NIC; NIV, TNT], 'good-hearted' [WBC], 'kind' [CEV], 'pitiful' [KJV], 'kindly' [REB], 'kind' [TEV], 'kindly disposed' [NAB], 'with tender hearts' [NLT]. Those that supply 'to have' as the implied imperative verb instead of 'to be' translate this adjective 'have a tender heart' [NRSV], 'have compassion' [NJB].
  f. ταπεινόφρων (LN **88.54**) (BAGD p. 804): 'humble' [BAGD, LN, NIC; CEV, NAB, NIV, REB, TEV, TNT], 'humble-minded' [BNTC], 'humble of mind' [WBC], 'a humble mind' [NRSV], 'with humble minds' [NLT], 'courteous' [KJV], 'self-effacing' [NJB].

QUESTION—What is the context of the exhortations in 3:8–9?
1. Verse 8 applies to relationships within the church, and 3:9 to relationships with society at large [BNTC, IVP, NCBC, NIBC, NIC, NTC, WBC].
2. Both verses apply to relationships with all people, whether in the church or in society at large [Sel].

QUESTION—What is the function of τὸ δὲ τέλος 'finally'?
1. It indicates a summary or recapitulation of exhortation just given [NIC; NAB], or a summary of what relationships within the fellowship should be like [NIBC]. It concludes the hortatory section begun at 2:17 [Alf]. It concludes the section on submission with a pattern for Christian conduct [NTC].
2. It begins a final, concluding section of general exhortation to all the believers [BNTC, ICC, IVP, NCBC, Sel, TH, TNTC, WBC]. It is moving toward a summary of teaching in the same way that love is the τέλος 'goal' or 'end' of the law [EGT].

QUESTION—What is the implied verb in this clause?
1. The imperatival participle ὄντες 'being' is implied [Alf, Sel].
2. The adjectives are used as imperatives [BNTC, ICC, NIC, WBC].

**3:9** not repaying[a] evil[b] for[c] evil nor abuse[d] for abuse,
LEXICON—a. pres. act. participle of ἀποδίδωμι (LN 38.16) (BAGD 3. p. 90): 'to repay' [NIV, NJB, NLT, NRSV, REB], 'to pay back' [TEV], 'to recompense' [BAGD, LN], 'to return' [BNTC, NIC, WBC; NAB, TNT], 'to render' [KJV]. The phrase 'not repaying evil' is translated 'don't be hateful' [CEV].
b. κακός (LN 88.106) (BAGD 3. p. 398): 'evil' [BAGD, BNTC, LN, NIC, WBC; all versions except CEV, NJB, REB], 'wrong' [NJB, REB], 'hateful' [CEV].
c. ἀντί (LN 57.145) (BAGD 2. p. 73): 'for' [BAGD, LN; KJV, NAB, NLT, NRSV, TNT], 'with' [NIV, NJB, REB, TEV], not explicit [CEV].
d. λοιδορία (LN 33.393) (BAGD p. 479): 'abuse' [BAGD, BNTC; NRSV, REB, TNT], 'abusive word' [NJB], 'insult' [LN, NIC, WBC; NAB, NIV], 'railing' [KJV], 'cursing' [TEV], 'reviling' [BAGD]. This noun is also translated as a verb phrase: 'to insult' [CEV], 'to say unkind things' [NLT].

but[a] on-the-contrary[b] blessing[c] (them) because to this you-were-called[d]
LEXICON—a. δέ (LN 89.124): 'but' [BNTC, LN, NIC, WBC; KJV, NIV, NRSV], not explicit [REB, TNT]. This word is also conflated with the following word and translated 'instead' [CEV, NAB, NJB, NLT, TEV].
b. τοὐναντίον (LN 89.134): 'on the contrary' [BNTC, LN, NIC, WBC; NRSV, REB], 'contrariwise' [KJV], 'rather' [LN], 'instead' [LN; CEV, NAB, NJB, NLT, TEV], not explicit [NIV]. This word is also translated as a verb phrase: 'to do the very opposite' [TNT].
c. pres. act. participle of εὐλογέω (LN 33.470) (BAGD 2.a. p. 322): 'to bless' [BAGD, BNTC, LN, NIC, WBC; KJV], 'to treat with kindness'

[CEV], 'to return a blessing' [NAB], 'to repay with a blessing' [NJB, NRSV], 'to pay back with a blessing' [NLT, TEV], 'to respond with blessing' [REB], 'to give a blessing' [TNT].
d. aorist pass. indic. of καλέω (LN 33.312) (BAGD 2. p. 399): 'to be called' [BAGD, BNTC, LN, NIC, WBC; KJV, NAB, NIV, NJB, NRSV, TEV, TNT], 'to be called to a task' [LN]. This verb is also translated as a verb phrase: 'you are God's chosen ones' [CEV], 'this is what God wants you to do' [NLT]. The verb phrase 'you were called so that you may inherit a blessing' is translated 'a blessing is what God intends you to receive' [REB], 'a blessing is what God promised to give you' [TEV]. See this word at 1:15, 2:9, 21.

QUESTION—What is meant by εὐλογοῦντες 'blessing (them)'?

It means to forgive those who abuse one and do good to them instead [NIC]. It means to speak well of enemies [Sel] and to intercede for them [NIBC, NTC, Sel, TG, TH]. It means to invoke God's graciousness upon them [NCBC]. It means offering the gospel [IVP], or to use words of kindness to offer the hope of salvation [WBC]. It means to seek the highest good for others [NIBC, NTC].

QUESTION—What relationship is indicated by εἰς τοῦτο 'to this'?

1. It refers back to what has just been stated [IVP, NCBC, NIBC, TG, TH, WBC; NAB, NIV, NJB, NLT]: they have been called to bless and not retaliate. They have been called to all the virtues of 3:8–9 [TNTC].
2. It refers to what follows [Alf, BNTC, EGT, ICC, NIC, Sel; CEV, REB, TEV, TNT]: they have been called to inherit a blessing.

**that/so-that[a] you-may-inherit[b] a blessing.[c]**

LEXICON—a. ἵνα (LN 89.59): 'so that' [BNTC, LN; NIV, NJB], 'that' [BNTC, NIC; KJV, NAB, NRSV], 'in order to' [LN], 'to' [TNT], 'because' [TEV], 'for' [REB], not explicit [CEV, NLT].
b. aorist act. subj. of κληρονομέω (LN 57.131) (BAGD 2. p. 435): 'to inherit' [BNTC, NIC, WBC; KJV, NIV, NJB, NRSV], 'to obtain' [BAGD], 'to receive' [LN; TNT], 'to receive as one's inheritance' [NAB], 'to be given' [LN; TEV], 'to gain possession of' [LN], 'to acquire' [BAGD]. 'So that you may inherit a blessing' is translated 'he will bless you' [CEV, NLT].
c. εὐλογία (LN 33.470) (BAGD 3.b.α. p. 323): 'blessing' [BAGD, BNTC, LN, NIC, WBC; all versions except CEV, NLT]. 'So that you may inherit a blessing' is translated 'he will bless you' [CEV, NLT].

QUESTION—What relationship is indicated by ἵνα 'that/so-that'?

1. It indicates the content of τοῦτο 'this' [Alf, BNTC, EGT, ICC, NIC, Sel, TG, TH; CEV, REB, TEV, TNT]: God called you to this, namely, that you inherit a blessing.
2. It indicates the purpose for believers to bless others, which is to receive a blessing [IVP, NCBC, NIBC, WBC; KJV, NAB, NIV, NJB, NLT]. It

indicates the purpose for believers to live righteously and bless others, which is to receive a blessing [TNTC].
3. It indicates that God's blessing comes both as a result of his call as well as of the fact that believers bless others [ICC], or that God's call is the basis both of blessing and of being blessed [TG].

QUESTION—What is meant by κληρονομήσητε 'that-you-may-inherit'?
It refers to a receiving a gift that is not merited or earned, but which is given freely [BNTC, NCBC, NIBC, NIC].

QUESTION—What is the blessing that is inherited?
It is final salvation [NCBC, NTC]. It is God's final pronouncement of eternal well-being and peace at the end of time [WBC]. It is blessing in this life, such as emotional, relational, psychological, or spiritual well-being, plus blessing in the life to come [TNTC]. It is blessing in general [TG].

**3:10** For[a] the-one-wanting[b] to-love[c] life and to-see good days let-him-stop[d] the tongue from evil and (the) lips not to-speak deceit,

LEXICON—a. γάρ (LN 89.23): 'for' [BNTC, LN, NIC, WBC; KJV, NIV, NJB, NRSV], 'because' [LN], not explicit [CEV, NAB]. Since this conjunction is used to introduce a scriptural quote, it is also translated 'as Scripture says' [REB, TNT], 'as the Scripture says' [TEV], 'for the Scriptures say' [NLT].

b. pres. act. participle of θέλω (LN 25.1) (BAGD 1. p. 355): 'to want' [BAGD, LN; CEV, REB, TEV, TNT], 'to wish' [BAGD, LN], 'to desire' [BNTC, LN, NIC], 'to choose' [WBC]. Ὁ θέλων 'the-one-wanting' is taken together with ἀγαπᾶν 'to love' and translated 'he that will love life' [KJV], 'he that cares for life' [NAB], 'whoever would love life' [NIV], 'who among you delights in life' [NJB], 'if you want a happy life' [NLT], 'those who desire life' [NRSV].

c. pres. act. infin. of ἀγαπάω (LN 25.104) (BAGD 2. p. 5): 'to love' [BAGD, LN, WBC; CEV, KJV, NIV, REB, TNT], 'to enjoy' [BAGD], 'to take pleasure in' [LN], 'to choose' [BNTC], 'to strive after' [NIC], not explicit [NAB, NJB, NLT, NRSV].

d. aorist act. impera. of παύω (LN **68.46**) (BAGD 1. p. 638): 'to stop' [BAGD, WBC; CEV], 'to keep from' [BAGD, NIC; NAB, NIV, NLT, NRSV, TEV], 'to cause to cease, to make stop' [LN], 'to restrain' [BNTC; REB, TNT], 'to refrain' [KJV], 'to guard' [NJB].

QUESTION—What relationship is indicated by 'for'?
It introduces a scriptural quote to support his teaching [Alf, NCBC, NIC, NTC, TG, TH, WBC; NLT, REB, TEV, TNT]. It introduces a quotation from Psalm 34 to support his assertions about nonretaliation [BNTC, IVP, NIBC]. It introduces a quotation from Psalm 34 as grounds for all the exhortations of 3:8–9 [ICC, TNTC]. It expresses the authority of the Word of God which he quotes [NTC].

QUESTION—What is meant by ζωή 'life'?
1. It refers to eternal life [BNTC, EGT, NCBC, Sel, TH, WBC].

2. It refers to this present life [Alf, ICC, IVP, NIC, TG, TNTC].
3. It refers to this present life as well as eternal life [NTC].

**3:11** and let-him-turn-away[a] from evil and let-him-do good, let-him-seek[b] peace[c] and let-him-pursue[d] it;

LEXICON—a. aorist act. impera. of ἐκκλίνω (LN 31.99) (BAGD p. 241): 'to turn away from' [BAGD, BNTC, LN, NIC; NJB, NLT, NRSV, TEV], 'to turn from' [WBC; NAB, NIV, REB], 'to give up' [CEV], 'to eschew' [KJV].
- b. aorist act. impera. of ζητέω (LN 13.19) (BAGD 2.a. p. 339): 'to seek' [BAGD, BNTC, NIC, WBC; KJV, NAB, NIV, NJB, NRSV, REB], 'to attempt to find' [LN], 'to find' [CEV]. The phrase 'let him seek peace and pursue it' is translated 'work hard at living in peace with others' [NLT], 'you must strive for peace with all your heart' [TEV].
- c. εἰρήνη (LN 22.42) (BAGD 1.b. p. 227): 'peace' [BAGD, BNTC, LN, NIC, WBC; all versions except CEV, NLT], 'the road that leads to peace' [CEV], 'peace with others' [NLT].
- d. aorist act. impera. of διώκω (LN 15.158) (BAGD 4.b. p. 201): 'to pursue' [BAGD, BNTC, LN, WBC; NIV, NJB, NRSV, REB], 'to chase after' [NIC], 'to follow' [CEV], 'to follow after' [NAB], 'to ensue' [KJV].

QUESTION—What is the εἰρήνη 'peace' they are to seek?
It is harmony in interpersonal relationships [IVP, NIBC, NIC, NTC, TG, TH, TNTC, WBC; NLT].

**3:12** For[a] (the) eyes of the Lord (are) on[b] (the) righteous[c] and his ears (open) to[d] their prayer,[e]

LEXICON—a. ὅτι (LN 89.33): 'for' [BNTC, LN, WBC; KJV, NIV, NJB, NRSV, TEV, TNT], 'because' [LN, NIC; NAB], not explicit [CEV, NLT, REB].
- b. ἐπί with accusative (LN 90.57): 'on' [BNTC, LN, NIC, WBC; NIV, NJB, NRSV], 'over' [KJV]. The phrase 'the eyes of the Lord are on' is translated 'the Lord watches over' [CEV, TEV], 'the eyes of the Lord watch over' [NLT], 'the Lord has eyes for' [NAB, REB], 'the Lord looks with favor on' [TNT].
- c. δίκαιος (LN 88.12) (BAGD 1.b. 195): 'righteous' [BAGD, BNTC, LN, NIC; KJV, NIV, NRSV, REB, TEV, TNT], 'upright' [BAGD; NJB], 'just' [BAGD, LN, WBC; NAB], 'everyone who obeys him' [CEV], 'those who do right' [NLT].
- d. εἰς with accusative (LN 90.59): 'open to' [BNTC, WBC; NLT, NRSV, REB], 'attentive to' [NIV], 'to' [LN; CEV], 'turned to' [NJB], 'toward' [LN], 'open for' [NIC], 'open unto' [KJV]. The phrase 'his ears (open) to' is translated 'has ears for' [NAB], 'listens to' [TEV], 'is always ready to hear' [TNT].
- e. δέησις (LN 33.171) (BAGD p. 171): 'prayer' [BAGD, BNTC, LN, WBC; NIV, NRSV], 'prayers' [CEV, KJV, NLT, REB, TEV, TNT], 'requests' [LN, NIC], 'cry' [NAB, NJB].

QUESTION—What relationship is indicated by ὅτι 'because'?
It indicates the grounds for the foregoing exhortations [IVP, WBC]. It gives the grounds for the exhortations just given as conditions of prosperity [Alf]. It introduces the grounds for the statements just made about Christian behavior, which is that nothing in life is hidden from God, and that this knowledge should govern all behavior [NCBC].

**but[a] (the) face of (the) Lord (is) against[b] the-ones-doing evil.**
LEXICON—a. δέ (LN 89.124): 'but' [BNTC, LN, NIC, WBC; all versions].
  b. ἐπί with accusative (LN 90.34): '(is) against' [BNTC, LN, NIC; KJV, NIV, NRSV], '(is set) against' [WBC; NJB, REB], '(sets his face) against' [NAB], '(turns his face) against' [NLT]. The phrase 'the face of the Lord is against' is translated 'he opposes' [CEV, TEV], 'he turns away from' [TNT].

**DISCOURSE UNIT: 3:13–5:11** [IVP] The topic is the Christian attitude toward hostility.

**DISCOURSE UNIT: 3:13–4:19** [NTC, Sel, TG]. The topic is the third doctrinal section [Sel], suffering [NTC], the Christian attitude toward persecution [TG].

**DISCOURSE UNIT: 3:13–4:6** [WBC]. The topic is the promise of vindication.

**DISCOURSE UNIT: 3:13–22** [Sel, TH; NAB, NLT]. The topic is Christian patience [Sel], further exhortations of Christian conduct [TH], Christian suffering [NAB], suffering for doing good [NLT].

**DISCOURSE UNIT: 3:13–17** [IVP, WBC; NJB]. The topic is the blessings and opportunities of the persecuted [IVP], suffering for doing good [WBC], persecution [NJB].

**3:13** **And who (is) the-one harming[a] you if[b] you-become zealous[c] (ones) of the good?**
TEXT—Instead of ζηλωταί 'zealous (ones)', some manuscripts have μιμηταί 'followers'. GNT does not mention this alternative. Only KJV reads 'followers'.
LEXICON—a. fut. act. participle of κακόω (LN 20.12) (BAGD 1. p. 398): 'to harm' [BAGD, BNTC, LN, NIC, WBC; all versions except NJB], 'to hurt' [NJB].
  b. ἐάν (LN 89.67): 'if' [LN; all versions except CEV], not explicit [CEV].
  c. ζηλωτής (LN 25.77) (BAGD 1.a.β. p. 338): 'enthusiast' [BAGD, LN], 'eager' [CEV, NIV, NLT, NRSV, TEV]. 'Zealous of the good' is translated 'committed deeply to doing what is right' [NAB], 'determined only to do what is right' [NJB], 'devoted to what is good' [REB], 'devoted to goodness' [TNT].

1 PETER 3:13

QUESTION—What relationship is indicated by καί 'and'?
It resumes the argument from 3:12 [NIC]. It provides a quick transition from the psalm quote to the next idea [Sel]. It introduces a logical conclusion to the last part of the psalm quotation [BNTC, WBC]. It is a typically Semitic use of a particle to preface an apodosis, stating the conclusion of an expressed or implied protasis which, in this case, would be the thought from the quotation from Psalms [BNTC].

QUESTION—What connection does this verse have with what precedes it?
1. The participle κακώσων 'doing harm' echoes the ποιοῦντας κακά 'doing evil' found at the end of the previous verse and gives continuity between the two verses [EGT, NCBC, NIBC, NIC, Sel, WBC]. The mention of 'evil/harm' and 'good' connects it with the thought of 3:11–12 [TH, WBC].
2. It is linked to the thought and argument of 3:9 regarding the Christian's doing good and not evil in the face of persecution [IVP].

QUESTION—What is meant by this rhetorical question?
1. It is proverbial, meaning that normally no one bothers a person who does good [IVP, NIC, NTC, TNTC].
2. It means that no matter what people do, they can't do you ultimate harm [BNTC, NCBC, NIBC, TG, TH, WBC]. If that happens you will even be blessed [BNTC, NIBC, WBC], or God will strengthen you [NTC], or you will grow in grace [NIBC]. No harm that is external can damage the inner character [BNTC, NCBC, TH] or touch you in the spiritual plane [NCBC, NIBC, TH].

**3:14** **But even if you-should-suffer**[a] **because-of**[b] **righteousness**[c] **(you are) blessed.**[d]

LEXICON—a. pres. act. opt. of πάσχω (LN 24.78) (BAGD 3.a.β. p. 634): 'to suffer' [BAGD, BNTC, LN, NIC, WBC; all versions].
b. διά with accusative (LN 89.26): 'because of' [BNTC, LN, NIC], 'on account of' [LN], 'in the cause of' [WBC], 'for' [all versions].
c. δικαιοσύνη (LN 88.13) (BAGD 4. p. 197): 'righteousness' [BAGD, LN, NIC; KJV], 'upright behavior' [BNTC], 'justice' [WBC; NAB], 'doing good things' [CEV], 'what is right' [NIV], 'doing what is right' [NLT, NRSV, TEV, TNT], 'doing right' [REB], 'being upright' [NJB].
d. μακάριος (LN 25.119) (BAGD 1.β. p. 486): 'blessed' [BAGD, BNTC, NIC, WBC; NIV, NJB, NRSV], 'fortunate' [BAGD; TNT], 'happy' [BAGD, LN; KJV, NAB, REB, TEV]. The phrase 'you are blessed' is translated 'God will bless you' [CEV], 'God will reward you' [NLT].

QUESTION—What is implied by the use of the optative verb πάσχοιτε 'you should suffer' with ἀλλ' εἰ καί 'but even if'?
1. It posits a possibility which is not necessarily an imminent probability or specific reality [Alf, EGT, NCBC, Sel]. It states a possibility which would be an exception to the general principle just stated in 3:13 [IVP]. It states

the case as being unlikely [TNTC], hypothetical [ICC], or only a remote possibility [BNTC, NIC, NTC, TG].
2. It is used to point out that Christians are not exempt from suffering and that it is a privilege to suffer for doing right [TH]. It strengthens the rhetorical device of 3:13, emphasizing that a believer who suffers is blessed anyway [WBC].

**But don't fear[a] the fear of-them, neither[b] be-perturbed.[c]**
LEXICON—a. aorist pass. (deponent = act.) subj. of φοβέομαι (φοβέω) (LN 25.252) (BAGD 1.a. or 1.b.γ. p. 863): 'to fear' [LN, NIC; NAB, NIV, NRSV], 'to be afraid' [BAGD, LN; CEV, KJV, NLT, TEV, TNT], 'to have fear' [BNTC, WBC; REB], 'to have dread' [NJB].
  b. μηδέ (LN 69.7) (BAGD 1.b. p. 517): 'neither' [LN; KJV], 'and do not' [NAB, NRSV, TEV, TNT], 'and don't' [CEV, NLT], 'do not' [NIV, REB], 'have no' [NJB].
  c. aorist pass subj. of ταράσσω (LN **25.244**) (BAGD 2. p. 805): 'to be perturbed' [REB], 'to be caused to be distressed' [LN], 'to worry' [CEV, NLT, TEV], 'to be troubled' [KJV], 'to stand in awe' [NAB], 'to be frightened' [NIV], 'to have fear' [NJB], 'to be intimidated' [NRSV], 'to be upset' [TNT].
QUESTION—What is meant by τὸν δὲ φόβον αὐτῶν μὴ φοβηθῆτε 'don't fear the fear of them'?
  1. They are not to have the same fears as other people who don't know Christ [NIBC; NAB, NIV, NRSV].
  2. They are not to fear other people [BNTC, IVP, NCBC, NIC, NTC, Sel, TG, TH, TNTC, WBC; CEV, NJB, REB, TEV, TNT].
  3. They are not to fear the threats or intimidation of other people [Alf, EGT, ICC].

**3:15** **But sanctify[a] the Lord Christ/Christ as Lord in your hearts, always[b] prepared[c] for a defense[d]**
TEXT—Instead of κύριον δὲ τὸν Χριστόν 'Christ as Lord/the Lord Christ' some manuscripts have κύριον δὲ τὸν θεόν 'the Lord God'. GNT selects the reading 'Christ as Lord/the Lord Christ' with an A rating, indicating that the text is certain. The reading 'the Lord God' is taken only by KJV.
LEXICON—a. aorist act. impera. of ἁγιάζω (LN 88.27) (BAGD 3. p. 9): 'to sanctify' [KJV, NRSV], 'to honor as holy' [LN], 'to reverence' [BAGD; TNT], 'to hold in reverence' [REB], 'to have reverence for' [TEV], 'to set apart' [NIV], 'to venerate' [NAB], 'to worship' [NLT], 'to honor' [CEV], 'to proclaim' [NJB].
  b. ἀεί (LN 67.86) (BAGD 1. p. 19): 'always' [BAGD, LN; all versions except NAB, TEV], 'ever' [NAB], 'at all times' [TEV].
  c. ἕτοιμος (LN 77.2) (BAGD 2. p. 316): 'prepared' [BAGD, LN, NIC; NIV], 'ready' [BAGD, BNTC, LN, WBC; all versions except NIV].
  d. ἀπολογία (LN 33.436) (BAGD 2.b. p. 96): 'defense' [BAGD, BNTC, LN, NIC; NRSV, REB, TNT], 'answer' [WBC; CEV, KJV, NIV, NJB,

TEV]. The noun ἀπολογία is also used as an infinitive and is translated '(ready) to answer' [WBC; TEV], '(ready) to reply' [NAB], '(ready) to explain' [NLT].

QUESTION—What is meant by ἁγιάσατε 'sanctify'?

It means to honor him as Lord [Alf], to have deep respect for him as Lord [TG]. It means to acknowledge or regard him as holy [BNTC, IVP, NCBC, NTC, Sel, TH, TNTC, WBC], to honor him as God [TH]. It means to reverence, honor, and obey him [NIC], or to hold him in reverence [ICC].

QUESTION—What is the relationship between 'Christ' and 'Lord' in this sentence?

1. Lord is predicative [Alf, IVP, NIC, NTC, Sel, TG, TNTC; CEV, NIV, NLT, NRSV, REB, TEV, TNT]: sanctify Christ as Lord.
2. Christ and Lord are appositional [BNTC, ICC, TH, WBC; NAB, NJB]: sanctify the Lord Christ.

**to-everyone asking<sup>a</sup> you (to give) account<sup>b</sup> concerning the hope in/among you,**

LEXICON—a. pres. act. participle of αἰτέω (LN **33.163**) (BAGD p. 26): 'to ask' [BAGD; KJV, NAB, NIV, NJB, TEV], 'to ask for' [BNTC, LN], 'to ask about' [CEV, NLT], 'to demand' [WBC; NRSV], 'to question' [NIC; TNT], 'to challenge' [REB].

b. λόγος (LN **89.18**) (BAGD 2.a. p. 478): 'account' [BAGD, BNTC], 'accounting' [WBC; NRSV], 'reason' [LN; KJV, NAB, NIV, NJB], not explicit [NIC; CEV, NLT, TNT]. This noun is also translated as a verb: 'to justify' [REB], 'to explain' [TEV].

QUESTION—How is the term 'hope' used in this context?

1. It refers to the hope that Christians have because of Christ [Alf, BNTC, NIBC, NTC, Sel, TNTC, WBC]. This hope is an inward hope that transforms the outlook [TNTC]. It is a future-oriented confidence or expectation [NTC]. This inner hope stood out as unusual in the society of that day, which was characterized by a widespread sense of frustration [Sel].
2. It is a metonymy and is used as a synonym for Christian faith [ICC, IVP, NCBC, NIC, TH]. It is faith that has a definite future expectation [IVP, NIC].

QUESTION—What is meant by ἐν ὑμῖν 'in/among you'?

1. It means the hope is in their hearts [BNTC, NIC; KJV, NRSV, REB, TEV].
2. It means the hope that is among them [TNT].

**3:16 but with meekness<sup>a</sup> and reverence/fear,<sup>b</sup> having a good conscience<sup>c</sup>**

TEXT—The phrase ἀλλὰ μετὰ πραΰτητος καὶ φόβου 'but with meekness and reverence/fear' is included with 3:15 by KJV, NIV, and REB.

LEXICON—a. πραΰτης (LN **88.59**) (BAGD 699): 'gentleness' [BAGD, BNTC, LN; NIV, NRSV], 'humility' [BAGD, WBC], 'courtesy' [BAGD; NJB, REB], 'meekness' [BAGD, LN, NIC; KJV]. This noun is also

translated as an adverb: 'gently' [NAB, TNT], 'in a gentle way' [NLT]; as an adjective: 'kind' [CEV].
  b. φόβος (LN 53.59): 'reverence' [BNTC, LN, WBC; NRSV], 'respect' [NIC; NIV, NJB, REB, TEV], 'fear' [KJV]. This noun is also translated as an adjective: 'respectful' [CEV]; as an adverb: 'respectfully' [NAB, TNT], 'in a respectful way' [NLT]. See this word at 1:17, 2:18, 3:2.
  c. συνείδησις (LN 26.13) (BAGD 2. p. 786): 'conscience' [BAGD, BNTC, LN, NIC, WBC; all versions].
QUESTION—What is meant by φόβος 'reverence/fear'?
  1. It means reverence for or fear of God [BNTC, EGT, ICC, IVP, NCBC, NIBC, NIC, WBC].
  2. It means respect for other people [TG; CEV, NAB, NIV, NJB, NLT, REB, TEV, TNT].
  3. It means reverence of God and respect for other people [Alf, NTC]. It is respect for others and reverence for the mystery entrusted to them [Sel].

**so-that when[a] you-are-spoken-against[b] the-ones-reviling[c] your good conduct in Christ may-be-ashamed.[d]**

TEXT—Instead of καταλαλεῖσθε 'you-are-spoken-against', some manuscripts have καταλαλοῦσιν ὑμῶν ὡς κακοποιῶν 'they speak evil of you as evildoers'. GNT selects the reading 'you-are-spoken-against' with an A rating, indicating that the text is certain. The reading 'they speak evil of you as evildoers' is taken only by KJV.

LEXICON—a. ἐν ᾧ (preposition ἐν with relative pronoun ὅ in the dative case) (LN 67.139): 'when' [NRSV, REB, TEV], 'in cases where' [BNTC], 'with respect to' [NIC], 'in a situation where' [WBC], 'whereas' [KJV], 'whenever' [NAB], 'if' [NLT], 'while' [LN], not explicit [CEV, NIV, NJB, TNT]. See this phrase at 2:12.
  b. pres. pass. indic. of καταλαλέω (LN 33.387) (BAGD p. 412): 'to be spoken against' [BAGD; TNT], 'to be spoken evil of' [BAGD, LN; KJV], 'to be slandered' [BAGD, LN, NIC; NJB], 'to be abused' [BNTC; REB], 'to be accused' [WBC], 'to be defamed' [NAB], 'to be maligned' [NRSV], 'to be insulted' [TEV]. This verb is also translated as a noun: 'slander' [NIV]. The phrase 'you are spoken against the ones reviling' is translated 'to say bad things about' [CEV], 'to speak evil against' [NLT].
  c. pres. act. participle of ἐπηρεάζω (LN 88.129) (BAGD 285): 'to revile' [BAGD, NIC], 'to mistreat' [LN], 'to vilify' [BNTC], 'to denounce' [WBC], 'to falsely accuse' [KJV], 'to libel' [NAB], 'to speak maliciously against' [NIV], 'to slander' [NJB], 'to abuse' [NRSV], 'to malign' [REB, TNT], 'to speak evil of' [TEV]. The phrase 'you are spoken against the ones reviling' is translated 'to have bad things said about' [CEV], 'speak evil against you' [NLT].
  d. aorist pass. subj. of καταισχύνω (LN 25.194) (BAGD 2. p. 410): 'to be ashamed' [KJV, NIV, NJB, NLT], 'to be put to shame' [BAGD, LN;

NRSV, REB, TNT], 'to be humiliated' [LN], 'to make ashamed' [CEV], 'to be shamed' [NAB], 'to become ashamed' [TEV].
QUESTION—Which verb governs 'your good conduct'?
1. 'Revile' governs 'your good conduct' [Alf, BNTC, EGT, ICC, NIC, NTC, TG, TH, TNTC, WBC; all versions except NLT, TNT]: they revile the good conduct.
2. 'Be ashamed' governs 'your good conduct' [NCBC; NLT, TNT]: because they are made ashamed by the good conduct.
QUESTION—What is meant by 'in Christ'?
1. It is a synonym for being a Christian [EGT, TG, TH; CEV, NLT, TEV]. It defines the good conduct as being Christian [WBC; REB, TNT].
2. It means that the Christian life has its source in the believer's relationship to Christ, who provides the power and motive for the way of life [BNTC, NIC]. It refers to a reciprocal indwelling of Christ and the believer [Sel].

**3:17** **For (it is) better, if the will of God wills,ᵃ to sufferᵇ doing-good than doing-evil.**
LEXICON—a. pres. act. opt. of θέλω (LN 25.1): 'to will' [NIC], 'to want' [LN; NLT, TNT], 'to be the will (of God)' [BNTC; all versions except CEV, NLT, TNT], 'to require' [WBC], not explicit [CEV].
b. pres. act. infin. of πάσχω (LN 24.78) (BAGD 3.a.α. p. 634): 'to suffer' [BAGD, BNTC, LN, NIC, WBC; all versions]. See this word at 2:19 and 3:14.
QUESTION—What is meant by the phrase 'if the will of God wills' used with the optative verb θέλοι?
The repetition of 'will' is pleonastic, and the phrase means simply 'if God wills' [EGT, ICC]. It is a devout cliché just as in English, and does not imply a conditional clause [BNTC]. The optative mood of the verb is used to state the proposition, and does not necessarily imply the unlikelihood of suffering [BNTC]. The optative mood of the verb suggests a possibility which would not normally be the case [Alf, ICC, NIC, TNTC]. The optative mood conveys indefiniteness [NCBC], contingency [Sel], or the hypothetical nature of the case [EGT]. It is used in the same way as 'if necessary' in 1:6 [ICC, NIC].
QUESTION—What is meant by suffering for doing evil?
1. It refers to the final judgment of God [NTC, WBC].
2. It means the same as in 2:20, that there is no special benefit in the suffering one deserves for having done evil [Alf, BNTC, NIBC, NIC, TNTC].

**DISCOURSE UNIT: 3:18–22** [IVP, WBC; NJB]. The topic is the significance of Christ's victory [IVP], the vindication of Christ [WBC], the resurrection and the descent into hell [NJB].

# 1 PETER 3:18

**3:18** For[a] Christ also suffered[b] for[c] sins once-for-all,[d]

TEXT—Instead of ἐπαθεν 'suffered', some manuscripts have ἀπέθανεν 'died'. GNT selects the reading 'suffered' with a B rating, indicating that the text is almost certain. The reading 'died' is taken by or translated by BNTC, CEV, NAB, NIV, NJB, TEV and TNT. NLT reads 'suffered when he died'.

LEXICON—a. ὅτι (LN 89.33): 'for' [BNTC, LN, WBC; KJV, NIV, NRSV, TEV, TNT], 'because' [LN, NIC], 'the reason why' [NAB], not explicit [CEV, NJB, NLT, REB].

    b. aorist act. indic. of πάσχω (LN 24.78) (BAGD 3.a.β. p. 634): 'to suffer' [BAGD, LN, NIC, WBC; KJV, NRSV, REB], 'to suffer when he died' [NLT], 'to die' [BNTC; CEV, NAB, NIV, NJB, TEV, TNT]. See this word at 2:19, 3:14, 17.

    c. περί with the genitive (LN **90.39**) (BAGD 1.g. p. 644): 'for' [BAGD, BNTC, NIC; all versions], 'on behalf of' [LN, NIC].

    d. ἅπαξ (LN 60.67; 60.68) (BAGD 1. p. 80): 'once for all' [BNTC; NAB, NIV, NRSV], 'once and for all' [LN (60.68); NJB, REB, TEV, TNT], 'once for all time' [NLT], 'once' [BAGD, LN (60.67), NIC, WBC; CEV, KJV].

QUESTION—What relationship is indicated by ὅτι 'for'?

It gives the basis for what has just been said about suffering for doing right, which is that Christ suffered [Alf, BNTC, NCBC, NIC, NTC, Sel, TG, TH, TNTC, WBC].

1. It indicates the grounds for what has just been said in 3:17 concerning suffering, which is that to endure wrongful suffering is a powerful testimony [TNTC].
2. It indicates the grounds for what has just been said in a way that parallels 2:21, which is that Christ's sufferings are exemplary, setting the pattern that the Christian should follow [NIC, Sel, TG, WBC].
3. It introduces a quotation of catechetical or hymnic material, which gives the entire passage that follows concerning Christ's death, resurrection, ascension and victory over evil as the basis for facing persecution courageously [BNTC].

QUESTION—What relationship is indicated by καί 'also'?

It relates Christ's experience of suffering to that of the believers who were suffering [Alf, BNTC, NIC, TG, TNTC, WBC]. This is to make Christ's sufferings exemplary to the believer [TG, TNTC, WBC]. It serves to encourage the believers to believe that just as Christ was triumphant over apparent defeat in his suffering, so also will they be [BNTC]. It points out that just as Christ suffered for sins, so also do Christians, but in a different way and with a different meaning [Alf].

QUESTION—What is meant by the temporal adverb 'once'?

It means 'once for all' [BNTC, ICC, IVP, NCBC, NIBC, NTC, Sel, TG, TH; all versions except CEV, KJV]. His suffering and death for sins is complete [TNTC, WBC] and their purpose fully accomplished, effective for all time [NIBC, TG, TH, WBC]. It is unique and secures final forgiveness [IVP]. It

# 1 PETER 3:18

emphasizes the brevity of the suffering that Christians will have to endure [Alf, NIC].

## a-righteous[a] (man) for[b] unrighteous[c] (ones), that[d] he-might-bring[e] you to God

TEXT—Instead of ὑμᾶς 'you', some manuscripts have ἡμᾶς 'us'. GNT selects the reading 'you' with a C rating, indicating difficulty in deciding which variant to place in the text. The reading 'us' is taken by BNTC, KJV, NJB, NLT, and REB.

LEXICON—a. δίκαιος (LN 88.12) (BAGD 1.b. p. 195): 'righteous' [BAGD, LN, NIC; NIV, NRSV], 'just' [BAGD, BNTC, LN, WBC; KJV, NAB, REB, TNT], 'upright' [BAGD; NJB], 'innocent' [CEV], 'good' [TEV]. This adjective is also translated as a verb phrase: 'he never sinned' [NLT].
- b. ὑπέρ with genitive object (LN 90.36) (BAGD 1.a.ε. p. 838): 'for' [BAGD; CEV, KJV, NIV, NLT, NRSV, REB, TNT], 'in behalf of' [BAGD], 'on behalf of' [BNTC, LN, NIC, WBC; TEV], 'for the sake of' [NAB, NJB].
- c. ἄδικος (LN 88.20) (BAGD 1. p. 18): 'unrighteous' [LN, NIC; NIV, NRSV, TNT], 'unjust' [BAGD, BNTC, LN, WBC; KJV, NAB, REB], 'guilty' [CEV, NJB], 'sinners' [NLT, TEV].
- d. ἵνα (LN 89.59): 'that (he might)' [WBC; KJV, NAB, NLT, REB, TNT], 'in order to' [BNTC, LN; NRSV, TEV], 'in order that' [NIC], 'so that' [LN], 'to' [CEV, NIV, NJB].
- e. aorist act. subj. of προσάγω (LN 15.172) (BAGD 1.b.α. p. 711): 'to bring to' [BAGD, BNTC, LN, WBC; CEV, KJV, NIV, NRSV, REB, TNT], 'to lead to' [NIC; NAB, NJB, TEV], 'to bring safely home to' [NLT].

## put-to-death[a] in-(the)-flesh[b] but[c] made-alive[d] in/by-(the)-spirit/Spirit;[e]

LEXICON—a. aorist pass. participle θανατόω (LN 20.65) (BAGD 1. p. 351): 'to be put to death' [BAGD, BNTC, NIC, WBC; all versions except NLT]. The passive is also expressed in the active voice: 'he suffered (physical) death' [NLT].
- b. σάρξ (LN 8.4, 58.10) (BAGD 2. p. 743): 'flesh' [BNTC, NIC, WBC; KJV, NRSV], 'body' [BAGD, LN (8.4); CEV, NIV, NJB, REB], 'physical nature' [LN (58.10)], 'fleshly existence' [NAB]. This noun is also translated as an adverb: 'physically' [TEV, TNT]; as an adjective: '(he suffered) physical death' [NLT].
- c. δέ (LN 89.136): 'but' [BNTC, NIC, WBC; all versions except CEV, NJB, REB], 'and' [CEV], not explicit [NJB, REB]. This word is part of the μέν ... δέ construction, the first word of which (μέν) often remains untranslated. See this construction at 1:20 and 2:4.
- d. aorist pass participle of ζῳοποιέω (LN 23.92) (BAGD 1. p. 341): 'to be made alive' [BAGD, BNTC, NIC, WBC; CEV, NIV, NRSV, TEV], 'to be given life' [NAB], 'to be raised to life' [NJB, NLT], 'to be brought to life' [REB, TNT], 'to be made to live' [LN], 'quickened' [KJV].

# 1 PETER 3:18

e. πνεῦμα (LN 12.18, 26.9) (BAGD 2. p. 675): 'spirit' [BAGD, BNTC, LN (26.9), NIC; CEV, NAB, NJB, NRSV, REB, TEV, TNT], 'Spirit' [LN (12.18), WBC; KJV, NIV, NLT].

QUESTION—What relationship is indicated by μέν . . . δέ 'but'?

It functions to mark contrast between the two clauses [BNTC, NCBC, NIC, NTC, TNTC, WBC]. The contrast subordinates the first clause 'put to death (in the) flesh' to the second clause 'made alive (in/by the) spirit/Spirit' [TNTC, WBC].

QUESTION—What is meant by πνεύματι '(in/by the) spirit/Spirit'?

In the phrase θανατωθεὶς μὲν σαρκὶ ζῳοποιηθεὶς δὲ πνεύματι 'put to death (in the) flesh but made alive (in/by the) spirit/Spirit', there are no prepositions 'in' or 'by', the dative case being that which indicates the grammatical relation of the nouns to the verbs.

1. It is a dative of reference indicating the sphere of the spirit/Spirit as the sphere of activity [ICC, IVP, NCBC, NIC, TG, TH, TNTC, WBC; NAB, NJB, NLT, NRSV, REB]. Πνεύματι refers to the sphere of Christ's existence in which the Holy Spirit was at work to effect bodily resurrection [TNTC, WBC]. The new life in the spiritual dimension was continuous with, but distinct from, the earthly physical life [ICC]. His new life was in a spiritual body and was supernatural or spiritual, determined by the Holy Spirit [Alf]. He was made alive as a complete person including his body, in the realm of the spiritual world [NIC]. It means he was resurrected as an immortal, spiritual being [TG].
2. It is a dative of agency, indicating the Spirit as the actor or agent who made Christ alive [NTC; KJV, NIV].
3. It is adverbial, indicating that Christ was put to death physically but made alive spiritually [TEV, TNT].
4. It indicates that though Christ's body was put to death, it was his spirit that was made alive [CEV].

**3:19 in which[a] also having-gone[b] he-preached[c] to the spirits in prison,[d]**

LEXICON—a. ἐν ᾧ (BAGD I.11.c p. 585): 'in which' [BNTC; NRSV], 'by which' [KJV], 'through whom' [NIV], 'in the spirit' [NIC; NJB, REB], 'in that state' [WBC], 'it was in the spirit that' [NAB], 'in his spiritual existence' [TEV], not explicit [CEV, NLT].

b. aorist pass. (deponent = act.) participle of πορεύομαι (LN 15.10): 'to go' [BNTC, LN, NIC, WBC; all versions except CEV], not explicit [CEV].

c. aorist act. indic. of κηρύσσω (LN **33.256**) (BAGD 2.b.β. p. 431): 'to preach' [BAGD, LN, NIC; all versions except NRSV, REB], 'to proclaim' [BAGD], 'to make proclamation' [BNTC, WBC; NRSV, REB].

d. φυλακή (LN 7.24) (BAGD 3. p. 867): 'prison' [BAGD, BNTC, LN, NIC; all versions except REB, TEV], 'refuge' [WBC]. The phrase ἐν φυλακῇ is translated 'imprisoned' [REB, TEV].

# 1 PETER 3:19

QUESTION—What is the meaning of ἐν ᾧ 'in which' and what is the antecedent to which it refers?
- 1. It refers to πνεύματι.
  - 1.1 It means as a spirit or spiritual being [EGT, TG, TH]. It means in his spiritual mode of existence or in the spiritual realm [Alf, BNTC, IVP, NIBC, NIC, TNTC; NAB, NJB, REB, TEV, TNT].
  - 1.2 It means through the instrumentality of the Holy Spirit [NTC; KJV, NIV].
- 2. It refers to ζῳοποιηθεὶς δὲ πνεύματι 'made alive in the Spirit' and means in his risen state [WBC].
- 3. It refers to the whole process of the passion and resurrection of 3:18 and means 'in the course of which' [Sel].

QUESTION—What relationship is indicated by καί 'also'?
- 1. It introduces another activity of Christ 'in the spirit', in addition to being resurrected [BNTC, NIBC, TNTC].
- 2. It means 'even' [Sel, WBC]: Christ even went to the spirits in prison.
- 3. It indicates sequence [NTC]: it was after the resurrection that Christ went and preached.

QUESTION—Who are the spirits he is referring to?
- 1. They are the spirits of the people of Noah's generation [Alf, ICC, TG, TNTC; NJB, TEV].
- 2. They are supernatural beings.
- 2.1 They are fallen angels [NTC].
- 2.2 They are the fallen angels of Genesis 6:1–4 who married human women and had offspring by them [BNTC, EGT, IVP, NCBC, NIBC, NIC, Sel].
- 2.3 They are evil spirit beings who are the spiritual offspring of the fallen angels of Genesis 6:1–4 who married human women and had offspring by them [WBC].

QUESTION—What was the nature of the preaching?
- 1. It was a proclamation of Christ's victory over the spiritual forces of darkness [BNTC, IVP, NIC, NTC, Sel, WBC].
- 2. It was evangelistic preaching urging repentance and offering forgiveness.
- 2.1 Christ was evangelizing the fallen angels [EGT, NCBC].
- 2.2 Christ was evangelizing people who had died [Alf, ICC, TG].
- 2.3 It was when the preincarnate Christ preached through Noah to the people of Noah's day [TNTC].

QUESTION—What is the prison, and where is it located?
- 1. It is the region of the dead [ICC]. It is that place of the dead known as Sheol in the OT or Hades in the NT [Alf, EGT, NIBC, Sel, TG].
- 2. It was the place where the spirits of fallen angels are bound in the underworld [NCBC].
- 3. It was a haunt of evil spirits where they attempted to take refuge [WBC].
- 4. It is a prison in the heavens [IVP]. It is a strata in the plurality of the heavens in the upper regions [BNTC].
- 5. It is hell [TNTC].

QUESTION—When did Christ preach?
1. He preached between the crucifixion and the resurrection [EGT, NCBC, Sel, TH].
2. He preached between the crucifixion and the ascension [ICC].
3. He preached after the resurrection [IVP, NIC, NTC, WBC].
4. He preached at the time of the ascension [BNTC].
5. During the time of Noah the preincarnate Christ preached through Noah to Noah's contemporaries [TNTC].

**3:20** the-ones-having-disobeyed[a] long-ago[b] in (the) days of Noah when[c] the patience[d] of God was-waiting[e]

LEXICON—a. aorist act. participle of ἀπειθέω (LN 36.23, 31.107) (BAGD 2., 3. p. 82): 'to disobey' [BAGD, LN (36.23); CEV, NAB, NIV, NLT], 'to not obey' [NRSV, TEV], 'to be disobedient' [BAGD, NIC, WBC; KJV], 'to refuse to obey' [BNTC; REB, TNT], 'to refuse to believe' [LN (31.107); NJB]. See this word also at 2:8 and 3:1.
  b. ποτε (LN 67.30): 'long ago' [WBC; NIV, NJB, NLT, TNT], 'when' [LN], 'once upon a time' [BNTC], 'once' [NIC], 'sometime' [KJV], 'in former times' [NRSV], 'in the past' [REB], 'as long ago as' [NAB], 'during' [TEV], not explicit [CEV].
  c. ὅτε (LN 67.30): 'when' [BNTC, LN, NIC; NIV, NLT, NRSV, TEV], 'while' [WBC; NAB, NJB, REB, TNT], 'when once' [KJV], not explicit [CEV].
  d. μακροθυμία (LN 25.167) (BAGD 2.b.α. p. 488): 'patience' [BAGD, BNTC, LN, NIC], 'forbearance' [BAGD], 'long-suffering' [KJV]. This noun is also translated as an adverb: 'patiently' [WBC; all versions except CEV, KJV]. The phrase 'the patience was waiting' is translated 'to be patient' [CEV].
  e. imperf. mid. (deponent = act.) indic. of ἀπεκδέχομαι (LN **13.28**) (BAGD p. 83): 'to wait' [BAGD, BNTC, NIC, WBC; all versions except CEV], 'to wait until' [LN], not explicit [CEV].

QUESTION—What was the reason for God's patient waiting?
God is slow to judge and was waiting to give people an opportunity to repent [BNTC, NCBC, NIBC, NIC, NTC, Sel, TH, TNTC, WBC; CEV, NJB, TNT]. He was waiting for the people to obey [TG]. He was also waiting on the completion of the ark [TH].

QUESTION—To what does ὅτε 'when' refer?
1. It relates ποτε ἀπειθήσασιν 'the-ones-having-disobeyed long-ago' to the specific period of time when God waited patiently and the ark was being constructed [Alf, BNTC, NIC, Sel, TG, WBC; all versions].
2. It refers to ἐκήρυξεν 'preached/proclaimed', that is, Christ went and preached through Noah to Noah's contemporaries when they formerly were disobedient [TNTC].

(when) (the) ark[a] was-being-built[b] in/into[c] which a few, that is eight souls were-saved[d] through[e] water.
LEXICON—a. κιβωτός (LN **6.44**) (BAGD 1. p. 431): 'ark' [BAGD, **BNTC, LN**, NIC, WBC; all versions except CEV, NLT, TEV], 'ship' [LN], 'boat' [LN; CEV, NLT, TEV].
- b. pres. pass. participle of κατασκευάζω (LN 45.1, 77.6) (BAGD 2. p. 418): 'to be built' [BAGD, BNTC, LN (45.1), NIC; all versions except KJV, TNT], 'to be prepared' [LN (77.6); KJV, TNT], 'to be fashioned' [WBC].
- c. εἰς (LN 83.13, 84.22): 'in' [BNTC, LN (83.13), NIC, WBC; all versions except CEV, KJV, NLT], 'into' [LN (84.22); CEV], not explicit [NLT]. This word is also conflated with 'which' and translated as 'wherein' [KJV].
- d. aorist pass. indic. of διασῴζω (LN **21.19**) (BAGD p. 189): 'to be saved' [BAGD, **BNTC, LN**, NIC, WBC; KJV, NIV, NJB, NRSV, TEV], 'to be rescued' [BAGD, LN], 'to be brought safely through' [BAGD; CEV, REB, TNT], 'to escape' [NAB], 'to be saved from drowning' [NLT].
- e. διά (LN 90.8, 84.29): 'through' [BNTC, LN (84.29), NIC, WBC; all versions except KJV, NLT, TEV], 'by' [LN (90.8); KJV, TEV], 'in' [NLT].

QUESTION—How is εἰς 'in/into' used in this context?
1. It means 'into'; that is, they were saved by going into the ark [ICC, TNTC; CEV].
2. It means 'in'; that is, they were saved by being in the ark [NIC, TG, WBC; all versions except CEV, NLT]. Εἰς is used instead of ἐν in order to make clear that the preposition is being used to express locality and not instrumentality [WBC].
3. It is used in both senses, that is, having entered into the ark, they were saved in it [Alf, BNTC, Sel, TH].

QUESTION—What does he mean by δι' ὕδατος 'through water'?
1. It is used locally; they were saved going through the water.
   1.1 They were saved as they were passing through the waters of the flood in the ark [EGT, IVP, NCBC, NIC, NTC, Sel; NAB].
   1.2 They were saved as they were wading through the water of the flood to get into the ark [ICC, TNTC].
2. It is used instrumentally; they were saved by means of the water [Alf, BNTC, EGT, NIC, NTC, Sel, TG, TH, WBC].
   2.1 The water was instrumental, in that it floated the ark to safety [BNTC, EGT, TH].
   2.2 The water was instrumental, in that it saved them from a flood of human wickedness [NTC].
3. It is used both instrumentally and locally [BNTC, EGT, NIC, NTC, Sel].

**3:21** Which (as) an-antitype[a] also now saves[b] you (even) baptism,
TEXT—Instead of ὑμᾶς 'you', some manuscripts have ἡμᾶς 'us'. GNT does not mention this alternative. The reading 'us' is taken by only by KJV.

LEXICON—a. ἀντίτυπος (LN **58.69**) (BAGD 1. p. 76): 'antitype' [LN, NIC], 'corresponding to' [BAGD; NJB], 'correspondence, fulfillment, representation' [LN], 'a symbol pointing to' [TEV], 'prefigured' [BNTC; NRSV], 'like' [CEV], 'the like figure whereunto' [KJV], 'a picture of' [NLT]. This noun is also translated as a verb phrase: 'which corresponds to' [**LN**, WBC; NAB], 'symbolizes' [NIV, REB], 'here stands for' [TNT].
   b. pres. act. indic. of σῴζω (LN 21.27) (BAGD 2.a.γ. p. 798): 'to save' [BAGD, BNTC, LN, NIC, WBC; all versions except REB], 'to be brought to safety' [REB].

QUESTION—To what does the relative pronoun ὅ 'which' refer?
   1. It refers to ὕδωρ 'water' [BNTC, EGT, NIC, WBC; CEV, NIV, NJB, REB, TEV, TNT]. It refers to water in general, not just the flood [Alf].
   2. It refers to baptism [TG; NRSV]. It refers to the water of baptism [Sel].
   3. It refers to escaping through water [TNTC; NAB].
   4. It refers to the entire previous sentence regarding the construction of the ark and of Noah's family being saved in it [NCBC, NTC].

QUESTION—How is the concept of the ἀντίτυπον 'antitype' used in this passage?
   1. The type is the water of the flood, and the corresponding antitype is baptism [BNTC, ICC, TG]. Water represents the evil life left behind and through which the believer passes into safety, and the antitype is baptism and all it represents of regeneration and cleansing [ICC].
   2. Noah and his family who are saved by water are the type and believers are the antitype corresponding to them [Sel].
   3. The deliverance of Noah is the type and baptism is the antitype. The point of correspondence is that in both instances the remnant is saved and sin is washed away [EGT].
   4. There is no formal type-antitype relationship, but a simple correspondence or comparison [Alf, IVP, NTC, TNTC, WBC]. The symbol is that of Noah being saved through the flood waters, which pre-figures the cleansing of baptism [NTC]. The point of correspondence is that of going through water to new life [TNTC]. The points of correspondence are that the people in the ark correspond to believers, their escape compares to salvation, the flood compares to baptism, and the people who died in the flood compare to unbelievers of Peter's day [IVP].

QUESTION—What is meant by the statement that baptism 'saves you'?
   'Baptism' is a synecdoche. Baptism represents the whole process by which people accept the gospel by faith and are saved by virtue of the resurrection [IVP]. Baptism is the public expression of what has already occurred inwardly and which is made effective by the resurrection [NIBC]. Baptism saves because of the faith and repentance which are antecedent to baptism, and because of the resurrection through which regeneration occurs [ICC]. Baptism saves because of the pledge of the good conscience and the inner cleansing of the believer through Christ's shed blood which the outward ceremony represents [NTC]. It is not baptism but the resurrection that saves,

## 1 PETER 3:21

and baptism is the instrument by which God makes known his saving activity [TH]. Baptism saves in the same way that faith 'saves', which is because it is an appeal to God who saves [WBC]. Salvation is God's action, but baptism brings salvation through the new believer's pledge of obedience to Jesus Christ and because of the resurrection [TG].

**not a removal[a] of dirt[b] of/from-(the)-body[c]**
LEXICON—a. ἀπόθεσις (LN 85.44) (BAGD p. 91): 'removal' [BAGD, BNTC, LN, NIC, WBC; NAB, NIV, NLT, NRSV, TNT], 'washing off' [NJB, TEV], 'washing away' [REB], 'putting away' [LN; KJV]. The phrase 'removal of dirt' is translated 'washing' [CEV].
   b. ῥύπος (LN **79.55**) (BAGD 1. p. 738): 'dirt' [BAGD, LN, NIC; NIV, NJB, NLT, NRSV, TEV, TNT], 'filth' [BNTC, WBC; KJV], 'stain' [NAB], 'impurities' [REB], not explicit [CEV].
   c. σάρξ (LN 8.4) (BAGD 2. p. 743): 'body' [BAGD, BNTC, LN, NIC; CEV, NIV, NLT, NRSV, TNT], 'flesh' [WBC; KJV]. This noun is also translated as an adjective: 'physical' [NAB, NJB], 'bodily' [REB, TEV]. In addition to being translated as an adjective, the genitive form of this noun is also translated 'of the (body)' [WBC; KJV], 'from the (body)' [BNTC, NIC; NIV, NLT, NRSV, TNT].

QUESTION—What is meant by οὐ σαρκὸς ἀπόθεσις ῥύπου 'removal of dirt of/from-the-body'?
   1. It refers to outward cleansing of a physical nature [Alf, EGT, ICC, IVP, NCBC, NIBC, NIC, NTC, Sel, TG, TH, TNTC; CEV, NAB, NIV, NJB, NLT, NRSV, REB, TEV, TNT].
   2. It refers to circumcision, which was the OT type of which baptism is the corresponding NT antitype [BNTC].
   3. It refers to the defilement of carnality, which is contrasted with the appeal to God of the conscience [WBC].

**but (the) pledge of[a]/appeal for[a] a good conscience to[b] God through[c] (the) resurrection of Jesus Christ,**
LEXICON—a. ἐπερώτημα (LN **33.162**) (BAGD 2. p. 285): 'pledge' [BAGD, BNTC; NAB, NIV, NJB], 'promise' [TEV, TNT], 'answer' [NIC; KJV], 'turning' [CEV], 'request' [BAGD, **LN** (33.162)], 'appeal' [BAGD, LN (33.162), WBC; NLT, NRSV, REB].
   b. εἰς (LN 90.59): 'to' [BNTC, LN, NIC, WBC; all versions except KJV, NIV], 'toward' [LN; KJV, NIV].
   c. διά (LN 89.76, 89.26): 'through' [BNTC, LN (89.76), NIC, WBC; NAB, NJB, NRSV, REB, TEV, TNT], 'by' [LN (89.76); KJV, NIV, NLT], 'because of' [LN (89.26)], 'because' [CEV].

QUESTION—What is the relationship between ἐπερώτημα 'pledge/appeal' and συνείδησις 'conscience'?
   1. Συνείδησις 'conscience' is taken subjectively, 'from' or 'out of' a good conscience.
      1.1 Ἐπερώτημα is a response of commitment toward God.

1.1.1 Baptism is a pledge or promise to God made from, with, or arising out of a good conscience [BNTC, ICC, NCBC, NIBC; NAB, NIV, NJB, TEV, TNT].
1.1.2 Baptism is an answer to God of a good conscience [NIC; KJV].
1.1.3 Baptism is a turning to God with a clear conscience [CEV].
1.2 Ἐπερώτημα is an appeal made to God, and baptism is an appeal to God that arises out of a good conscience [EGT, WBC; NLT, REB].
1.3 Ἐπερώτημα is the seeking after God that comes from a good conscience [Alf].
2. Συνείδησις 'conscience' is taken objectively, 'for' or 'regarding' a good conscience.
2.1 Ἐπερώτημα is an appeal made to God, and baptism is an appeal to God for a good or clear conscience [TNTC; NRSV]
2.2. Ἐπερώτημα is a pledge or response made to the Christian community when questioned at baptism. The baptismal candidate makes a pledge about a good conscience and faith in God, and is brought safe to God through baptism [ICC].

QUESTION—What is the function of the phrase 'through the resurrection of Jesus Christ'?

1. It relates to the statement that 'baptism saves', and indicates that the resurrection is the power by which salvation occurs [Alf, BNTC, ICC, IVP, NCBC, NIBC, NIC, NTC, Sel, TG, TH, WBC; all versions except CEV, NAB, NJB].
2. It is the reason a person turns to God with a clear conscience [CEV]. It is the means by which the pledge of a good conscience is made to God [NAB, NJB].

**3:22** who is at (the) right[a] of God having-gone[b] into heaven, angels and authorities[c] and powers[d] having-been-subjected[e] to-him.

LEXICON—a. δεξιά (LN 8.32, 87.36) (BAGD 2.a.α. p. 174): 'right hand' [BAGD, BNTC, LN (8.32), NIC, WBC; all versions except CEV, NLT], 'right side' [CEV], 'place of honor' [LN (87.36); NLT].
  b. aorist pass. (deponent = act.) participle of πορεύομαι (LN 15.10): 'to go' [BNTC, LN, NIC, WBC; KJV, NAB, NIV, NLT, NRSV] 'to enter' [NJB, REB, TNT], 'to be in' [CEV].
  c. ἐξουσία (LN 12.44) (BAGD 4.c.β. p. 278): 'authorities' [BAGD, BNTC, LN, NIC, WBC; CEV, KJV, NIV, NLT, NRSV, REB], 'heavenly authorities' [TEV, TNT], 'rulers, wicked forces' [LN], 'angelic rulers' [NAB], 'ruling forces' [NJB].
  d. δύναμις (LN 12.44) (BAGD 6. p. 208): 'powers' [BAGD, BNTC, LN, NIC, WBC; all versions].
  e. aorist pass. participle of ὑποτάσσω (LN 36.18) (BAGD 1.b.α. p. 848): 'to be subjected' [BAGD; NAB], 'to be made subject' [BNTC, NIC; KJV, NRSV, TNT], 'to submit to' [LN], 'in submission to' [WBC; NIV], 'subject to' [NJB], 'to be under the control of' [CEV], 'to bow before'

[NLT]. This passive participle is also translated actively with Jesus Christ as the subject and the angels, authorities, and powers as the object: 'to receive the submission of' [REB], 'to rule over' [TEV].

**DISCOURSE UNIT: 4:1–19** [TH; REB]. The topic is Christian suffering and service [TH]; the final testing [REB].

**DISCOURSE UNIT: 4:1–11** [NIC; CEV, NIV, NLT, NRSV]. The topic is exhortation to firmness in the end times [NIC], being faithful to God [CEV], living for God [NIV, NLT], good stewards of God's grace [NRSV].

**DISCOURSE UNIT: 4:1–6** [IVP, Sel, TH, WBC; NAB, NJB, TEV]. The topic is the obligations of Christians, living in view of the coming judgment [Sel], living for the promise [WBC], readiness to suffer as a result of obeying Christ [TH]; in Christian faithfulness [NAB], the break with sin [NJB], changed lives [TEV].

**4:1** Therefore[a] Christ having-suffered[b] in-the-flesh[c] you also arm-yourselves[d] (with) the same way-of-thinking,[e]

TEXT—Some manuscripts include ὑπὲρ ἡμῶν 'for us' after παθόντος 'having-suffered'. It is omitted by GNT with an A rating, indicating that the text is certain. It is included only by KJV.

LEXICON—a. οὖν (LN 89.50): 'therefore' [LN, WBC; NAB, NIV], 'since then' [BNTC, NIC], 'since therefore' [NRSV], 'since' [REB, TEV], 'forasmuch then' [KJV], 'so then, since' [NLT], 'we see then' [TNT], 'as' [NJB], not explicit [CEV].

b. aorist act. participle of πάσχω (LN 24.78) (BAGD 3.a.β. p. 634): 'to suffer' [BNTC, NIC, WBC; all versions except NJB, REB, TNT], 'to undergo suffering' [NJB, TNT], 'to endure suffering' [REB]. See this word at 3:14, 17, 18.

c. σάρξ (LN 8.4) (BAGD 2. p. 743): 'flesh' [BNTC, NIC, WBC; KJV, NAB, NRSV], 'body' [BAGD, LN; NIV]. The dative form σαρκί 'in-the-flesh' is also translated adverbially: 'here on earth' [CEV], 'bodily' [NJB, REB, TNT], 'physically' [TEV]; as the object of 'suffered': 'physical pain' [NLT]. See this word at 3:18, 21.

d. aorist mid. imperf. of ὁπλίζω (LN **77.10**) (BAGD 575): 'to arm oneself' [BAGD, BNTC, NIC, WBC; all versions except CEV, TEV], 'to make ready' [LN], 'to be ready' [CEV], 'to strengthen oneself' [TEV].

e. ἔννοια (LN **30.5**) (BAGD 267): 'way of thinking' [**LN**; TEV], 'insight' [BAGD, NIC], 'thought' [BAGD, BNTC], 'attitude' [LN; NIV, NLT], 'disposition' [REB], 'resolve' [WBC], 'resolution' [TNT], 'intention' [NRSV], 'mind' [KJV], 'mentality' [NAB], 'conviction' [NJB]. The phrase 'you also arm yourselves with the same way of thinking' is translated 'you must be ready to suffer as he did' [CEV].

1 PETER 4:1

QUESTION—What relationship is indicated by οὖν 'therefore'?
It resumes the thought of 3:18 regarding the suffering of Christ and draws a conclusion from it [Alf, BNTC, EGT, ICC, IVP, NCBC, NIBC, NIC, NTC, Sel, TG, TH, TNTC, WBC].

**because/that[a] the-one having-suffered in-(the)-flesh has-finished-with[b] sin**
LEXICON—a. ὅτι (LN 89.43; 90.21): 'because' [LN (89.43); CEV, NIV, TEV], 'for' [LN (89.43), WBC; KJV, NLT, NRSV, TNT], 'that' [BNTC, LN (90.21), NIC; NJB], not explicit [NAB, REB].
  b. perf. mid. indic. of παύομαι (παύω) (LN 68.34) (BAGD 2. p. 638): 'to finish with' [BNTC, NIC; NRSV, REB, TNT], 'to cease' [LN], 'to cease from' [KJV], 'to stop' [LN; CEV, NLT], 'to be through with' [WBC], 'to break with' [NAB, NJB], 'to be done with' [NIV], 'to be no longer involved with' [TEV].
QUESTION—What relationship is indicated by ὅτι 'because/that'?
  1. It marks discourse content contained in the statement that follows [BNTC, EGT, NIC, NTC; NJB]: you must arm yourself with the insight that one having suffered in the flesh has finished with sin.
  2. It gives the grounds for the statement just made [Alf, ICC, IVP, NCBC, TG, TH, TNTC, WBC; CEV, KJV, NIV, NLT, NRSV, TEV, TNT]: you must arm yourself with the same way of thinking as Christ because the person who has suffered in the flesh has finished with sin.
QUESTION—What does it mean that 'the one having suffered in the flesh has finished with sin'?
  1. Christ is the subject of the aorist participle παθών 'having suffered', and is the one who has suffered in the flesh [NIBC, NTC, WBC]. Christ is through with sin, in that he has dealt with it finally and completely, and since he has put it behind him, so should believers [WBC]. Christ suffered in his flesh that believers might be free from sin by identification with and imitation of Christ [NIBC, NTC].
  2. The subject of the aorist participle παθών 'having suffered' is the believer who suffers in the flesh.
  2.1 The thought is parallel to Romans 6:7 and refers to death to the old life of sin [Alf, EGT, NCBC]. Sin is conquered when the flesh, as the seat of sin, is disciplined and purified through suffering [NCBC]. The flesh is mortified by suffering, but believers are also separated from sin by union and identification with Christ [Alf]. Suffering for what is right purifies the sinner in that it diminishes the desire to sin [TH].
  2.2 The person who endures persecution and continues to obey God demonstrates the fact of having broken with sin [ICC, IVP, Sel, TG, TNTC; all versions].
  3. Christ as well as the believer suffer in the flesh [BNTC, NIC]. Christ finished with sin when he suffered, and the Christian who suffers can follow Christ's example and gain freedom from sin when the flesh is disciplined through suffering [NIC]. Christ was freed from the forces of

evil which caused his unjust suffering and death and, by virtue of identification with him in baptism, the believer is delivered from spiritual slavery to sin [BNTC].

**4:2** so-as[a] to-live[b] the remaining time[c] in (the) flesh no-longer for-(the)-lusts[d] of men but for-(the)-will[e] of God.

LEXICON—a. εἰς (LN 89.48): 'so as (to)' [WBC; NRSV], 'so that as a result' [LN], 'so that' [BNTC; REB], 'that' [KJV], 'as a result' [NIV], 'with the result that' [NIC], 'it means' [CEV], 'then' [TNT], 'from now on, then' [TEV], 'because' [NJB], not explicit [NAB, NLT, TEV].

b. aorist act. infin. of βιόω (LN **41.18**) (BAGD p. 142): 'to live' [BAGD, BNTC, LN, NIC, WBC; KJV, NIV, NRSV, REB, TEV], 'to spend one's life' [NAB, NLT], not explicit [CEV, NJB, TNT].

c. χρόνος (LN 67.78) (BAGD 888): 'time' [BAGD, BNTC, LN, WBC; KJV], 'life' [NIC; all versions except KJV, REB], 'days' [REB]. The phrase 'the remaining time in the flesh' is translated 'the rest of your lives' [NIC], 'the rest of your life' [CEV, NLT], 'the rest of his earthly life' [NIV], 'what remains of your earthly life' [NAB], 'the rest of your earthly lives' [TEV, TNT], 'the rest of your earthly life' [NRSV], 'the rest of his days on earth' [REB], 'the rest of life on earth' [NJB].

d. ἐπιθυμία (LN 25.20) (BAGD 3. p. 293): 'lust' [BAGD, LN; CEV], 'desire' [BAGD, LN, NIC; CEV, NAB, NRSV, TEV], 'evil desires' [NIV, NLT], 'passion' [BNTC; NJB, TNT], 'impulse' [WBC], 'appetite' [REB]. The grammatical relation of the dative case of this noun is variously expressed: 'for' [NIC, WBC; NIV], 'in accordance with' [BNTC], '(to spend) on' [NAB], 'by' [NRSV], 'to' [KJV]; or by the use of a verb: 'ruled by' [NJB], 'controlled by' [TEV], 'chasing after' [NLT], 'to satisfy' [REB], 'to indulge' [TNT], not explicit [CEV]. See this word at 1:14, 2:11.

e. θέλημα (LN **25.2**) (BAGD 1.c.γ. p. 354): 'will' [BAGD, BNTC, NIC, WBC; all versions except REB], not explicit [CEV]. The phrase 'the will of God' is translated 'what God wills' [REB], 'what God desires' [LN]. The grammatical relation of the dative case of this noun is variously expressed: 'for' [NIC; NIV], 'in accordance with' [BNTC], '(to spend) on' [NAB], 'by' [NRSV, TEV], 'to' [KJV]; or by the use of a verb: 'to do' [WBC; REB], 'ruled by' [NJB], 'you will be anxious to do' [NLT], 'you will do' [TNT], not explicit [CEV]. See this word at 2:15.

QUESTION—What relationship is indicated by εἰς 'so-as'?

1. It indicates the purpose of the imperative verb ὁπλίσασθε 'arm yourselves' [Alf, BNTC, NCBC, NIBC, NIC, WBC; NRSV, TEV, TNT].
2. It indicates the result of having ceased from sin [EGT, ICC, Sel; KJV, NIV, NJB, REB].
3. It indicates the purpose of having broken with sin [TNTC].

# 1 PETER 4:3

**4:3** For[a] the time having-passed[b] (is) sufficient[c] to-have-done[d] the desire[e] of the Gentiles[f]

TEXT—Some manuscripts include τοῦ βίου 'of life' after χρόνος 'time'. GNT does not mention this alternative. It is included only by KJV.

TEXT—Some manuscripts include ὑμῖν '(to) us' after ἀρκετός 'sufficient'. GNT does not mention this alternative. It is included only by KJV.

LEXICON—a. γάρ (BAGD 2. p. 152): 'for' [BAGD, BNTC, NIC; KJV, NIV], 'you see' [BAGD], not explicit [WBC; all versions except KJV, NIV].

    b. perf. act. participle of παρέρχομαι (LN 67.85) (BAGD 1.a.β. p. 626): 'to pass' [BAGD, LN], 'to go by, pass by' [BAGD], 'past' [KJV], 'that is past' [BNTC], 'in the past' [WBC; NIV, NJB, NLT, REB, TEV, TNT], 'already past' [NIC], 'already spent' [NRSV], 'already' [NAB], not explicit [CEV].

    c. ἀρκετός (LN **59.45**) (BAGD p. 107): 'sufficient' [BAGD, **BNTC, LN**, NIC], 'to suffice' [KJV], 'enough' [BAGD, WBC; NAB, NIV, NLT, NRSV, REB, TEV], 'adequate' [BAGD, LN], 'long enough' [CEV, TNT], 'quite long enough' [NJB].

    d. perf. mid. (deponent = act.) infin. of κατεργάζομαι (LN 90.47) (BAGD 1. p. 421): 'to do' [BAGD, LN, NIC, WBC; NIV, NRSV, REB, TEV, TNT], 'to accomplish' [BAGD, BNTC], 'to work' (represented as a past participle 'to have wrought') [KJV], 'to live (the sort of life)' [NJB], not explicit [CEV, NAB, NLT].

    e. βούλημα (LN **25.4**) (BAGD p. 145): 'desire' [BAGD, LN], 'will' [LN, NIC; KJV], 'intention' [BAGD], not explicit [CEV]. The phrase 'the will of the Gentiles' is translated 'what the pagans wish to do' [BNTC], 'what the Gentiles wanted' [WBC], 'what the pagans enjoy' [NAB], 'what the pagans choose to do' [NIV], 'the sort of life that Gentiles choose to live' [NJB], 'the evil things that godless people enjoy' [NLT], 'what the Gentiles like to do' [NRSV], 'what pagans like to do' [REB], 'what the heathen like to do' [TEV], 'what the heathen desire to do' [**LN**], 'what pagans want' [TNT].

    f. ἔθνη (LN 11.37): 'Gentiles' [WBC; KJV, NJB, NRSV], 'heathen' [LN; TEV], 'pagans' [BNTC, LN; NAB, NIV, REB, TNT], 'nations' [NIC], 'people who don't know God' [CEV], 'godless people' [NLT]. See this word at 2:12.

**having-lived[a] in licentiousness,[b] lusts,[c] drunkenness,[d] revelries,[e] drinking-parties,[f] and lawless/disgusting[g] idolatries.[h]**

LEXICON—a. perf. mid. (deponent = act.) participle of πορεύομαι (πορεύω) (LN 41.11) (BAGD 2.c. p. 692): 'to live' [BAGD, BNTC, LN, NIC; NIV, NRSV, REB], 'walk' [BAGD; KJV], 'to behave' [LN; NJB], 'to go about doing' [LN], 'to go around doing' [CEV], 'to go along with' [NIC], 'to live a life of' [NAB, TNT], 'to spend one's life in' [TEV], not explicit [NLT].

b. ἀσέλγεια (LN 88.272) (BAGD p. 114): 'licentiousness' [BAGD; NRSV, TNT], 'licentious behavior' [LN], 'license' [REB], 'extreme immorality' [LN], 'acts of immorality' [WBC; NLT], 'debauchery' [BAGD; NAB, NIV], 'sensuality' [BAGD, BNTC, NIC], 'lasciviousness' [KJV], 'indecency' [TEV]. This noun is also translated as a predicate adjective: '(to be) immoral' [CEV]; as an adverb: '(behaving) in a debauched way' [NJB].

c. ἐπιθυμία (LN 25.20) (BAGD 3. p. 293): 'lust' [BAGD, LN, WBC; KJV, NIV, NLT, TEV], 'desire' [BAGD, LN, NIC], 'passion' [BNTC; NJB, NRSV], 'evil desires' [CEV, NAB], 'debauchery' [REB], 'self-indulgence' [TNT]. See this word at 1:14, 2:11, and 4:2.

d. οἰνοφλυγία (LN **88.284**) (BAGD p. 562): 'drunkenness' [BAGD, LN, NIC; all versions except CEV, KJV, NJB], 'intoxications' [BNTC], 'drunken orgies' [WBC], 'drinking' [CEV], 'drinking to excess' [NJB], 'excess of wine' [KJV].

e. κῶμος (LN **88.287**) (BAGD p. 461): 'revelry' [BAGD, BNTC; TNT], 'revel' [NRSV], 'reveling' [LN; KJV], 'carousing' [BAGD, LN], 'orgy' [**LN**, NIC; NAB, NIV, REB, TEV], 'feasting' [NLT], 'feast' [WBC], 'partying' [CEV], 'wild party' [NJB].

f. πότος (LN **88.287**) (BAGD p. 696): 'drinking party' [BAGD, NIC; TEV, TNT], 'drunken party' [BNTC], 'carousal' [BAGD; REB], 'carousing' [LN; NAB, NIV, NRSV], 'reveling' [**LN**], 'orgy' [LN], 'drunken orgy' [NJB], 'wild party' [NLT], 'revelry' [WBC], 'carrying on' [CEV], 'banqueting' [KJV].

g. ἀθέμιτος (LN 13.144, **88.143**) (BAGD p. 20): 'lawless' [BAGD, BNTC, WBC; NRSV], 'unlawful' [BAGD, NIC], 'forbidden' [LN (13.144); REB, TNT], 'disgusting' [LN (88.143); CEV, TEV], 'wanton' [BAGD; NAB], 'abominable' [KJV], 'detestable' [NIV], 'terrible' [NLT]. This adjective is also translated as an adverb: 'sacrilegiously' [NJB].

h. εἰδωλολατρία (LN 53.63) (BAGD p. 221): 'idolatry' [BAGD, BNTC, LN, NIC, WBC; KJV, NAB, NIV, NRSV, TNT], 'worship of idols' [NLT, REB, TEV], 'worshipping false gods' [NJB]. This noun is also translated as a verb phrase: 'to worship idols' [CEV].

QUESTION—What is meant by describing idolatry as ἀθέμιτος 'lawless/disgusting'?

1. It was lawless in that it was forbidden by the Mosaic law [ICC, NIBC]. It was lawless in that it was not authorized by God [NIC]. It was an offense against the most sacred law of God [Alf, Sel]. It violated the Mosaic law against idolatry and was accompanied by detestable acts of gross sin [NTC]. It was contrary to Jewish law and therefore repugnant to God [WBC]. Certain forms of idol worship were contrary to civil law because of the gross evils associated with them [EGT, TNTC].
2. It was detestable because it was contemptuous of the only true God [IVP]. It was shameful, disgusting, and clearly evil [NCBC, TG, TH]. It was disgusting in that it was outrageous and indecent [NIBC].

QUESTION—Why are all these vices described by plural nouns?
The plural nouns show that the sinful acts were habitual [NTC]. They indicate the variety and frequency of the acts named [Sel]. The plural noun ἀσελγείαις refers to multiple acts of immorality [EGT, ICC, WBC], or to various sorts of lasciviousness [ICC]. Οἰνοφλυγία refers to habitual drinking or drunkenness [NIBC, TH].

**4:4** Wherein[a] they-think-it-strange[b] (that) you (are) not running-with[c] (them) into the same flood[d] of dissipation[e] blaspheming,[f]

LEXICON—a. ἐν ᾧ (BAGD I.11.c. p. 585): 'wherein' [KJV], 'in this' [BNTC], 'with reference to which' [NIC], 'therefore' [WBC], 'so' [NJB], 'of course' [NLT], 'now' [CEV, REB, TNT], 'and now' [TEV], not explicit [NAB, NIV, NRSV].

b. pres. pass. indic. of ξενίζω (LN 25.206): 'to think it strange' [NIC; KJV, NIV], 'to be surprised' [LN, WBC; NAB, NLT, NRSV, TEV, TNT], 'to be astonished' [BNTC], 'to wonder' [CEV], 'to be taken aback' [NJB], 'to be unable to understand' [REB].

c. pres. act. participle of συντρέχω (LN 15.133, **41.15**) (BAGD 2. p. 793): 'to run with' [NIC; KJV], 'to run together' [BAGD, LN (15.133)], 'to run around with' [CEV], 'to rush with' [BNTC], 'to plunge with' [WBC; NIV, REB], 'to plunge' [NAB], 'to hurry with' [NJB], 'to join in living' [**LN** (41.15)], 'to be closely associated with' [LN (41.15)], 'to join in' [NLT, NRSV, TEV, TNT].

d. ἀνάχυσις (LN **78.26**) (BAGD p. 63): 'flood' [BAGD, NIC, WBC; NIV, NJB], 'swamp' [NAB], 'excess' [KJV, NRSV, TNT], not explicit [CEV, NLT, TEV]. This noun is also translated as an adjective: 'dissolute' [BNTC], 'excessive' [**LN**], 'reckless' [REB].

e. ἀσωτία (LN 88.96) (BAGD p. 119): 'dissipation' [BAGD, WBC; NIV, NRSV, REB], 'debauchery' [BAGD, NIC], 'profligacy' [BAGD, BNTC; NAB], 'recklessness' [LN], 'riot' [KJV], 'loose living' [TNT], 'wild and reckless living' [TEV], 'the wicked things they do' [NLT], not explicit [CEV]. This noun in the genitive case is also translated as a verb phrase: 'which is rushing down to ruin' [NJB].

f. pres. act. participle of βλασφημέω (LN 33.400) (BAGD 2.b.α. p. 142): 'to blaspheme' [BAGD, LN; NRSV], 'to revile' [LN], 'to vilify' [BNTC], 'to slander' [NIC; TNT], 'to insult' [TEV], 'to curse' [CEV], 'to speak evil of' [KJV], 'to say evil things about' [NLT], 'to heap abuse on' [NIV], 'to abuse' [NJB, REB]. This participle is also translated as a verbal adjective modifying the unbelievers: 'blasphemers' [WBC; NAB].

QUESTION—What relationship is indicated by ἐν ᾧ 'wherein'?
1. It refers to the previously stated fact of having ceased from these various vices [Alf, BNTC, EGT, TH]. It shifts the focus from the sins of the past to the present refusal to sin, which is what surprises and offends unbelievers [WBC].
2. It refers to the manner of life describes by the vices named [ICC].

# 1 PETER 4:4

QUESTION—Who is the implied object of the participle βλασφημοῦντες 'blaspheming'?
1. Christians are being vilified [Alf, IVP, NTC, TG, TH, TNTC; CEV, KJV, NIV, NJB, NLT, NRSV, REB, TEV, TNT].
2. The abuse is directed toward Christians but is also blasphemy because it does not give glory to God [EGT]. They blaspheme Christians and God, because it is God's will the Christians are keeping [NCBC]. They also blaspheme God because to insult believers is to insult God [BNTC].
3. It is blasphemy of God, because it makes virtue out to be vice, and faith to be impiety [ICC]. It is blasphemy because it calls what is good evil [Sel]. It is primarily blasphemy against God because God is the one who called the believers out of that darkness into his light, and so to blaspheme them is to blaspheme God [WBC].

**4:5** who will-give$^a$ account$^b$ to-the (one) being ready$^c$ to-judge$^d$ (the) living and (the) dead.

LEXICON—a. fut. act. indic. of ἀποδίδωμι (LN 90.46) (BAGD 1. p. 90): 'to give (account)' [BNTC, LN, NIC; KJV, NAB, NIV, NRSV, REB, TEV]. The phrase ἀποδίδωμι λόγον 'to give account' is translated 'to answer' [WBC; TNT], 'to have to answer' [CEV, NJB], 'to have to face God' [NLT].
b. λόγος (LN 57.228) (BAGD 2.a. p. 478): 'account' [BAGD, BNTC, LN, NIC; KJV, NIV, REB, TEV], 'accounting' [NAB, NRSV], not explicit [WBC; CEV, NJB, NLT, TNT].
c. ἑτοίμως (LN 77.2) (BAGD p. 316): 'ready' [BAGD, BNTC, LN, NIC, WBC; all versions except CEV, NJB, NLT], 'prepared' [LN], not explicit [CEV, NJB, NLT].
d. aorist act. infin. of κρίνω (LN 56.20) (BAGD 4.b.α. p. 452): 'to judge' [BAGD, BNTC, NIC, WBC; all versions except REB], 'to pass judgment' [REB], 'to act as a judge' [LN]. See this verb at 1:17 and 2:23.

**4:6** For$^a$ to this-end$^b$ he/it-was-preached$^c$ also$^d$ to-the-dead,

LEXICON—a. γάρ (BAGD 2. p. 152): 'for' [BAGD, BNTC, NIC, WBC; KJV, NAB, NIV, NRSV], 'and' [NJB], not explicit [CEV, NAB, NLT, REB, TEV, TNT].
b. εἰς (LN 89.57): 'for this purpose' [LN]. The expression εἰς τοῦτο 'to this end' is translated 'this is why' [BNTC], 'that is why' [NLT, TEV], 'that was why' [REB], 'for this reason' [NIC], 'for this cause' [KJV], 'the reason was' [NAB], 'for this is the reason' [NIV, NRSV], 'and this was why' [NJB], not explicit [WBC; CEV, TNT].
c. aorist pass. indic. of εὐαγγελίζομαι (LN 33.215) (BAGD 2.b.α. p. 317): 'to be preached' [BAGD; all versions except NJB, NRSV], 'to be told the good news' [LN], 'to be proclaimed' [WBC; NRSV], 'to be brought' [NJB]. The εὐ- prefix normally identifies what is being preached as the gospel [WBC; KJV, NAB, NIV, NJB, NRSV, REB] or the good news [NIC; CEV, NLT, TEV, TNT]. The English cognate of this verb,

'evangelize', takes the person or persons being evangelized as the subject of the verb when used in the passive voice, but in Greek the subject is normally either the content of the message, 'Christ' [BNTC], or the message itself, i.e., the good news [NIC, WBC; all versions].
- d. καί (LN 89.93): 'also' [BNTC, LN; KJV, TEV], 'even' [LN; CEV, NAB, NIV, NLT, NRSV, REB], 'as well' [NJB], not explicit [NIC, WBC; TNT]

QUESTION—What relationship is indicated by γάρ 'for'?

It indicates the grounds for the statement about judgment in 4:5 [Alf, ICC, NCBC]. It refers to the judgment mentioned in 4:5 [BNTC, NTC, Sel, TNTC]. It is a reference to general judgment in order to make a statement about Christians who have died [NIC].

QUESTION—What relationship is indicated by εἰς τοῦτο 'to this end'?
1. It refers forward to the ἵνα 'so that' clause; 'this is why . . .' [Alf, BNTC, Sel, TG, WBC; CEV, KJV, NAB, TNT].
2. It refers backwards to the content of 4:5, 'that was why . . .' [TH; NLT, REB, TEV].

QUESTION—What or who is the implied subject of the passive verb εὐηγγελίσθη 'was preached'?
1. It is the gospel message that was preached [Alf, EGT, ICC, IVP, NCBC, NIBC, NIC, NTC, TG, TH, TNTC, WBC; all versions].
2. It is Christ that was preached [BNTC, Sel].

QUESTION—Who are the dead that are being preached to?
1. The dead are those who heard and believed during their lifetime, and then died [BNTC, IVP, NIBC, NIC, NTC, Sel, TNTC, WBC; NIV].
2. The dead are not only those who heard the gospel of Christ during their lifetime, but also the faithful of the OT period who believed God's promises during their lifetime, and then died [WBC].
3. They are those who heard the gospel after their death [Alf, EGT, ICC, NCBC, TG, TH; NJB, NRSV, TEV, TNT]. The dead are all the dead in Hades [ICC]. They are all the dead in Sheol to whom Christ preached [TG]. They are all who died before Christ came [TH]. The dead are all who had died [Alf, EGT]; Christ preached in Hades, and the apostles did the same after him [EGT]. The dead are all who never heard the gospel while alive [NCBC].

**so-that[a] they-might-be-judged[b] as/according-to[c] men in-(the)-flesh[d]**
- LEXICON—a. ἵνα (LN 89.49): 'so that' [LN, WBC; CEV, NIV, NJB, NLT, NRSV, TEV, TNT], 'that' [LN; KJV, NAB], 'in order that' [BNTC, NIC; REB].
  - b. aorist. pass. subj. of κρίνω (LN 56.30) (BAGD 6.a. p. 452): 'to be judged' [BAGD, BNTC; CEV, KJV, NIV, NRSV, TEV, TNT], 'to be condemned' [LN, WBC; NAB, REB], 'to undergo judgment' [NJB], 'to be found guilty' [NIC], 'to be punished' [NLT].
  - c. κατά with accusative object (LN 89.4): 'according to' [KJV, NIV], 'with regard to' [LN], not explicit [CEV, NLT, TNT]. The phrase κατά

ἀνθρώπους 'as/according to men' is translated 'in the eyes of men' [BNTC; NAB], 'by human standards' [NIC], 'among people generally' [WBC], 'that faces all humanity' [NJB], 'as everyone is (judged)' [NRSV, TEV], '(to die) as everyone does' [REB].

d. σάρξ (LN 8.4) (BAGD 2. p. 743): 'flesh' [BNTC, NIC, WBC; KJV, NAB, NRSV], 'body' [BAGD, LN; NIV, NJB, NLT, REB]. Σαρκί 'in the flesh' (dative case) is also translated 'in their physical existence' [TEV], 'in this life' [CEV], 'while on earth' [TNT]. See this word at 2:11, 3:18, 21, 4:1.

QUESTION—What is the judgment that is referred to here?
1. It is physical death, which comes to all men [Alf, BNTC, EGT, ICC, IVP, NCBC, Sel, TG, TH, TNTC; NJB, NLT, NRSV, REB, TEV].
2. It is physical suffering and persecution of the Christian by unbelievers [NTC]. It is rejection and condemnation by unbelievers [NIC, WBC]. People viewed Christians as being no better off for having believed because they died just like everyone else [NIC].

QUESTION—What relationship is indicated by κατά 'as/according-to'?
1. It means 'as men': they experienced the judgment of death as all men do as a consequence of sin [Alf, EGT, ICC, NIBC, TG, TH, TNTC; NJB, NLT, REB]. They are judged for what they do in this life [CEV], they are judged as everyone is judged [NRSV, TEV]. They are judged while on earth [TNT].
2. It means according to the standards of man: they are viewed as guilty in the eyes of men [BNTC, IVP, NIC, NTC, Sel, WBC; NAB].

**but[a] live as/according-to[b] God in-(the)-spirit/Spirit[c].**

LEXICON—a. δέ (LN 89.124, 89.136): 'but' [BNTC, LN (89.124); KJV, NIV, TNT], 'yet' [REB], not explicit [NIC, WBC; CEV, NAB, NJB, NLT, NRSV, TEV]. This enclitic is part of the μέν ... δέ construction serving as a marker of contrast. While μέν is normally untranslatable, the contrast may be shown either by translating δέ as 'but', or by a concessive adverb, such as 'though' [WBC; NJB, NRSV], 'although' [NIC; NAB, NLT, REB].

b. κατά with accusative object (LN 89.4): 'according to' [KJV, NIV], 'with regard to' [LN]. The phrase κατὰ θεόν 'as/according to God' is translated 'in the eyes of God' [BNTC; NAB], 'by God's standard' [NIC], 'before God' [WBC], 'with God' [CEV], '(the life) of God' [NJB], 'as God does' [NLT, NRSV], 'as God lives' [REB], 'in God's way' [TNT].

c. πνεῦμα (LN 12.18, 26.9) (BAGD 2. p. 675): 'spirit' [BAGD, BNTC, LN (26.9); all versions except TEV, TNT], 'Spirit' [LN (12.18), NIC, WBC]. Πνεύματι (dative case) 'in the spirit/Spirit' is also translated 'in their spiritual existence' [TEV], 'spiritually' [TNT].

QUESTION—What relationship is indicated by the μέν ... δέ construction?
The μέν ... δέ construction sets up a set of contrasts in two balanced clauses, the first clause being concessive and the second indicating the real

152  1 PETER 4:6

purpose of the ἵνα 'so that' statement. That is, the gospel was preached that they might live in the spirit, even though they were judged in the flesh [Alf, BNTC, EGT, NCBC, NIC, Sel, TG, TH, TNTC, WBC; NAB, NJB, NLT, NRSV, REB]. The μέν … δέ construction sets up a contrast between the two clauses, part of the contrast being a sequence of time as indicated by the different tenses of 'judged' (aorist) and 'live' (present) [ICC, TG, TH; CEV, TEV, TNT]. It sets up a contrast between what appears to men, but what is actually true as God sees it [BNTC, IVP, NIC, NTC, Sel, WBC; NAB].

QUESTION—What relationship is indicated by κατά 'as/according to'?
1. It means as God lives, or in the way in which God lives [EGT, ICC, NCBC, Sel, TG, TH, TNTC; TNT]. It is eternally [Sel]. 'As God lives' is in the realm of the spirit [TNTC; NLT, NRSV, REB, TEV]. It means 'before God in the realm of the spirit' [WBC]. It is a life with God [Alf; CEV], it is the life of God [NJB].
2. It means according to God's standards of judgment [BNTC, IVP, NIC, NTC; NAB].

**DISCOURSE UNIT: 4:7–11** [IVP, Sel, TH, WBC; NAB, NJB, TEV]. The topic is the imminence of the judgment [Sel], mutual love: the key to Christ community in the end time [WBC], Christian service [TH]; mutual charity [NAB], the revelation of Christ is close [NJB], good managers of God's gifts [TEV].

**4:7** But[a] the end[b] of-all-things has-come-near.[c] Therefore be-soberminded[d] and be-self-controlled[e] for-the-purpose-of/in[f] prayers.

LEXICON—a. δέ (LN 89.124): 'but' [BNTC, LN, NIC; KJV], not explicit [WBC; all versions except KJV].
  b. τέλος (LN 67.66) (BAGD 1.a. 811): 'end' [BAGD, BNTC, LN, NIC, WBC; all versions except NAB], 'consummation' [NAB]. The phrase 'the end of all things' is translated: 'the end of the world' [NLT]. See this word at 1:9.
  c. perf. act. indic. of ἐγγίζω (LN 67.21) (BAGD 5.b. p. 213): 'to come near' [BAGD, LN], 'to be at hand' [BNTC; KJV], 'to be close at hand' [NAB], 'to be near' [NIC, WBC; NIV, NJB, NRSV, TEV, TNT], 'to come (to an end) soon' [CEV], 'to come soon' [NLT], 'to be upon us' [REB].
  d. aorist act. impera. of σωφρονέω (LN 30.22, 32.34) (BAGD 2. p. 802): 'to be sober' [KJV], 'to be clear-minded' [NIV], 'to keep one's mind calm' [NJB], 'to be unperturbed' [NAB], 'to keep sane' [NIC], 'to be sane, to think straight' [LN (30.22)], 'to be sensible, to have sound judgment' [LN (32.34)], 'to be self-controlled' [BNTC; TEV], 'to lead a self-controlled life' [REB], 'to be self-restrained' [TNT], 'to prepare oneself mentally' [WBC], 'to be earnest' [NLT], 'to be serious' [BAGD; CEV, NRSV].
  e. aorist act. impera. of νήφω (LN 30.25, 88.86) (BAGD p. 538): 'to be self-controlled' [BAGD, LN (88.86); NIV], 'to discipline oneself' [NRSV], 'to be sober' [LN (88.86); TNT], 'to lead a sober life' [REB], 'to be soberminded' [LN (30.25)], 'to keep your mind sober' [NJB], 'to keep clear-

headed' [BNTC], 'to be clear-headed' [NIC], 'to be alert' [TEV], 'to be sensible' [CEV], 'to remain calm' [NAB], 'to attend (to prayer)' [WBC], 'to watch (unto prayer)' [KJV], 'to be disciplined' [NLT].

f. εἰς with accusative (LN 89.57, 90.23): 'for the purpose of' [LN (89.57)], 'for the sake of' [NRSV], 'for' [BNTC], 'so that' [NIC; NIV], 'in' [LN (90.23); NLT]. The phrase εἰς προσευχάς 'for the purpose of/in prayers' is translated '(attend) to prayers' [WBC], 'so that you will be able to pray' [NAB], 'so that you can pray' [NIC; NIV], 'to help you to pray' [REB], 'to be able to pray' [TEV, TNT].

QUESTION—What is the function of δέ 'but'?

It marks a new section or new thought which refers back to the idea of judgment in 4:5 [Alf, ICC, TH, WBC]. It links this section closely with the previous one [BNTC]. It continues the idea of judgment [Sel]. It is a weak conjunction that makes 4:1–6 a basis for what follows [IVP]. It is a bridge between 4:6 and the exhortations that follow [NTC].

QUESTION—What relationship is indicated by εἰς 'for-the-purpose-of/in'?

1. It indicates the purpose of the command, which is to be mentally prepared in order to be able to pray [Alf, BNTC, IVP, NCBC, NIBC, NIC, NTC, TH, TNTC, WBC; all versions except NLT].
2. It indicates the sphere of activity within which the command is to be carried out, which is 'in your prayers' [NLT].

QUESTION—Is εἰς προσευχάς 'for the purpose of/in prayers' linked to both imperative verbs or only to νήψατε 'be self-controlled', which immediately precedes it?

1. It is linked to both verbs [IVP, NIC, NTC, TH, TNTC, WBC; NIV, NJB, NLT, REB, TEV, TNT]: be sober-minded for the purpose of prayer, and be self-controlled for that reason as well.
2. It is linked only to νήψατε 'be self-controlled' [BNTC; KJV]: be self-controlled for the purpose of prayer, and be sober minded also.

QUESTION—What is the relationship between the idea of the end of all things and being soberminded?

The idea of the end of all things should not shake people out of the normal routine of the responsibilities of living [BNTC, ICC, NCBC, NIC]. Attachment to earthly commitments should not absorb the attention of the believer [NIBC]. One ought to have a realistic perception of the world as it is, in order to pray properly [IVP, TNTC].

**4:8 Above[a] all keeping[b] love for one-another fervent,[c] because love covers[d] a-multitude of sins.**

TEXT—Instead of καλύπτει 'covers', some manuscripts have καλύψει 'shall cover'. GNT does not mention this alternative. Only KJV reads 'shall cover'.

LEXICON—a. πρό with genitive object (LN 65.54) (BAGD 3. p. 702): 'above' [BAGD, BNTC, LN, NIC, WBC; all versions except CEV, NLT], 'more important than' [**LN**], 'most important (of all)' [CEV, NLT].

b. pres. act. participle of ἔχω (LN 90.65) (BAGD I.2.e. β. p. 332): 'to keep' [BNTC], 'to maintain' [NIC; NRSV, REB], 'to preserve' [NJB], 'to have' [BAGD, LN; KJV], 'to remain (constant) in' [WBC], 'to continue to show' [NLT], 'to let (love) be (constant)' [NAB], not explicit [CEV, NIV, TEV, TNT]. The participial phrase 'keeping love for one another (constant)' is translated 'love one another' [NIV, TEV], 'to be (wholehearted) in your love for one another' [TNT].

c. ἐκτενής (LN **25.71, 68.12**) (BAGD p. 245): 'fervent' [KJV], 'without ceasing' [**LN** (68.12)], 'earnest' [BAGD, LN (25.71)], 'at full strength' [BNTC], 'constant' [WBC; NAB, NRSV], 'intense' [NJB], 'deep' [NLT], 'whole-hearted' [TNT]. This word is also translated as an adverb: 'earnestly' [**LN** (25.71), NIC; TEV], 'sincerely' [CEV], 'deeply' [NIV]; as a noun: 'fervor' [REB]. See the adverbial form of this word at 1:22.

d. pres. act. indic. of καλύπτω (LN 79.114) (BAGD 2.a. p. 401): 'to cover' [BAGD, BNTC, LN, NIC, WBC; KJV, NAB, NLT, NRSV], 'to cover over' [LN; NIV, NJB, TEV], 'to wipe away' [CEV], 'to cancel' [REB], 'to cause to be forgiven' [TNT].

QUESTION—How is the adjective ἐκτενής 'fervent' used in relation to the noun it modifies, 'love'?

1. It is used as a predicate adjective [Alf, BNTC, ICC, Sel; NAB]: let the love that you already have be fervent.
2. It is used adverbially [NIC, TNTC; CEV, NIV, TEV]: love fervently.
3. It is used attributively [NTC; KJV, NJB, NLT, NRSV]: have fervent love.

QUESTION—Whose sins are covered by love, and who covers the sins?

1. The person who loves 'covers' or forgives the sins of others [Alf, EGT, IVP, NCBC, NIC, NTC, TG, TH, TNTC]. The Christian community loves and forgives sins [WBC].
2. The forgiving love of Christ is referred to because only Christ's love forgives sins [NIBC]. The love of Christ atones for sins, but as believers become a channel of his atoning love, then their love for others becomes a kind of secondary atonement [ICC].
3. Those who love have their own sins covered or forgiven by God [BNTC, Sel].

**4:9** (Be) hospitable[a] to one-another without complaint,[b]

LEXICON—a. φιλόξενος (LN **34.58**) (BAGD p. 860): 'hospitable' [BAGD, LN; NAB, NRSV, REB, TNT]. This adjective is also translated as a noun with the implied imperative verb expressed: 'practice hospitality' [BNTC], 'use hospitality' [KJV], 'offer hospitality' [NIC; NIV], 'show hospitality' [WBC]. The phrase 'be hospitable' is translated 'welcome people into your home' [CEV], 'welcome each other into your houses' [NJB], 'share your home with those who need a meal or a place to stay' [NLT], 'open your homes to each other' [TEV].

b. γογγυσμός (LN 33.382) (BAGD 1. p. 164): 'complaint' [BAGD, LN], 'complaining' [WBC; NAB], 'grumbling' [BNTC; NIV], 'grudging'

[KJV]. The phrase 'without complaint' is translated 'ungrudgingly' [NIC], 'don't grumble about it' [CEV], 'do not grumble' [TNT], 'cheerfully' [NLT].

**4:10** **according-as/as**[a] **each-one received a-gift**[b] **ministering**[c] **it to each-other**
LEXICON—a. καθώς (LN 78.53, 89.34) (BAGD 2. p. 391): 'as' [BAGD; KJV], 'inasmuch as, because' [LN (89.34)], 'just as' [LN (78.53)], 'in the measure' [NAB], 'with respect to' [NIC], not explicit [CEV, NJB, NLT, REB, TEV, TNT]. The clause 'according-as each-one received a gift' is also translated 'whatever gift each has received' [BNTC, WBC; NIV, NRSV].
  b. χάρισμα (LN 57.103) (BAGD 2. p. 879): 'gift' [BAGD, BNTC, LN, NIC; all versions except CEV, NJB, TEV], 'gracious gift' [LN], 'spiritual gift' [WBC], 'wonderful gifts' [CEV], 'special gift' [TEV], 'grace' [NJB].
  c. pres. act. participle of διακονέω (LN 35.19) (BAGD 2. p. 184): 'to serve' [BAGD, LN, NIC; NIV, NRSV], 'to use in service' [BNTC; CEV, REB, TNT], 'to use in ministry' [WBC], 'to use for the good (of others)' [TEV], 'to minister' [KJV], 'to put at the service' [NAB, NJB], not explicit [NLT].
QUESTION—What relationship is indicated by καθώς 'according-as/as'?
  1. It is an affirmation of the fact of having received gifts [BNTC, NTC, TG, TH, WBC; CEV, KJV, NJB, NLT, TNT]: since you have received gifts, use them.
  2. It refers to the particular nature of the gift that was received [Alf, NIC; NIV, NRSV, REB, TEV]: whatever gift it is you have received, then use that one in service.
  3. It refers to the manner in which the gift was received [TNTC]: you received freely, so freely serve others.
  4. It refers to the measure of how the gift was received [NAB]: use however many gifts you have been granted for serving others.

**as good stewards**[a] **of-(the) varied**[b] **grace of-God.**
LEXICON—a. οἰκονόμος (LN **37.39**) (BAGD 2. p. 560): 'steward' [BAGD, BNTC, NIC; KJV, NJB, NRSV, REB], 'manager' [BAGD, **LN**, WBC; TEV], 'administrator' [LN], 'distributors' [NAB], not explicit [CEV]. This noun is also translated as a verb: 'to administer' [NIV], 'to manage' [NLT], 'to fulfill your trust' [TNT].
  b. ποικίλος (LN 58.45) (BAGD 1. p. 683): 'varied' [BNTC; NJB, REB], 'manifold' [BAGD, BNTC; KJV, NAB, NRSV], 'diversified' [BAGD, LN, WBC], 'different' [TEV], 'of various kinds' [BAGD, LN], 'variety of' [NLT], 'in its various forms' [NIV], 'in many forms' [TNT], 'many (wonderful gifts)' [CEV]. See this word at 1:6.

**DISCOURSE UNIT: 4:11–5:12** [NIC]. The topic is coming to grips with Christian suffering.

**4:11** If anyone speaks,ᵃ (let it be) as-thoughᵇ (it were) (the) oraclesᶜ of-God

LEXICON—a. pres. indic. act. of λαλέω (LN 33.70): 'to speak' [BNTC, LN, NIC; KJV, NAB, NIV, NLT, NRSV], 'to do the speaking' [WBC], 'to have something to say' [TNT], 'to preach' [TEV], 'to have the gift of speaking' [CEV], 'to be a speaker' [NJB, REB].
  b. ὡς (LN 64.12) (BAGD III.1.a. p. 898): 'as though' [NLT], 'as if' [BAGD], 'as' [BAGD, BNTC, LN, NIC, WBC; KJV, NIV, NJB, NRSV, REB], not explicit [CEV, NAB, TEV, TNT].
  c. λόγιον (LN 33.97) (BAGD p. 476): 'oracle' [BNTC, LN; KJV, REB], 'message' [LN; CEV, NAB, TEV], 'saying' [BAGD, LN], 'words' [TNT], 'the words' [NJB], 'the very words' [NIC; NIV, NRSV], 'as bringing words from' [WBC]. The clause 'as though (it were) the oracles of God' is also translated 'as though God himself were speaking through you' [NLT].

QUESTION—What is meant by ὡς λόγια θεοῦ 'as though the oracles of God'?
  A person who exercises a speaking gift should recognize the responsibility of speaking God's message and not just his own [Alf, EGT, IVP, TG, TH, WBC]. God will provide the words just as he provides strength for service [IVP]. God will speak through them if they are faithful [BNTC, NTC]. It means speaking God's truth and not just one's own opinion [NCBC, Sel], speaking with a seriousness of purpose [TNTC], being aware of a divine commission [NIBC]. Scripture is God's oracles, and one who speaks as God's oracles would speak in the manner that Scripture speaks, that is with sincerity and seriousness [ICC].

**if anyone serves,ᵃ as byᵇ (the) strengthᶜ which God supplies,ᵈ**

LEXICON—a. pres. indic. act. of διακονέω (LN 35.19) (BAGD 2. p. 184): 'to serve' [BAGD, LN, NIC, WBC; NAB, NIV, NJB, NRSV, TEV, TNT], 'to render service' [BNTC], 'to give service' [REB], 'to minister' [KJV]. The clause 'if anyone serves' is translated 'if you have the gift of helping others' [CEV], 'are you called to help others?' [NLT].
  b. ἐξ with genitive object (LN 90.16): 'by' [LN], 'from' [BNTC, LN, NIC], 'with' [CEV, NAB, NIV, NLT, NRSV, TEV], 'of' [KJV], 'in' [NJB, REB]. 'As by' is translated 'let him rely on' [TNT].
  c. ἰσχύς (LN 79.62) (BAGD p. 383): 'strength' [BAGD, BNTC, LN, NIC, WBC; all versions except KJV, NLT], 'ability' [KJV], 'strength and energy' [NLT].
  d. pres. act. indic. of χορηγέω (LN 35.31) (BAGD p. 883): 'to supply' [BAGD, BNTC, NIC; CEV, NLT, NRSV, REB, TNT], 'to provide' [BAGD, WBC; NAB, NIV], 'to give' [KJV, TEV], 'to grant' [NJB], 'to provide for, to supply the needs of' [LN].

QUESTION—What is meant by διακονεῖ 'serves'?
  It refers to general ministry of a practical nature not involving prophecy and teaching [WBC], such as caring for the needy [BNTC, IVP, NIBC, NIC, TG], caring for travelers or the persecuted [NIBC], leadership [BNTC, NIC],

healing [NIC], almsgiving or hospitality [EGT], helping or encouraging [TNTC], or caring for any physical need [Sel]. It is the work of anyone who serves, but specifically the work of deacons [NTC]. It is the service offered by any Christian, including those with gifts of preaching and teaching [NCBC].

**so-that[a] in all-things God may-be-glorified[b] through[c] Jesus Christ,**

LEXICON—a. ἵνα (LN 89.52): 'so that' [BNTC, LN, WBC; NIV, NJB, NRSV, TEV], 'in order that' [NIC], 'that' [KJV], not explicit [CEV, NAB, NLT]. The clause 'so that God may be glorified' is translated 'should be done in a way that will bring glory to God' [CEV], 'thus God is to be glorified' [NAB], 'then God will be given glory' [NLT], 'let God be glorified' [REB, TNT].

b. pres. pass. subj. of δοξάζω (LN 87.24): 'to be glorified' [BNTC, LN, NIC, WBC; KJV, NAB, NRSV, REB, TNT], 'to receive the glory' [NJB], 'to be given glory' [NLT], 'to be praised' [NIV], 'to have praise given to' [TEV], 'to bring honor to' [CEV].

c. διά with genitive object (LN 90.4): 'through' [BNTC, LN, NIC, WBC; all versions except CEV], 'because of' [CEV].

QUESTION—What relationship is indicated by ἵνα 'so that'?

1. It indicates the purpose of the exercise of the spiritual gifts, which is that God be glorified (ἐν πᾶσιν being taken to refer to the gifts, not the believers themselves) [Alf, IVP, NIC, TG, TH, WBC]. It indicates that the motive and purpose of the believer should be to let God be glorified through what is done in ministry [BNTC, NIBC; REB, TNT].
2. It indicates that the purpose of the believers themselves should be that God is to be glorified, with ἐν πᾶσιν being taken to mean 'in all of you' instead of 'in all things' [NAB].
3. It indicates the result of using one's spiritual gift, which is that God will be glorified [NLT].

QUESTION—To what does ἐν πᾶσιν 'in all things' refer?

1. It refers to the ministry done by believers [Alf, BNTC, IVP, NIC, NTC, TG, TH, TNTC, WBC; all versions except NAB].
2. It refers to the believers themselves [NAB]: in all of you.

**to whom/him[a] is the glory and the power[b] forever and ever, amen.**

LEXICON—a. ᾧ (relative pronoun in the dative case): 'to whom' [BNTC, WBC; KJV, TEV], 'to him' [NIC; NAB, NIV, NJB, NLT, NRSV, REB, TNT]. 'To whom is the glory' is translated 'who is glorious' [CEV].

b. κράτος (LN 76.6) (BAGD 4. p. 449): 'power' [BAGD, BNTC, NIC; all versions except CEV, KJV, NAB], 'might' [BAGD, LN, WBC], 'dominion' [KJV, NAB]. This noun is also translated as an adjective: 'powerful' [CEV].

QUESTION—Does ᾧ 'to whom/him' refer to God or Jesus Christ?

1. It refers to Jesus Christ [EGT, ICC, IVP, NTC, Sel, TNTC, WBC; CEV].
2. It refers to God [Alf, BNTC, NCBC, NIC, TH].

**DISCOURSE UNIT: 4:12–5:11** [WBC]. The topic is the responsibility of a church and its elders.

**DISCOURSE UNIT: 4:12–19** [IVP, NIC, Sel, TH, WBC; CEV, NAB, NIV, NJB, NLT, NRSV, TEV]. The topic is suffering, joy, and judgment [IVP], suffering for Christ's sake [Sel], the fiery trial [WBC], further words of encouragement of suffering Christians [TH], suffering for being a Christian [CEV, NIV, NLT], blessings of persecution [NAB], suffering for Christ [NJB], suffering as a Christian [NRSV, TEV].

**DISCOURSE UNIT: 4:12–14** [WBC]. The topic is suffering and glory.

**4:12** Beloved[a] (do) not be-surprised[b] (at) the fiery-ordeal[c] coming[d] among you as[e] a test[f]

LEXICON—a. ἀγαπητός (LN 25.45) (BAGD 2. p. 6): 'beloved' [BAGD, LN, NIC; KJV, NAB, NRSV], 'dear friends' [BNTC, WBC; CEV, NIV, NLT, REB, TNT], 'my dear friends' [NJB, TEV]. See this word at 2:11.
  b. pres. pass. impera. of ξενίζω (LN **25.206**) (BAGD 2. p. 548): 'to be surprised' [BAGD, BNTC, LN, WBC; all versions except KJV, NJB, REB], 'to wonder' [BAGD], 'to be shocked' [NIC], 'to think it strange' [KJV], 'to be taken aback' [NJB, REB]. See this word at 4:4.
  c. πύρωσις (LN 24.91, 78.37) (BAGD 2. p. 731): 'fiery ordeal' [BAGD, BNTC, NIC, WBC; NRSV, REB], 'painful suffering' [LN (24.91)], 'intensity' [LN (78.37)]. This noun is also translated as an adjective describing πειρασμός 'test': 'fiery' [KJV, NLT], 'painful' [NIV, TEV]; as a prepositional phrase or clause: 'that is like walking through fire' [CEV], 'trial by fire' [NAB, TNT], 'testing by fire' [NJB].
  d. pres. mid. (deponent = act.) participle of γίνομαι (LN 13.107): 'to come' [REB], 'to come upon one' [BNTC, NIC], 'to happen, to occur' [LN], 'to take place' [NJB, NRSV, TNT], 'to break out' [WBC], not explicit [KJV, NAB]. The experiential aspect of the participle 'coming among you' is also is also expressed 'to be going through' [CEV, NLT], 'to be suffering' [NIV, TEV].
  e. πρός with accusative object (LN 89.60): 'for the purpose of' [LN], 'in order to' [LN], 'for' [BNTC], not explicit [CEV, NIV, NJB, NLT, TEV]. The prepositional phrase πρός πειρασμόν 'as a test' is translated 'it is a test' [NAB], 'to test (you)' [NIC; NRSV, REB, TNT], 'to put (you) to the test' [WBC], 'to try (you)' [KJV].
  f. πειρασμός (LN **27.46**) (BAGD 1. p. 640): 'test' [BAGD, NIC, WBC; NRSV, REB, TEV], 'testing' [BNTC; CEV, NJB], 'painful testing' [LN], 'trial' [BAGD; NAB, NIV, NLT, TNT]. This noun is also translated as a verb: 'to try' [KJV].

QUESTION—What is meant by πύρωσις 'fiery ordeal'?
  This metaphor refers to the refining of precious metals by intense heat [Alf, BNTC, ICC, IVP, NIBC, NIC, NTC, Sel, TG, TH, TNTC, WBC].

**as (though) a strange-thing<sup>a</sup> (were) happening<sup>b</sup> to-you,**
LEXICON—a. ξένος (LN **28.34**) (BAGD 1.b.β. p. 548): 'strange' [BAGD, BNTC, NIC, WBC; KJV, NIV, NJB, NLT, NRSV], 'unheard of' [BAGD, LN], 'extraordinary' [REB], 'unusual' [TEV], 'unexpected' [TNT], not explicit [CEV, NAB].
  b. pres. act. participle of συμβαίνω (LN 13.111) (BAGD p. 777): 'to happen' [BAGD, BNTC, LN, NIC, WBC; all versions except CEV, NAB, REB], not explicit [CEV, NAB, REB].

**4:13 but<sup>a</sup> in-so-far-as<sup>b</sup> you-share<sup>c</sup> in-the sufferings of-Christ rejoice,<sup>d</sup>**
LEXICON—a. ἀλλά (LN 89.125): 'but' [BNTC, LN, NIC; KJV, NIV, NJB, NRSV], 'instead' [LN; NAB, NLT], 'no' [WBC], 'on the contrary' [REB], 'rather' [TEV], not explicit [CEV, TNT].
  b. καθό (LN **78.53**) (BAGD 2. p. 390): 'in so far as' [BAGD, BNTC; NJB, NRSV, REB, TNT], 'to the degree that' [BAGD, **LN**], 'just as' [LN], 'as' [NIC], 'to the extent' [WBC], 'inasmuch as' [KJV], 'in the measure that' [NAB], 'that' [NIV], not explicit [CEV, NLT, TEV].
  c. pres. act. indic. of κοινωνέω (LN 57.98) (BAGD 1.b.α. p. 438): 'to share' [BAGD, BNTC, LN, NIC, WBC; NAB, NJB, NRSV], 'to be a partaker' [KJV], 'to participate in' [NIV]. The phrase 'to share in the sufferings of Christ' is translated 'the chance to suffer as Christ suffered' [CEV], 'it will make you partners with Christ in his suffering' [NLT], 'it gives you a share in Christ's sufferings' [REB].
  d. pres. act. impera. of χαίρω (LN 25.125) (BAGD p. 874): 'to rejoice' [BAGD, BNTC, LN, NIC; KJV, NAB, NIV, NRSV, REB], 'to be glad' [BAGD, LN, WBC; CEV, NJB, NLT, TEV, TNT].
QUESTION—What relationship is indicated by καθό 'in so far as'?
  1. It refers to extent, and means 'in as much as, to the degree that' [Alf, BNTC, TH, TNTC], 'in the measure in which' [Sel; NAB], or 'to the extent that' [WBC].
  2. It means 'just as', balancing the ideas of the two clauses [IVP; TEV]: just as you suffer, so also you can rejoice.
  3. It means 'so far as', and states a condition that the suffering must be undeserved and must be for Christ [EGT].
QUESTION—In what way do they share in the sufferings of Christ?
  They share in Christ's sufferings in that they experience what he did [Alf, BNTC, NIBC, NIC, TG]. They experience the same kinds of sufferings as Christ's, and which come for the same reason as Christ's, that is, the persecution of the righteous by the wicked [IVP]. They suffer as representing Christ [EGT]. They suffer as Christ did and produce similar results, but to a lesser degree [ICC]. They experience similar rejection and persecution, and endure it in the same manner as he did [Sel, TH, WBC]. They share the sufferings of Christ because Christ identifies with his people and suffers when they do [NTC].

**so-that[a] also you-may-rejoice[b] being-glad[c] at[d] the revelation of his glory.**
LEXICON—a. ἵνα (LN 89.49): 'so that' [BNTC, LN, WBC; NIV, NJB, TEV], 'that' [LN; KJV], 'in order that' [NIC], not explicit [CEV, NAB, NLT, NRSV, REB, TNT].
  b. aorist pass. (deponent = act.) subj. of χαίρω (LN 25.125) (BAGD p. 873): 'to rejoice' [BAGD, BNTC, LN, NIC, WBC; NAB], 'to be glad' [BAGD, LN; KJV, NJB, NRSV, TNT]. The phrase χαρῆτε ἀγαλλιώμενοι 'rejoice being glad' is translated 'rejoice with exultation' [BNTC], 'rejoice all the more' [WBC], 'even greater happiness' [CEV], 'enjoy a much greater gladness' [NJB], 'be overjoyed' [NIV], 'have wonderful joy' [NLT] 'your joy will be unbounded' [REB], 'be full of joy' [TEV].
  c. pres. mid. participle of ἀγαλλιάω (LN 25.133) (BAGD p. 4): 'to be glad' [BAGD, NIC], 'to shout for joy' [NRSV], 'to be full of happiness' [TNT], 'to be overjoyed' [BAGD, LN], 'to rejoice greatly' [LN]. This participle is also treated as an adverb or adverbial phrase modifying and intensifying the verb χαρῆτε 'rejoice': 'with exceeding joy' [KJV], 'exultantly' [NAB]. See this word at 1:6.
  d. ἐν with dative object (LN 67.33): 'when' [LN, NIC, WBC; all versions], 'at the time of' [LN], 'at' [BNTC].
QUESTION—What relationship is indicated by ἐν 'at'?
  1. It is temporal, referring to the point in time when Christ will be revealed [Alf, BNTC, ICC, NIBC, NTC, TG, TH, TNTC, WBC; all versions].
  2. It refers to believers rejoicing in the fact of Christ's glorification [IVP].

**4:14** **If[a] you-are-insulted[b] for[c] the name of-Christ, (you are) blessed,[d] because the Spirit of-glory and of-God rests[e] upon you.**
TEXT—Some manuscripts include κατὰ μὲν αὐτούς βλασφημεῖται, κατὰ δὲ ὑμᾶς δοξάζεται 'on their part he is evil spoken of, but on your part he is glorified' at the end of the sentence. It is omitted by GNT with an A rating, indicating that the text is certain. The reading 'on their part he is evil spoken of, but on your part he is glorified' is taken by WBC and KJV.
LEXICON—a. εἰ (LN 89.65): 'if' [BNTC, LN, NIC; all versions except CEV, NAB], 'when' [WBC; CEV, NAB].
  b. pres. pass. indic. of ὀνειδίζω (LN 33.389) (BAGD 1. p. 570): 'to be insulted' [BNTC, LN, NIC; all versions except CEV, KJV, NRSV], 'to be ridiculed' [WBC], 'to be reproached' [BAGD; KJV], 'to be reviled' [BAGD; NRSV, REB], 'to suffer' [CEV].
  c. ἐν with dative object (LN 89.26): 'for' [BNTC, WBC; CEV, KJV, NAB, NJB, NLT, NRSV, REB, TNT], 'because of' [LN, NIC; NIV], 'because (you are)' [TEV], 'on account of' [LN]. The phrase ἐν ὀνόματι Χριστοῦ 'for the name of Christ' is translated 'for being a Christian' [CEV, NLT], 'for being Christians' [REB], 'for the sake of Christ' [NAB], 'for Christ's sake' [TNT], 'for bearing Christ's name' [NJB], 'because you are Christ's followers' [TEV].

d. μακάριος (LN 25.119) (BAGD 1.b. p. 486): 'blessed' [BAGD, BNTC, NIC, WBC; NIV, NJB, NRSV], 'fortunate' [BAGD; TNT], 'happy' [BAGD, LN; KJV, NAB, NLT, REB, TEV]. The statement 'you are blessed' with the implied present indicative of the verb 'to be' is also treated as an imperative '(count it) a blessing' [CEV], 'be happy' [NLT], 'count yourselves happy' [REB], 'count yourselves fortunate' [TNT].

e. pres. mid. indic. of ἀναπαύω (LN 23.80) (BAGD 1. p. 59): 'to rest' [BNTC, LN, NIC, WBC; all versions except CEV, NAB, NLT], 'to come to rest' [NAB], 'to come upon' [NLT], 'to be with' [CEV].

QUESTION—What is meant by ἐν ὀνόματι Χριστοῦ 'for the name of Christ'?

It means because of or on account of Christ [BNTC, NIC, TH], for Christ's sake [NAB, TNT], for allegiance to Christ [WBC], for association with Christ and his followers [NIBC], or for being a Christian [TG; CEV, NJB, NLT, REB, TEV]. It means on account of your confession of Christ in word and action [Alf]. 'The name' signified the Christian religion to early believers, and 'for the name of Christ' refers to Christian ministry, such as preaching and teaching, baptizing, praying and healing [NTC].

QUESTION—What is meant by 'the Spirit of glory and of God (literally 'the of-glory and of-God Spirit') rests on you'?

Since 'the glory' is a circumlocution for the name of God, the Spirit of glory is the Spirit of God [EGT, Sel]. The glory is the communicable presence of God among his people by his Spirit in the shekinah [NIBC, Sel]. This glory of God rests on the church [Sel]. The Spirit of God rests on the Christian like the shekinah of the OT [ICC, TNTC]. Persecution of believers proves the presence of God among them because the wicked are really reacting against God [NIBC]. The Spirit brings a foretaste of the glory that is to come [BNTC, ICC, IVP, TNTC], especially for those who are persecuted [BNTC, NIC]. When the Spirit of God rests on a believer, the glory of God rests on him as well, and conveys a share of the glory he will have when Christ appears [IVP]. It refers to the Spirit of Christ's glory [WBC]. The Spirit of glory is the Spirit of Christ [NTC]. This phrase is a citation from or is influenced by the wording of Isaiah 11:2 [EGT, ICC, NIBC, NTC, TNTC].

QUESTION—What is the relationship between the nouns τῆς δόξης 'of glory' and τοῦ θεοῦ 'of God' in the phrase 'the of glory and of God Spirit'?

1. They are appositional. The Spirit of glory is the Spirit of God [Alf, BNTC, ICC; NRSV]. The Spirit of God is the Spirit of glory [WBC; NJB].

2. The noun τῆς δόξης 'the of glory' is attributive, modifying 'Spirit', and τοῦ θεοῦ 'the of God' is objective; together they form an attributive statement, 'God's glorious Spirit' [CEV], or 'the glorious Spirit of God' [TH; NLT].

3. 'Of glory' is attributive, 'that glorious Spirit' and stands in apposition to 'Spirit of God'. 'That glorious Spirit, which is the Spirit of God' [TNT].

4. 'Of glory' is the sphere within which the Spirit of God is described, 'the Spirit of God in all his glory' [REB], 'God's Spirit in its glory' [NAB].

5. The Spirit of God is neither fully identified with nor fully differentiated from the shekinah, the glory [Sel].
   6. They form a trinitarian formula: 'the glory' refers to Christ, so he is saying that the Spirit of the glorious Christ and of God rests upon you [NTC].

**DISCOURSE UNIT: 4:15–19** [WBC]. The topic is suffering as a Christian.

**4:15** **For let not any of-you suffer**[a] **as a murderer**[b] **or thief**[c] **or evildoer**[d] **or as a meddler;**[e]

LEXICON—a. pres. act. impera. of πάσχω (LN 24.78) (BAGD 3.a.β. p. 634): 'to suffer' [BAGD, BNTC, LN, NIC, WBC; all versions]. The imperative aspect of μὴ γάρ τις ὑμῶν πασχέτω 'for let not any of you suffer' is translated 'let none of you' [BNTC; KJV, NRSV], 'none of you should' [NIC; TNT], 'none of you should ever deserve' [NJB], 'none of you must' [WBC], 'see to it that none of you' [NAB], 'if you suffer it should not be as' [NIV], 'if you suffer it must not be for' [NLT, REB], 'if any of you suffers it must not be because' [TEV], 'you deserve to suffer if you' [CEV]. See this word at 2:19, 3:14, 17, 18.

   b. φονεύς (LN 20.85) (BAGD p. 864): 'murderer' [BAGD, BNTC, LN, NIC, WBC; all versions except NLT, REB]. The phrase 'as a murderer' is translated 'for murder' [NLT, REB].

   c. κλέπτης (LN 57.233) (BAGD p. 434): 'thief' [BAGD, BNTC, LN, NIC, WBC; all versions except NLT, REB]. The phrase 'as a thief' is translated 'for stealing' [NLT], 'for theft' [REB].

   d. κακοποιός (LN 88.114) (BAGD p. 397): 'evildoer' [BAGD, LN; KJV], 'criminal' [BAGD, NIC, WBC; NIV, NJB, NRSV, TEV, TNT], 'wrongdoer' [LN], 'malefactor' [BNTC; NAB], 'crook' [CEV]. The phrase 'as an evildoer' is translated 'for making trouble' [NLT], 'for any other crime' [REB].

   e. ἀλλοτριεπίσκοπος (LN **88.245**) (BAGD p. 40): 'meddler' [BAGD, LN, NIC; NIV], 'meddler in others' affairs' [**LN**], 'busybody' [BAGD, LN, WBC; CEV], 'busybody in other men's matters' [KJV], 'mischief-maker' [BNTC; NRSV, TNT], 'destroyer of another's rights' [NAB], 'informer' [NJB]. The phrase 'as a meddler' is translated 'for prying into other people's affairs' [NLT], 'for meddling in other people's business' [REB], 'because he meddles in other people's affairs' [TEV].

QUESTION—What relationship is indicated by γάρ 'for'?
   It introduces a caveat, referring back to 'for the name of Christ'. That is, the suffering must be for Christ, and not for crimes committed [BNTC, EGT, NIC, WBC].

**4:16** **but if as**[a] **a Christian, (let) him not be-ashamed,**[b] **but let-him-glorify God in**[c] **this name.**[d]

TEXT—Instead of ὀνόματι 'name' some manuscripts have μέρει 'matter/behalf'. GNT does not mention this alternative. The reading 'matter/behalf' is taken by WBC, KJV.

LEXICON—a. ὡς (LN 89.37): 'as' [BNTC, NIC; KJV, NIV, NRSV, REB], 'because' [LN], 'because you are' [TEV], 'for being' [WBC; CEV, NAB, NJB, NLT, TNT].
  b. pres. pass. impera. of αἰσχύνομαι (αἰσχύνω) (LN 25.190) (BAGD 1. p. 25): 'to be ashamed' [BAGD, LN, NIC, WBC; CEV, KJV, NAB, NIV, TEV], 'to feel disgrace' [BNTC; REB], 'to consider it a disgrace' [NRSV]. The negative imperative μὴ αἰσχυνέσθω 'let him not be ashamed' is translated 'there must be no shame' [NJB], 'it is no shame' [NLT], 'that is no cause for shame' [TNT].
  c. ἐν with dative object (LN 89.26): 'in' [BNTC, WBC], 'because of' [LN], 'on account of' [LN], 'by' [NIC], 'on' [KJV], 'in virtue of' [NAB], 'that you bear' [NIV, TEV], 'because you bear' [NRSV], 'for bearing' [NJB], 'that he is called by' [TNT], 'for the privilege of being called by' [NLT], not explicit [CEV, REB].
  d. ὄνομα (LN 33.126, 58.22) (BAGD II. p. 573): 'name' [BNTC, LN (33.126), NIC; NAB, NIV, NJB, NRSV, REB, TNT], 'his wonderful name' [NLT], 'Christ's name' [TEV], 'capacity' [BAGD], 'category, being of the type that' [LN (58.22)], not explicit [CEV]. The LN 33.126 definition refers to the proper name of a person or object, such as 'Christ', whereas LN 58.22 refers to a categorization or classification, such as 'Christian'.

QUESTION—What relationship is indicated by δέ 'but'?

It is an adversative conjunction, indicating contrast with what has just been said [Alf, BNTC, ICC, IVP, NIC, NTC, TG, TH, TNTC, WBC; KJV, NIV, NJB, NLT, NRSV, REB, TEV, TNT].

QUESTION—What is meant by ἐν τῷ ὀνόματι τούτῳ 'in this name'?

1. It refers to the name 'Christian' [Alf, ICC, IVP, NIC, NTC, Sel, TG, TH; NAB, NIV, NJB, NRSV, REB, TNT].
2. It refers to the name of Christ [EGT, TNTC; NLT, TEV].
3. It is a semitic idiom [BNTC, NIBC]. It could refer to one's standing or capacity as a believer [BNTC, NTC; CEV], or the fact of being called to suffer for being a believer [BNTC]. 'The name' refers to the presence of God [NIBC].

**4:17** **For**[a] **the time**[b] **(has come for) the judgment**[c] **to begin from**[d] **the house**[e] **of God;**

LEXICON—a. ὅτι (LN 89.33): 'for' [BNTC, LN, WBC; KJV, NIV, NLT, NRSV], 'because' [LN, NIC], not explicit [CEV, NAB, NJB, REB, TEV, TNT].

## 1 PETER 4:17

b. καιρός (LN 67.1) (BAGD 2.b. p. 395): 'time' [BAGD, BNTC, LN, NIC, WBC; all versions except CEV, NAB], 'season' [NAB], not explicit [CEV].
c. κρίμα (LN 30.110) (BAGD 3. p. 450): 'judgment' [BAGD, LN], 'judging' [BAGD]. The phrase τὸ κρίμα 'the judgment' is translated 'the judgment' [BNTC, NIC, WBC; NJB, REB], 'judgment' [KJV, NAB, NIV, NLT, NRSV, TEV, TNT]. The phrase 'the time (has come for) the judgment to begin' is translated 'God has already begun judging' [CEV].
d. ἀπό with genitive object (LN 84.3): 'from' [LN, WBC], 'with' [BNTC, NIC; NAB, NIV, NRSV, REB, TNT], 'at' [KJV, NJB], 'among' [NLT], not explicit [CEV, TEV].
e. οἶκος (LN 10.8) (BAGD 1.b.α. p. 560): 'house' [BAGD, BNTC, NIC, WBC; KJV], 'household' [LN; NAB, NJB, NRSV, REB, TNT], 'family' [LN; NIV], '(his) own people' [CEV], '(God's) own children' [NLT], '(God's) own people' [TEV].

QUESTION—What relationship is indicated by ὅτι 'for'?

This passage is being linked to the previous paragraph, especially 4:12 [IVP]. A new clause, introduced by ὅτι, explains 4:15–16, that suffering as a Christian really is going to occur [WBC]. It indicates the grounds for the exhortation 'let him glorify God' in the previous verse [Alf, BNTC]. It introduces another reason for enduring persecution; the first is to glorify God and the second is that the present difficulties indicate the beginning of the end [ICC].

QUESTION—What is the judgment of which he speaks?

This is a judgment intended to separate the true believer from the false and to purify the true [IVP]. This is universal judgment in which God will reward or punish as necessary and in which he will refine his own people [NIBC, TNTC]. This is the time of judgment just prior to the end which will include all people [WBC]. It is the beginning of birth pangs [BNTC, WBC]. It is the final judgment [BNTC, ICC, TG] which begins with God's own people [BNTC, NIC, TH]. Judgment for believers is exoneration in Christ, and present adversities will draw them even closer to God [NTC]. It is the time for all people to be judged; the people of God will be chastised and the rest will be condemned [Alf].

QUESTION—What metaphor is in view when he speaks of judgment beginning 'from the house of God'?

1. Drawing from passages such as Ezekiel 9 and Malachi 3, he is depicting the church as the temple of God, at which God begins judgment with his own people and moves outward [Alf, BNTC, EGT, IVP, NIBC, NIC, Sel, TNTC, WBC].
2. The 'house of God' is the church as the family or household of God [ICC, NTC]. This parallels the story from Luke 19 where the master first judges the servants of his household and then executes his enemies [ICC]. The household of God is the community of God's own people [TG, TH].

**and if first[a] from[b] us, what (will be) the end[c] of-those not-obeying[d] the gospel[e] of God?**

LEXICON—a. πρῶτον (LN 67.18): 'first' [BNTC, NIC, WBC; KJV, NLT]. This adverb is also translated as a verb phrase: 'it begins with' [CEV, NAB, NIV, NJB, NRSV, TNT], 'it is starting' [REB], 'it starts' [TEV].

b. ἀπό with genitive object (LN 84.3): 'from' [LN, WBC], 'with' [BNTC, NIC; all versions except KJV, NLT], 'at' [KJV], not explicit [NLT].

c. τέλος (LN 89.40) (BAGD 1.c. p. 811): 'end' [BAGD, BNTC, LN, WBC; all versions except CEV, NIV, NLT], 'outcome' [BAGD, LN; NIV], 'result' [LN, NIC], 'fate' [NLT]. This rhetorical question is also expressed as an indicative statement: 'imagine how terrible it will be' [CEV], 'what terrible fate awaits' [NLT]. See this word at 1:9, 3:8, and 4:7.

d. pres. act. participle of ἀπειθέω (LN 36.23, 31.107) (BAGD 1. or 3. p. 82): 'to not obey' [BNTC, NIC; KJV, NIV, NRSV], 'to disobey' [BAGD, LN (36.23); TNT], 'to be disobedient' [BAGD, WBC], 'to refuse to obey' [CEV, REB], 'to refuse obedience' [NAB], 'to refuse to believe' [LN (31.107); NJB], 'to not believe' [NLT, TEV]. See this word at 2:8, 3:1, and 3:20.

e. εὐαγγέλιον (LN 33.217) (BAGD 2.b.β. p. 318): 'gospel' [BNTC, LN, NIC, WBC; KJV, NAB, NIV, NJB, NRSV, REB], 'good news' [BAGD, LN; NLT, TEV, TNT], 'message' [CEV].

**4:18 And[a] if the righteous (person) is-saved[b] with-difficulty,[c] where will-appear[d] the ungodly[e] and sinner[f]?**

LEXICON—a. καί (LN 89.92): 'and' [BNTC, LN, NIC, WBC; KJV, NAB, NIV, NLT], not explicit [NJB, NRSV]. This word is also translated as introducing a Scriptural quote: 'the Scriptures say' [CEV], 'Scripture says' [REB], 'as the Scripture says' [TEV], 'as Scripture says' [TNT].

b. pres. pass. indic. of σῴζω (LN 21.27) (BAGD 2.b. p. 798): 'to be saved' [BAGD, BNTC, LN, WBC; all versions except CEV], 'to be delivered' [NIC], 'to escape' [CEV].

c. μόλις (LN 22.33) (BAGD 1. p. 526): 'with difficulty' [BAGD, BNTC, LN; NAB], 'scarcely' [NIC; KJV], 'barely' [WBC; CEV, NLT]. This adverb is also translated as a verb phrase: 'it is hard' [NIV, NJB, NRSV, REB], 'it is difficult' [TEV].

d. fut. mid. indic. of φαίνομαι (φαίνω) (LN **13.118**) (BAGD 2.b. p. 851): 'to appear' [BAGD, BNTC, NIC; KJV]. The phrase 'where will appear' is translated 'what will happen to' [LN; CEV, NJB, TNT], 'what will become of' [BAGD, WBC; NIV, NRSV, REB, TEV], 'what is to become of' [NAB], 'what chance will (they) have' [NLT].

e. ἀσεβής (LN 53.11) (BAGD 1. p. 114): 'ungodly' [LN, NIC; KJV, NIV, NRSV], 'godless' [BAGD, WBC; NAB, NLT, TEV], 'impious' [BAGD, BNTC; REB], 'wicked' [NJB], 'others who don't respect God' [CEV], 'irreligious' [TNT].

f. ἁμαρτωλός (LN 88.295) (BAGD 2. p. 44): 'sinner' [BAGD, LN, NIC, WBC; all versions except REB, TNT], 'sinful man' [BNTC; TNT], 'sinful' [REB].

QUESTION—In what way can it be said that the righteous are saved 'with difficulty'?

The use of this word here comes as a result of the fact that this verse is quoted almost verbatim from the LXX of Proverbs 11:31 [Alf, BNTC, EGT, ICC, IVP, NIC, NTC, Sel, WBC]. This adverb signifies that the righteous are saved only by grace, and not without suffering [IVP]. The road to final salvation is rough [NIBC]. It is 'with difficulty' because it is not easy or without cost [WBC]. It is with difficulty because of the severe trials the believer must endure [Sel]. It is through difficulty and out of hardship and tribulation that believers come to final salvation [ICC, NIC, TG, TH]. We enter the kingdom through many hardships and through a process of spiritual growth that requires exertion [NTC]. The trial is hard, the believer is weak, and the wonder is that anyone is saved at all [Alf]. Even the righteous feel the pain of the discipline of God's intense holiness [TNTC]. God's fire will separate the true believers from those whose commitment is shallow [NIC].

QUESTION—What is the relationship between ἀσεβής 'ungodly' and ἁμαρτωλός 'sinner'?
1. 'Godless' describes 'sinner' [TG, TH]. It relates two aspects of the same person [Alf, BNTC, NTC; TEV, TNT].
2. These are two categories of disobedient people, 'the ungodly and the sinner' [NIC, WBC; KJV, NAB, NIV, NJB, NLT, NRSV].

**4:19** Therefore[a] also the-ones-suffering according-to[b] the will of-God let-them-entrust[c] their souls[d] to a faithful[e] creator[f] in doing-good.[g]

LEXICON—a. ὥστε (LN 89.52) (BAGD 1.b. p. 900): 'therefore' [BAGD, BNTC, LN; NRSV], 'wherefore' [KJV], 'for this reason' [BAGD], 'accordingly' [LN; NAB], 'so then' [LN, NIC, WBC; NIV, TEV, TNT], 'so' [NJB, NLT, REB], not explicit [CEV].

b. κατά (LN 89.8) (BAGD II.5.δ. p. 407): 'according to' [BNTC, NIC; KJV, NIV, NLT, REB], 'in accordance with' [BAGD, LN; NRSV, TNT], 'because of' [BAGD]. The phrase κατὰ τὸ θέλημα τοῦ θεοῦ 'according to the will of God' is translated 'because it is God's will' [TEV], 'when God requires' [WBC], 'as God's will requires' [NAB], '(whom) God allows to suffer' [NJB], 'for obeying God' [CEV].

c. pres. mid. impera. of παρατίθημι (LN 35.47) (BAGD 2.b.β. p. 623): 'to entrust' [BAGD, BNTC, LN, NIC, WBC; NAB, NRSV, REB], 'to trust oneself to' [NLT, TEV], 'to put oneself in the care of' [TNT], 'to commit oneself to the care of' [LN], 'to commit' [KJV, NIV, NJB], 'to have complete faith in' [CEV].

d. ψυχή (LN 9.20) (BAGD 1.c. p. 893): 'soul' [BAGD, BNTC; KJV, REB]. The expression τὰς ψυχὰς αὐτῶν 'their souls' is translated 'themselves'

[NIC; NIV, NJB, NRSV, TEV, TNT], 'their lives' [WBC; NAB], 'yourself' [NLT], not explicit [CEV]. See this word at 1:9 and 2:11.

e. πιστός (LN 31.87) (BAGD 1.a.β. p. 664): 'faithful' [BAGD, BNTC, LN, NIC, WBC; CEV, KJV, NAB, NIV, NRSV], 'trustworthy' [BAGD, LN; NJB], 'to be trusted' [TNT]. The adjective πιστός 'faithful' is also translated as a verb phrase: 'for he will never fail you' [NLT], '(he) will not fail them' [REB], 'he always keeps his promise' [TEV].

f. κτίστης (LN **42.40**) (BAGD p. 456): 'creator' [BAGD, BNTC, LN, NIC, WBC; all versions except NLT, REB], 'maker' [REB], 'the God who made you' [NLT].

g. ἀγαθοποιΐα (LN **88.3**) (BAGD p. 2): 'doing good' [BAGD, NIC; NJB], 'doing of good' [WBC], 'to continue to do good' [NIV, NRSV, REB, TNT], 'doing right' [CEV, NLT], 'well doing' [KJV], 'good actions' [TEV], 'good deeds' [LN; NAB], 'active well-doing' [BNTC].

QUESTION—What relationship is indicated by ὥστε 'therefore'?

It sums up what has already been said [NIBC]. It summarizes the teaching of the entire epistle up to this point [TNTC]. It introduces a conclusion to the discussion on suffering [NTC, TH]. It draws a conclusion about trusting God in suffering [BNTC]. It draws a conclusion about suffering for doing good [WBC]. It returns to the theme of comfort and encouragement after having digressed concerning the judgment [ICC]. It draws a conclusion from 4:17–18, that since their sufferings are a sign of God's favor in saving them from his judgment of the wicked, they can trust him fully [Alf]. It concludes the section 4:12–19 [NIC].

QUESTION—What relationship is indicated by καί 'also'?

None of the English versions translate this conjunction.

1. It is paired with ὥστε to indicate a conclusion being drawn about suffering for doing good [WBC].
2. It goes with 'entrust'. That is, they should glorify God, and they should also entrust their souls to God [ICC]. It introduces a new thought, which is the call to serene faith in God [Sel].
3. It goes with 'suffering'. That is, even the ones who suffer, as well as everybody else, should entrust their souls to God [Alf, BNTC, EGT; NJB].

QUESTION—What is meant by κατὰ τὸ θέλημα τοῦ θεοῦ 'according to the will of God'?

1. It means that it happens because it is God's will [BNTC, TG, TH; TEV], that God requires it to occur [WBC; NAB] or that God allows it to occur [NJB]. It is not by accident or by fate, but because God has decided it to be so [TNTC]. It is a reminder that nothing happens outside of the providential control of God [NTC].
2. It means in the course of following God's will [Alf, NIBC]. It means that the suffering should be for doing God's will, not for doing wrong [IVP, NIC]. It is suffering for obeying God [CEV].

QUESTION—What relationship is indicated by the preposition ἐν 'in' used with ἀγαθοποιΐα 'doing good'?
1. The preposition is temporal [WBC]: entrust their lives to their creator while, or as, they are doing good.
2. It is instrumental [ICC, NIC, NTC, TG; TEV]: trust is demonstrated by doing good.
3. The phrase ἐν ἀγαθοποιΐα is viewed as the second imperative of the sentence along with παρατιθέσθωσαν 'let them entrust' [CEV, NAB, NIV, NJB, NLT, NRSV, REB, TNT].

**DISCOURSE UNIT: 5:1–14** [NTC]. The topic is the conclusion.

**DISCOURSE UNIT: 5:1–11** [Sel, TG, TH, WBC; CEV, NIV, NLT, NRSV, REB, TEV]. The topic is the third hortatory section [Sel], the responsibilities of a church under judgment [WBC], exhortation to church leaders and to all Christians [TG], admonitions to the church [TH], helping Christian leaders [CEV], to elders and young men [NIV], advice for elders and young men [NLT], tending the flock of God [NRSV], the Christian community [REB], the flock of God [TEV].

**DISCOURSE UNIT: 5:1–7** [TNTC]. The topic is living as church members and officers.

**DISCOURSE UNIT: 5:1–5** [IVP, NIC, TH]. The topic is leadership in the church [IVP], the inner-church response to suffering [NIC], admonitions to church leaders [TH].

**DISCOURSE UNIT: 5:1–4** [Sel, WBC; NAB, NJB]. The topic is the church's ministers [Sel], the elders [WBC], the ministry [NAB], instructions to the elders [NJB].

**5:1** Therefore I-urge[a] (the) elders[b] among you, (I) the co-elder[c] and witness[d] of-the sufferings of-Christ and sharer[e] of the glory about to-be-revealed;

TEXT—The word οὖν 'therefore' does not occur in some manuscripts. GNT does not mention this omission. It is omitted or not translated by CEV, KJV, NAB, NIV, NJB, TEV.

LEXICON—a. pres. act. indic. of παρακαλέω (LN 33.168) (BAGD 2. p. 617): 'to urge' [BAGD; NJB], 'to appeal' [BAGD, BNTC, LN, WBC; NIV, REB, TEV], 'to make an appeal' [NAB], 'to exhort' [BAGD, NIC; KJV, NRSV], 'to encourage' [BAGD; CEV], 'to speak' [TNT]. This verb is also translated as a clause: 'this is my appeal' [NLT]. See this word at 2:11.

b. πρεσβύτερος (LN 53.77) (BAGD 2.b.α. p. 700): 'elder' [BAGD, LN; all versions except CEV, TEV], 'church elder' [TEV], 'church leader' [CEV], 'presbyter' [BAGD].

c. συμπρεσβύτερος (LN **53.78**) (BAGD p. 780): 'fellow elder' [BAGD, BNTC, LN, NIC, WBC; NAB, NIV, NJB, REB, TNT], 'also an elder'

[KJV], 'as an elder myself' [NRSV]. This noun is also translated by the verb phrase: 'I too am an elder' [NLT], 'I, who am an elder myself' [TEV], 'I too am a leader' [CEV].
  d. μάρτυς (LN 33.270) (BAGD 2.c. p. 494): 'witness' [BAGD, BNTC, LN, NIC, WBC; all versions except TNT], 'one who actually saw' [TNT], 'one who testifies' [LN].
  e. κοινωνός (LN 34.6) (BAGD 1.b.α. p. 439): 'sharer' [BAGD, WBC; NAB], 'partaker' [BNTC, NIC; KJV], 'partner' [BAGD, LN], 'companion' [BAGD]. This noun is also translated by a verb phrase: 'I will share in' [CEV, TEV], 'one who will share in' [NIV], 'one who is to have a share in' [NJB], 'I will share his glory and his honor' [NLT], 'one who shares in' [NRSV], 'one who has shared in' [REB], 'one who hopes to share in' [TNT].

QUESTION—What relationship is indicated by οὖν 'therefore'?
  1. It is a loose connective 'now', which Peter uses to shift to a new subject [NLT, NRSV, REB, TNT].
  2. It connects the thought of what has been said to the exhortation he is about to make [ICC]. It links the thoughts regarding suffering in 4:12–19 to what he is about to say [NCBC]. It takes up the exhortation in 4:19 about doing good even in suffering [Alf]. The appeal to elders is based on what he has just said previously about suffering while doing the will of God [EGT, NTC]. It connects his comments about suffering in 4:12–19 and 5:6–11 with this exhortation to the leaders, since leadership is vitally important to a church under the pressure of persecution [NIC]. It links 4:12–19 with what he says to elders, since judgment will begin with the house of God, a matter of great importance to leaders [WBC]. It links what he has said about judgment beginning with the house of God with the need for purity in relationships in the church, beginning with leaders [TNTC]. The advice and encouragement that he has given throughout the entire letter serves as the basis of the exhortation that now follows [BNTC].

QUESTION—What is Peter communicating when he uses the unique word συμπρεσβύτερος 'co-elder'?
  He is expressing humility [BNTC, IVP, NCBC, NIC, NTC, Sel]. He is showing his identification with the leaders in the responsibilities they carry [BNTC, EGT, IVP, NCBC, NIBC, NIC, Sel, TH]. It is a claim to their affection [ICC]. He is classing himself with those among whom judgment will begin, giving himself as an example of restoration by grace in case any of them may stand in need of that [TNTC].

QUESTION—In what way is Peter a μάρτυς 'witness' of the sufferings of Christ?
  The συν- 'co-' prefix of 'elder' is also carried over to μάρτυς 'witness', as in 'also a witness' [Alf, BNTC, IVP, NIC, WBC].

1. He is a witness in the sense of testifying or telling about Christ's sufferings [NCBC, NIBC, NTC, WBC]. He is both an eyewitness and one who testifies, but the primary focus is on bearing testimony [NIBC].
2. He was an eyewitness of some or all of the events of Christ's passion [Alf, EGT, ICC, NIBC, NTC, Sel, TG, TNTC]. His claim to be an eyewitness affirms and reinforces his apostolic office [ICC]. The nature of Peter's eyewitness of Christ's passion, during which time he had hidden, is a testimony of his restoration by grace [TNTC].
3. He is a witness in the sense that he participates in the sufferings of Christ because of the testimony he bears [BNTC, IVP, NIC, WBC]. Both he and the elders to whom he writes are co-witnesses in the sense that they share his sufferings because they bring his message [BNTC, NIC, WBC].

QUESTION—Is Peter's being a κοινωνός 'sharer' in glory, a reference to the future as expressed by μελλούσης ἀποκαλύπτεσθαι 'about to be revealed' or to his past experience?

1. It is a reference to the future [Alf, EGT, ICC, IVP, NCBC, NIBC, TG, TH, TNTC, WBC]. Although he had seen Christ's glory, and all believers share it now in part, it is primarily a future experience [NTC]. It is a future experience which will also be shared by the readers [IVP].
2. It is a reference to Peter's past experience as one who 'has shared in the glory to be revealed' [REB]. It speaks of Peter's experience of the glory of Christ at the transfiguration [Sel].
3. He is a partaker now of the future glory through his faithfulness [NIC].

**5:2 shepherd<sup>a</sup> the flock<sup>b</sup> of God among<sup>c</sup> you overseeing<sup>d</sup>**

LEXICON—a. aorist act. impera. of ποιμαίνω (LN 44.3) (BAGD 2.a.α. p. 683): 'to shepherd' [LN, NIC, WBC], 'to be shepherds of' [TEV], 'to take care of' [LN; TNT], 'to care for' [NLT], 'to tend' [BAGD, BNTC, LN; NRSV], 'to look after' [REB], 'to feed' [KJV], 'to give a shepherd's care' [NIV, NJB]. The phrase 'shepherd the flock of God' is translated 'just as shepherds watch over their sheep, you must watch over everyone God has placed in your care' [CEV].

b. ποίμνιον (LN 11.31) (BAGD 2.b. p. 684): 'flock' [BAGD, BNTC, NIC, WBC; all versions except CEV], 'sheep' [CEV], 'people who are like a flock' [LN].

c. ἐν (LN 83.9): 'among' [LN; KJV], 'with' [LN], 'in (your) midst' [NAB], 'which is round about (you)' [TNT]. The prepositional phrase ἐν ὑμῖν 'among you' is also translated as implying the responsibility given to the elders: 'in your charge' [BNTC; NRSV], 'under your care' [NIC; NIV], 'in your care' [WBC; CEV], 'entrusted to you' [NJB, NLT], 'that God gave you' [TEV], 'whose shepherds you are' [REB].

d. pres. act. participle of ἐπισκοπέω (LN 53.70, 35.39) (BAGD 2. p. 299): 'to oversee' [BAGD], 'to serve as overseer' [NIV], 'to exercise oversight' [BNTC; NRSV], 'to take the oversight' [KJV], 'to watch over' [NIC, WBC; CEV, NAB, NJB, NLT, TNT], 'to look after' [LN (35.39); REB], 'to take care of' [LN (35.39); TEV], 'to minister unto' [LN (53.70)], 'to care for' [BAGD, LN (53.70)].

QUESTION—How is the prepositional phrase ἐν ὑμῖν 'among you' used in this verse?
1. It is used locally, 'among you' [ICC, Sel; KJV, NAB, TNT].
2. It is used in the sense of what has been entrusted to their care [BNTC, NIC, TG, TH; CEV, NIV, NJB, NLT, NRSV, REB, TEV]. It refers to local presence but also being under the charge or care of the elders [Alf, WBC].

**not by compulsion,[a] but willingly,[b] according-to[c] God, nor for-sordid-gain[d] but eagerly,[e]**

TEXT—The words κατὰ θεόν 'according to God' do not occur in some manuscripts. It is included in GNT with a C rating, indicating difficulty in deciding whether or not to place it in the text. It is omitted only by KJV.

LEXICON—a. ἀναγκαστῶς (LN **71.31**) (BAGD p. 52): 'by compulsion' [BAGD], 'out of compulsion' [WBC], 'under compulsion' [NRSV, REB], 'out of obligation' [LN], 'under constraint' [BNTC; NAB], 'by constraint' [KJV], 'because you must' [NIC; NIV, TNT], 'because you think you must' [CEV], 'as a duty' [NJB], 'grudgingly' [NLT], 'unwillingly' [TEV].

b. ἑκουσίως (LN **25.65**) (BAGD p. 243): 'willingly' [BAGD, BNTC, LN, WBC; CEV, KJV, NAB, NLT, NRSV, REB, TEV], 'because you are willing' [NIV], 'without compulsion' [BAGD], 'voluntarily' [NIC], 'gladly' [NJB, TNT].

c. κατά (BAGD II.5.δ. p. 407): 'according to'. The phrase κατὰ θεόν 'according to God' is translated 'as God would have it' [BNTC; REB], 'in a godly manner' [NIC], 'before God' [WBC], 'in order to please God' [CEV], 'as God would have you do' [NAB, NRSV], 'as God would want you to do' [TNT], 'as God wants' [NJB], 'as God wants you to be' [NIV], 'as God wants you to' [TEV]. This phrase is also conflated with προθύμως 'eagerly' and translated 'eager to serve God' [NLT].

d. αἰσχροκερδῶς (LN **25.26**) (BAGD p. 25): 'for sordid gain' [NRSV], 'for sordid money' [NJB], 'greedy for money' [NIV], 'greedily' [BAGD, LN, WBC], 'shamefully greedy' [LN], 'for gain' [REB], 'in fondness for dishonest gain' [BAGD], 'for shameful gain' [BNTC], 'merely to make money' [CEV], 'for the money' [TNT], 'for shameful profit' [NAB], 'for profit' [NIC], 'for filthy lucre' [KJV], 'for what you will get out of it' [NLT], 'for mere pay' [TEV].

e. προθύμως (LN **25.69**) (BAGD p. 706): 'eagerly' [BAGD, BNTC, LN, NIC; NRSV], 'eager to serve' [NIV, NLT], 'eager to do it' [NJB], 'willingly' [BAGD, LN], 'with enthusiasm' [WBC], 'something you want to do' [CEV], 'of a ready mind' [KJV], 'generously' [NAB], 'out of sheer devotion' [REB], 'from a real desire to serve' [TEV], 'from a real eagerness to serve' [LN], 'because your heart is in it' [TNT].

**5:3** nor as lording-it-over[a] the (ones) allotted[b] (to your care) but being examples[c] of-the flock;

LEXICON—a. pres. act. participle of κατακυριεύω (LN 37.50) (BAGD 2. p. 412): 'to lord it over' [BAGD, LN, WBC; NAB, NIV, NJB, NLT, NRSV, REB], 'to domineer' [BNTC, NIC; TNT], 'to be bossy' [CEV], 'to be lord over' [KJV], 'to try to rule over' [TEV].
- b. κλῆρος (LN 35.49) (BAGD 2. p. 435): 'the charges allotted to you' [BNTC], 'those in your charge' [NRSV], 'your charges' [REB], 'the group which is in your charge' [NJB], 'people who are in your care' [CEV], 'people assigned to your care' [NLT], 'those who have been put in your care' [TEV], 'responsibility to care for' [LN], 'that which is assigned by lot, share' [BAGD], 'those assigned to you' [NAB], 'those entrusted to you' [NIV, TNT], 'respective congregations' [WBC], 'God's heritage' [KJV], 'portion' [BAGD, NIC].
- c. τύπος (LN 58.59) (BAGD 5.b. p. 830): 'example' [BAGD, BNTC, LN, NIC, WBC; all versions except KJV], 'ensample' [KJV], 'model' [LN], 'pattern' [BAGD].

QUESTION—How is the term κλῆρος 'allotted (to your care)' used in this context?
1. It refers to the church members as the portion assigned or allotted to the elders for care [Alf, EGT, NCBC, NIC, NTC, Sel, TH]
2. It refers to duties and responsibilities assigned or allotted to the elders [IVP].
3. It refers to the believers as being God's portion or lot, as quoted in the LXX of Deuteronomy 9:29 [NIBC].
4. It refers to offices and functions in the church which the leaders are not to allocate autocratically [BNTC].
5. It refers to individual churches as portions of the universal flock of God, and which are under the care of elders [WBC].

**5:4** and (after) the chief-shepherd[a] having-been-revealed[b] you-will-receive[c] the unfading[d] crown[e] of-glory.

LEXICON—a. ἀρχιποίμην (LN 44.5) (BAGD p. 113): 'chief shepherd' [BAGD, BNTC, LN, NIC, WBC; all versions except NLT], 'head shepherd' [LN; NLT].
- b. aorist pass. participle of φανερόω (LN 24.19) (BAGD 2.b.β. p. 853): 'to be revealed' [BAGD], 'to appear' [LN, NIC, WBC; all versions except CEV, NLT], 'to be manifested' [BNTC], 'to return' [CEV], 'to come' [NLT].
- c. fut. mid. indic. of κομίζω (LN **57.126**) (BAGD 2.a. p. 442): 'to receive' [BAGD, **BNTC, LN**, NIC, WBC; KJV, NIV, REB, TEV, TNT], 'to obtain' [LN], 'to be given' [CEV, NJB], 'to win' [NRSV], 'to win for oneself' [NAB]. This verb is also translated as a verb phrase 'your reward will be' [NLT].

d. ἀμαράντινος (LN **79.23**) (BAGD p. 42): 'unfading' [BAGD, BNTC, LN, WBC; NAB, NJB], 'unwithering' [NIC], 'not losing its brightness' [**LN**], 'that will never lose its brightness' [TEV], 'that will never lose its glory' [CEV], 'that fadeth not away' [KJV], 'that will never fade away' [NIV], 'that never fades away' [NRSV], 'that never fades' [REB, TNT], 'never-ending' [NLT]. See a form of this word at 1:4.

e. στέφανος (LN 6.192) (BAGD 2.a. p. 767): 'crown' [BAGD, LN, NIC, WBC; all versions except NLT], 'garland' [BNTC]. Τῆς δόξης στέφανον 'the crown of glory' is translated 'a share in his glory and honor' [NLT], 'a crown that will never lose its glory' [CEV], 'glory, a crown' [REB], 'the glorious crown' [TEV], 'the glorious crown of victory' [TNT].

**DISCOURSE UNIT: 5:5–11** [Sel, TH; NAB, NJB]. The topic is humility, sobriety, and watchfulness [Sel], admonitions to the whole Christian community [TH]; counsel to the laity [NAB], instructions to the faithful [NJB].

**DISCOURSE UNIT: 5:5** [WBC]. The topic is the rest of the congregation.

**5:5** **Likewise,**[a] **younger-ones,**[b] **be-subject-to**[c] **elders;**[d] **and all-of-you clothe-yourselves-with**[e] **humility,**[f]

LEXICON—a. ὁμοίως (LN 64.1) (BAGD p. 568): 'likewise' [BAGD, LN, NIC; KJV], 'in the same way' [BAGD, BNTC; NAB, NIV, NJB, NRSV, REB, TEV], 'so' [BAGD], 'in turn' [WBC], 'also' [TNT], not explicit [CEV, NLT]. See this word at 3:1, 3:7.

b. νέος (LN 67.116) (BAGD 2.b.β. p. 536): 'younger' [LN], 'ye younger' [KJV], 'younger people' [NJB], 'you younger people' [BNTC], 'you young people' [CEV], 'you who are younger' [NIC, WBC; NRSV], 'younger men' [REB], 'you younger men' [NAB, NLT, TEV, TNT], 'young men' [BAGD; NIV].

c. aorist pass. impera. of ὑποτάσσομαι (ὑποτάσσω) (LN 36.18) (BAGD 1.b.β. p. 848): 'to be subject to' [BNTC, NIC; NJB], 'subject oneself' [BAGD], 'to submit to' [LN; REB], 'to submit oneself to' [KJV, TEV], 'to be submissive to' [NIV], 'to defer to' [WBC], 'to obey' [BAGD, LN; CEV], 'to be obedient to' [NAB], 'to accept the authority of' [NLT, NRSV, TNT]. See this word at 2:13, 2:18, 3:1, 3:5, and 3:22.

d. πρεσβύτερος (LN 53.77, 67.102) (BAGD 1.a. p. 699, 2.b.α. p. 700): 'elder' [LN (53.77); all versions except NIV, REB, TEV], 'older' [LN (67.102); NIV, REB, TEV]. Πρεσβύτερος 'elder' is translated with the definite article 'the elders' [NIC; NJB, NLT, NRSV], 'the elder' [KJV], or 'the authority of elders' [WBC], probably indicating that this is the church office of presbyter. It is also translated with the possessive pronoun, 'your elders' [BNTC; CEV, NAB, TNT], which can be taken to refer to anyone with seniority, whether by office or by age.

e. aorist mid. (deponent = act.) impera. of ἐγκομβόομαι (LN **49.9**) (BAGD p. 216): 'to clothe' [NIC, WBC; KJV, NAB, NIV, NRSV, REB], 'to

dress' [LN], 'to put on oneself' [BAGD], 'to gird' [BNTC], 'to put on an apron' [TEV], not explicit [CEV, NLT, TNT]. The command τὴν ταπεινοφροσύνην ἐγκομβώσασθε 'clothe yourselves with humility' is translated 'be humble' [CEV], 'humility must be the garment you wear' [NJB], 'serve each other in humility' [NLT], 'take the humblest role and wait upon each other' [TNT].
- f. ταπεινοφροσύνη (LN 88.53) (BAGD p. 804): 'humility' [BAGD, BNTC, LN, NIC, WBC; all versions except CEV, TNT]. This noun is translated as an adjective: 'humble' [CEV], 'humblest' [TNT].

QUESTION—What relationship is indicated by ὁμοίως 'likewise'?

It is a transitional device loosely linking sections [NIC, Sel]. It transitions to a new item of instruction [NCBC, NTC]. It is a transition between successive exhortations [BNTC]. It marks the shift in exhortation from one group of people to another [TG, WBC]. It transitions to a new subject with the same general theme of submission [TH]. It refers to the similarity between the responsibilities of the two groups in acting appropriately according to their station, whether that be exercising authority graciously or submitting to it [IVP]. It refers to the similarity in principle between one section and another, which is the need for unselfishness [ICC]. It refers to the common ideas between the two sections of recognizing positions and duties [Alf].

QUESTION—Who are the νεώτεροι 'younger-ones' and what is their relationship to the πρεσβύτεροι 'elders'?

1. Both terms are a reference to age groups [ICC, Sel, TG; NIV, REB, TEV].
2. 'Younger' refers to younger people, whereas 'elder' refers to church officers [IVP, NIC], or to age and church office [NTC]. 'Younger' refers to age, and 'elders' also refers to the group of older people, from which officers were also chosen [BNTC].
3. 'Elders' refers to church officers, but 'younger' likewise refers to church officers who are more recently appointed, and who need to submit to the others [NIBC].
4. 'Elders' refers to church officers, and 'younger' refers to everyone else [Alf, WBC].

**because[a] God opposes[b] (the) proud-ones,[c] but gives[d] grace to (the) humble-ones.[e]**

LEXICON—a. ὅτι (LN 89.33): 'because' [LN; NAB, NIV, NJB, REB], 'for' [BNTC, LN, NIC, WBC; KJV, NLT, NRSV]. This conjunction is also used as introducing an OT quotation, 'the Scriptures say' [CEV], 'for the scripture says' [TEV], 'for, as Scripture says' [TNT].
- b. pres. mid. indic. of ἀντιτάσσω (LN 39.1) (BAGD p. 76): 'to oppose' [BAGD, LN, NIC, WBC; CEV, NIV, NJB, NRSV, TNT], 'to resist' [BAGD; KJV, TEV], 'to be opposed to' [BNTC], 'to be stern with' [NAB], 'to set oneself against' [NLT], 'to set one's face against' [REB].

c. ὑπερήφανος (LN 88.214) (BAGD p. 841): 'proud' [BAGD, NIC; KJV, NIV, NJB, NLT, NRSV, TEV, TNT], 'proud people' [CEV], 'arrogant' [BAGD, BNTC, LN, WBC; NAB, REB], 'haughty' [BAGD].
d. pres. act. indic. of δίδωμι (LN 57.71) (BAGD 1.b.β. p. 193): 'to give' [BAGD, BNTC, LN, NIC, WBC; KJV, NIV, NRSV, TNT], 'to grant' [BAGD]. The phrase 'gives grace' is translated 'helps' [CEV], 'shows kindness' [NAB], 'shows favor' [NLT, REB, TEV], 'accords his favor' [NJB].
e. ταπεινός (LN 88.52) (BAGD 2.b. p. 804): 'humble' [BAGD, BNTC, LN, NIC, WBC; all versions], 'lowly' [BAGD].

**DISCOURSE UNIT: 5:6–11** [IVP, NIC]. The topic is concluding practical advice and encouragement [IVP], final exhortation on standing firm under pressure [NIC].

**DISCOURSE UNIT: 5:6–7** [WBC]. The topic is humility and trust in God.

**5:6** **Humble-yourselves[a] therefore[b] under the mighty[c] hand[d] of-God, so-that you may-be-exalted[e] in time,[f]**
LEXICON—a. aorist pass. impera. of ταπεινόω (LN 88.56) (BAGD 2.b. p. 804): 'to humble oneself' [BAGD, BNTC, LN, NIC, WBC; KJV, NIV, NLT, NRSV, REB, TEV, TNT], 'to be humble' [CEV], 'bow down beneath' [BAGD], 'to bow humbly' [NAB], 'to bow down' [NJB]. This verb in the passive voice is translated with the meaning of the middle voice: 'humble yourselves' [BNTC, NIC, WBC; KJV, NIV, NLT, NRSV, REB, TEV, TNT].
b. οὖν (LN 89.50): 'therefore' [BNTC, LN; KJV, NIV, NRSV], 'so' [LN], 'then' [LN, NIC; NJB, REB, TEV, TNT], not explicit [WBC; CEV, NAB, NLT].
c. κραταιός (LN **76.9**) (BAGD p. 448): 'mighty' [BAGD, **BNTC, LN**, NIC, WBC; all versions except NJB], 'powerful' [BAGD, LN], not explicit [NJB].
d. χείρ (LN 76.3, 8.30) (BAGD 2.a.β. p. 880): 'hand' [BAGD, BNTC, LN (8.30), NIC, WBC; KJV, NAB, NIV, NRSV, REB, TEV, TNT], 'power' [BAGD, LN (76.3); CEV, NJB, NLT].
e. aorist act. subj. of ὑψόω (LN 87.20, 81.5) (BAGD 2. p. 851): 'to exalt' [BAGD, BNTC, LN (87.20), NIC; KJV, NRSV], 'to raise up' [LN (81.5); NJB, TNT], 'to lift up' [BAGD, LN (81.5), WBC; NIV, REB, TEV], 'to lift high' [NAB], 'to raise high' [BAGD], 'to honor' [CEV, NLT]. This aorist subjunctive is also translated as a future indicative: 'and he will lift you up' [WBC; REB], 'and he will honor you' [CEV, NLT].
f. καιρός (LN 67.1) (BAGD 3. p. 395): 'time' [BAGD, LN, WBC], 'due time' [NIC; KJV, NAB, NIV, NJB, NRSV, TNT], 'his good time' [NLT], 'his own good time' [TEV], 'the appointed time' [BNTC]. The phrase 'in time' is translated by a verb phrase: 'when the time comes' [CEV].

QUESTION—What is meant by ταπεινώθητε 'humble yourselves'?
It means to submit to the difficulties and trials that God providentially allows [Alf, IVP, NCBC, NIC, TNTC]. It means to recognize God's sovereignty in difficulty and testing [BNTC]. It is acceptance of the humiliations that would come to believers in those difficult times [Sel]. It is an attitude of dependence on God [NIBC], submission to God's care and protection [WBC], or acceptance of suffering as his plan for them [TH]. It means to be subject to God and confident in him alone [NTC].

QUESTION—What relationship is indicated by οὖν 'therefore'?
It indicates an exhortation based on the quotation from Proverbs 3:34 in 5:5 [BNTC, NCBC, NIC, NTC, TH, TNTC, WBC].

QUESTION—What is implied by the image of the hand of God?
It refers to deliverance as well as discipline by God [ICC, IVP, NCBC, NIC, NTC, TG, TH]. It refers to God's wise providence [TNTC]. It is the picture of deliverance in the OT [BNTC, NIBC, Sel, WBC]. It refers to the fact that affliction and suffering are allowed by God [Alf].

QUESTION—What is meant by ἐν καιρῷ 'in time'?
1. It refers to the parousia [BNTC, IVP, NIC, Sel], the last time [NCBC, NIBC, TH, WBC].
2. It means the right time as God sees it, which may or may not be the return of Christ [Alf, NTC, TNTC]. It is the time God chooses [TG].

**5:7 casting[a] all your cares[b] upon him, because it-matters[c] to-him concerning you.**

LEXICON—a. aorist act. participle of ἐπιρίπτω (LN **25.250, 90.18**) (BAGD 2. p. 298): 'to cast (one's cares) upon' [BAGD, BNTC, NIC; KJV, NAB, NIV, NRSV, REB, TNT], 'to throw' [WBC], 'to put (one's cares) upon' [LN (25.250)], 'to put (responsibility) on' [LN (90.18)], 'to turn (worries) over to' [CEV], 'to give (worries and cares) to' [NLT], 'to leave (worries) with' [TEV], 'to unload (your burden) on to' [NJB].

b. μέριμνα (LN 25.224) (BAGD p. 504): 'care' [KJV, NAB], 'anxiety' [BAGD, BNTC, LN, NIC, WBC; NIV, NRSV, REB, TNT], 'worry' [BAGD, LN; CEV, TEV], 'burden' [NJB], 'worries and cares' [NLT].

c. pres. act. indic. third person impersonal verb of μέλει (LN 30.39) (BAGD 2. p. 500): 'to be concerned about' [LN; NJB], 'it is a care or concern to someone about someone' [BAGD], 'to care about someone' [BNTC, NIC, WBC], 'to care for someone' [all versions except NJB, NLT], 'to care about what happens to someone' [NLT].

QUESTION—What is the function of the aorist participle ἐπιρίψαντες 'having cast'?
1. It functions imperatively [all versions except KJV].
2. It is subordinate to and dependent on the imperative verb ταπεινώθητε 'humble yourselves' in the previous verse and explains how that is done [Alf, BNTC, NCBC, NIC, TH, TNTC, WBC]: humble yourselves by casting your cares upon him.

## 1 PETER 5:8

**DISCOURSE UNIT: 5:8–11** [TNTC, WBC]. The topic is warfare against the devil [WBC], living as Christians in spiritual conflict [TNTC].

**5:8** **Be-sober,**[a] **watch.**[b] **Your adversary**[c] **the devil as a roaring**[d] **lion walks-about**[e] **looking-for**[f] **someone to-devour.**[g]

TEXT—Some manuscripts include ὅτι 'because' after γρηγορήσατε 'watch'. GNT does not mention this variant. It is included only by KJV and NJB.

TEXT—Instead of τινα καταπιεῖν 'someone to devour', some manuscripts have τίνα καταπίῃ 'whom he may devour'. GNT selects the reading 'someone to devour' with a C rating, indicating difficulty in deciding which variant to place in the text. The reading 'whom he may devour' is taken by KJV.

LEXICON—a. aorist act. impera. of νήφω (LN 30.25) (BAGD p. 538): 'to be sober' [BNTC; KJV, TNT], 'to stay sober' [NAB], 'to keep sober' [NJB], 'to be sober-minded' [LN], 'to be self-controlled' [BAGD; NIV], 'to be clear-headed' [NIC], 'to pay attention' [WBC], 'to be on one's guard' [CEV], 'to be careful' [NLT], 'to discipline oneself' [NRSV], 'to be alert' [TEV], 'to be on the alert' [REB]. See this word at 1:13 and 4:7.

    b. aorist act. impera. of γρηγορέω (LN 27.56) (BAGD 2. p. 167): 'to be on watch' [TEV], 'to be watchful' [BAGD, BNTC, LN; TNT], 'to watch out for' [NLT], 'to be vigilant' [LN; KJV], 'to be alert' [LN, NIC; NIV], 'to be on the alert' [BAGD], 'to stay alert' [NAB], 'to keep alert' [NJB, NRSV], 'to wake up' [WBC; REB], 'to stay awake' [CEV].

    c. ἀντίδικος (LN **39.9**) (BAGD p. 74): 'adversary' [BNTC, **LN**, NIC; KJV, NRSV], 'enemy' [BAGD, LN; CEV, NIV, NJB, NLT, REB, TEV, TNT], 'opponent' [BAGD, WBC; NAB].

    d. pres. mid. (deponent = act.) participle of ὠρύομαι (LN **14.78**) (BAGD p. 897): 'to roar' [BAGD, BNTC, LN, NIC, WBC; all versions].

    e. pres. act. indic. of περιπατέω (LN 15.227) (BAGD 1.c. p. 649): 'to walk about' [KJV], 'to go about' [TNT], 'to walk, to go' [LN], 'to roam around' [TEV], 'to prowl' [BNTC, NIC; NAB, NIV, NLT, NRSV, REB], 'to be on the prowl' [NJB], 'to be on the move' [WBC], 'to sneak around' [CEV].

    f. pres. act. participle of ζητέω (LN 27.41): 'to look for' [LN; all versions except CEV, KJV], 'to seek' [BNTC, NIC; KJV], 'to find' [CEV], 'to be ready' [WBC].

    g. aorist act. infin. of καταπίνω (LN **20.52**) (BAGD 1.b. p. 416): 'to devour' [BAGD, BNTC, NIC; all versions except CEV], 'to swallow' [WBC], 'to destroy' [LN], 'to attack' [CEV].

QUESTION—What is meant by γρηγορήσατε 'watch'?

It means to be watchful and ready to respond to external influences [NTC]. It means to focus one's attention and be alert for sin or attacks of evil [TNTC], to be on the alert for spiritual attack [NIBC]. The two verbs taken together mean to prepare the mind and spirit for battle [WBC]. The two verbs express one thought, which is to be alert for dangers and temptation [TG]. It means to be alert to the spiritual danger of being deceived [IVP]. It means to be ready for whatever may come [TH].

QUESTION—What is meant by καταπιεῖν 'devour'?

It means to annihilate [NIC], or bring to spiritual ruin [TG]. It means to destroy faith [TH], to cause believers to apostatize [IVP, TH], to renounce their allegiance to Christ and so come to spiritual death [NIBC, WBC]. It means to demoralize through persecution so that believers would deny the faith [BNTC]. It refers to the fact that Satan is the one who provokes persecution [EGT, ICC].

**5:9** Resist[a] him firm[b] (in) the faith, knowing the same (kind) of-sufferings to-be-accomplished/laid-upon[c] your brotherhood[d] in the world.

LEXICON—a. aorist act. impera. of ἀνθίστημι (LN 39.18) (BAGD 1. p. 67): 'to resist' [BAGD, BNTC, LN, NIC, WBC; CEV, KJV, NAB, NIV, NRSV, TEV], 'to oppose' [BAGD], 'to stand up to' [NJB, REB, TNT], 'to take a firm stand against' [NLT].

b. στερεός (LN **74.21**) (BAGD 2. p. 766): 'firm' [BAGD, BNTC, NIC, WBC; REB], 'strong' [NJB], 'steadfast' [BAGD; KJV, NRSV], 'solid' [NAB]. This adjective is also translated as a verb: 'to be firm' [LN; TEV, TNT], 'to stand firm' [NIV], 'to be strong' [**LN**; CEV, NLT].

c. pres. mid. or pass. infin. of ἐπιτελέω (LN **13.108**) (BAGD 4. p. 302): 'to be accomplished' [BAGD, BNTC, LN, WBC; KJV], 'to be laid on' [NIC], 'to be brought about' [BAGD, LN], 'to undergo (suffering)' [NAB, NIV, NJB, NRSV], 'to go through' [NLT, REB, TEV], 'to have to bear' [TNT], 'to happen' [**LN**], not explicit [CEV].

d. ἀδελφότης (LN 11.22) (BAGD 1. p. 16): 'brotherhood' [BAGD, BNTC, LN, NIC, WBC], 'brotherhood of believers' [NAB], 'fellow believers' [LN; TEV, TNT], 'the Lord's followers' [CEV], 'brethren' [KJV], 'brothers' [NIV], 'the community of your brothers' [NJB], 'brothers and sisters' [NRSV], 'fellow Christians' [REB], 'Christians' [NLT]. See this word at 2:17.

QUESTION—What is meant by τῇ πίστει 'the faith'?

1. This is a reference to the believer's personal trust and faith [BNTC, EGT, NCBC, NIBC, NIC, Sel, TG, TH, WBC; CEV, NAB, NJB, NLT, NRSV, REB, TEV]: be firm in your faith.
2. The article indicates that it refers to the Christian faith [Alf, ICC, IVP, NTC; KJV, NIV, TNT]: be firm in the faith.

QUESTION—What is meant by ἐπιτελεῖσθαι 'to be accomplished/laid upon'?

1. It refers to suffering as something being accomplished in the lives of the believers [Alf, BNTC, ICC, NTC, Sel, TNTC, WBC; KJV].
2. It means that believers go through, undergo, or experience suffering [TG, TH, TNTC; NAB, NIV, NJB, NLT, NRSV, REB, TEV], or experience it because it is laid upon them [NIC].
3. It means to pay the 'dues' or 'tax' of suffering [EGT, NCBC].

QUESTION—What is implied in the use of the term ἀδελφότης 'brotherhood' instead of the more customary 'brothers'?

The collective term emphasizes unity and solidarity [BNTC, NIC] or their common bond of experience [NIBC]. It is a collective noun used in place of 'the brothers' [Sel].

**5:10** **And/but<sup>a</sup> the God of-all grace, the (one) having-called<sup>b</sup> you into his eternal glory in<sup>c</sup> Christ Jesus,**

TEXT—Instead of ὑμᾶς 'you', some manuscripts have ἡμᾶς 'us'. GNT selects the reading 'you' with an A rating, indicating that the text is certain. Only KJV reads 'us'.

TEXT—The word Ἰησοῦ 'Jesus' does not occur in some manuscripts. It is included by GNT with a C rating, indicating difficulty in deciding whether or not to place it in the text. It is omitted by BNTC, WBC; NAB, NIV, NJB, NRSV, TEV, TNT.

LEXICON—a. δέ (LN 89.94): 'and' [LN, NIC; NIV, NRSV], 'but' [BNTC, WBC; CEV, KJV, TEV], not explicit [NAB, NJB, NLT, REB, TNT].
  b. aorist act. participle of καλέω (LN 33.307) (BAGD 2. p. 399): 'to call' [BAGD, BNTC, LN, NIC, WBC; all versions except CEV], 'to choose' [CEV]. See this word at 1:15, 2:9, 21, and 3:9.
  c. ἐν with dative object (LN 90.6, 89.119): 'in' [BNTC, LN (89.119), NIC, WBC; NAB, NIV, NJB, NRSV, REB, TNT], 'in union with' [LN (89.119)], 'with' [TEV], 'by' [LN (90.6); KJV], 'by means of' [NLT]. Agency is also indicated by the translation 'he had Christ Jesus choose you' [CEV].

QUESTION—What relationship is indicated by δέ 'and/but'?
  1. It is additive 'and' [NIC; NIV, NRSV] or 'moreover' [Sel].
  2. It is contrastive or adversative [Alf, BNTC, EGT, TH, TNTC, WBC; CEV, KJV, TEV]: but. It contrasts the difficulty of suffering with the fact that it won't last long [TNTC]. It contrasts eternal glory with temporary suffering [WBC]. It contrasts God with the adversary [EGT].
  3. It serves as a transitional device without definite additive or contrastive meaning [NAB, NJB, NLT, REB, TNT]: now.

QUESTION—What relationship is indicated by ἐν 'in'?
  1. It refers to God's glory, which is in Christ [ICC, NIBC], or the means by which God's glory is shared, which is union with Christ [TG, TH; TEV].
  2. It refers to Christ as the means by which God called the believers [Alf, BNTC, EGT, IVP, NCBC, NTC, WBC; CEV, KJV, NLT]. Christ is the means of the call as well as the sphere of the Christian's existence [WBC].
  3. It refers to the sphere in which the believer has both the calling and the glory, which is in union with Christ [NIC, Sel, TNTC].

**(after) having-suffered a-little-while, will himself restore,<sup>a</sup> make-firm<sup>b</sup> strengthen,<sup>c</sup> (and) establish<sup>d</sup> (you).**

TEXT—Instead of καταρτίσει, στηρίξει, σθενώσει, θεμελιώσει 'he will restore, confirm, strengthen, and establish' (future indicative), some manuscripts have καταρτίσαι, στηρίξαι, σθενώσαι, θεμελιώσαι 'may he restore, confirm, strengthen, and establish' (aorist optative). GNT selects the reading 'he will restore, etc.' (future indicative) with a B rating, indicating that the text is almost certain. The reading 'may he restore' is taken only by KJV.

LEXICON—a. fut. act. indic. of καταρτίζω (LN 75.5) (BAGD 1.b. p. 417): 'to restore' [BNTC, NIC; NAB, NIV, NJB, NLT, NRSV, REB, TNT], 'to prepare' [WBC], 'to complete' [BAGD], 'to make complete' [BAGD; CEV], 'to perfect' [TEV], 'to make perfect' [KJV].

b. fut. act. indic. of στηρίζω (LN 74.19) (BAGD 2. p. 768): 'to make firm' [TNT], 'to make more firm' [LN], 'to give firmness' [TEV], 'to confirm' [BAGD; NAB, NJB], 'to strengthen' [BAGD, LN], 'to make strong' [NIV], 'to make steady' [CEV], 'to establish' [BAGD, BNTC, NIC; REB], 'to stablish' [KJV], 'to support' [WBC; NLT, NRSV].

c. fut. act. indic. of σθενόω (LN 74.14) (BAGD p. 749): 'to strengthen' [BAGD, BNTC, LN, NIC, WBC; KJV, NAB, NJB, NLT, NRSV, REB, TNT], 'to make strong' [BAGD; CEV], 'to give strength' [TEV], 'to make firm' [NIV].

d. fut. act. indic. of θεμελιόω (LN 31.94) (BAGD 2.a. p. 356): 'to establish' [BAGD, WBC; NAB, NRSV], 'to strengthen' [BAGD], 'to cause to be steadfast in' [LN], 'to make steadfast' [NIV], 'to settle' [BNTC, NIC; KJV], 'to make firm' [CEV], 'to support' [NJB], 'to place on a firm foundation' [NLT], 'to set on a solid foundation' [TNT], 'to give a sure foundation' [TEV]. This verb is also translated adverbially with reference to one or more of the preceding verbs '(strengthen you) on a firm foundation' [REB].

QUESTION—What is the function of the pronoun αὐτός 'himself'?

It is emphatic [Alf, WBC]. It emphasizes that God himself and no one else will personally do this [NCBC, NIC]. It gives special force, connoting intimacy and tenderness on God's part [Sel].

QUESTION—What is meant by καταρτίσει 'restore'?

1. It means to restore, repair, or mend what is broken, to make complete [BNTC, NTC, TH]. It means to be restored by establishing and confirming character [NIC]. It means to be renewed or re-equipped after the wearing effect of hostility [NIBC]. It means to perfect [NCBC, TG], to make complete and whole [TG], to re-establish and make whole [Sel].
2. It means to correct or amend sins and shortcomings [EGT, ICC], to perfect by removing defects [Alf].
3. It means to prepare [TNTC, WBC]. Believers are prepared and completed in any resource they may have lost in suffering [TNTC].

**5:11** To-him (be/is)ᵃ the powerᵇ forever, amen.

TEXT—Some manuscripts include ἡ δόξα καί 'the glory and' before τὸ κράτος 'the power'. It is omitted by GNT with a B rating, indicating that the text is almost certain. It is included only by KJV.

TEXT—Some manuscripts include τῶν αἰώνων 'and ever' (literally 'of ages') after εἰς τοὺς αἰῶνας 'forever' (literally 'to the ages'). It is omitted by GNT with an A rating, indicating that the text is certain. It is included by BNTC; KJV, NIV, NJB, NLT, NRSV, REB.

LEXICON—a. There is no lexical entry in the Greek text corresponding to the verb 'to be'. It is supplied and represented either as an optative 'to him be' [KJV, NIV, NRSV, TEV, TNT], 'dominion be his' [NAB], or as an indicative statement 'to him is' [NIC], 'is his' [NLT], 'to him belongs' [BNTC, WBC], 'belongs to him' [REB], 'God will be in control' [CEV], 'his power lasts' [NJB].
- b. κράτος (LN 76.6) (BAGD 4. p. 449): 'power' [BAGD, LN, NIC; NIV, NJB, NLT, NRSV, REB, TEV, TNT], 'might' [LN, WBC], 'rule' [BAGD], 'sovereignty' [BAGD], 'dominion' [BNTC; KJV, NAB]. This sentence is also translated 'God will be in control forever' [CEV].

QUESTION—What is the mood of the implied verb 'to be' in this doxology?
1. It is optative 'be' [TH; KJV, NAB, NIV, NRSV, TEV, TNT].
2. It is indicative 'is' [BNTC, EGT, IVP, NIC, Sel, WBC; CEV, NJB, NLT, REB].

**DISCOURSE UNIT: 5:12–14** [IVP, NIC, Sel, TG, TH, TNTC, WBC; CEV, NAB, NIV, NJB, NLT, NRSV, REB, TEV]. The topic is closing greetings [IVP, Sel, WBC], final greetings and benediction [WBC; NRSV], conclusion and greetings [NIC], closing words [TG], concluding greetings and the closing blessing [TH]; final greetings [CEV, NIV, REB, TEV], farewell [NAB], last words, greetings [NJB], Peter's final greetings [NLT].

**5:12 Through[a] Silvanus the faithful[b] brother, as I-consider[c] (him), I-wrote to-you briefly**

LEXICON—a. διά with genitive object (LN 90.4): 'through' [LN, WBC; NAB, NJB, NRSV, REB], 'by' [BNTC, LN; KJV], 'by means of' [NIC], 'with the help of' [NIV, NLT, TEV, TNT]. The phrase is also translated as a verb phrase: '(Silvanus) helped me' [CEV].
- b. πιστός (LN 31.87) (BAGD 1.a.α. p. 664): 'faithful' [BAGD, BNTC, LN, NIC, WBC; CEV, KJV, NAB, NIV, NLT, NRSV, TEV], 'trustworthy' [BAGD, LN; NJB, REB]. This adjective is also translated as a phrase: 'whom I can trust' [TNT].
- c. pres. mid. (deponent = act.) indic. of λογίζομαι (LN 31.1) (BAGD 3. p. 476): 'to consider' [LN, WBC; CEV, NLT, NRSV], 'to regard' [LN, NIC; NIV, TEV], 'to suppose' [KJV], 'to take to be' [NAB], 'to account' [BNTC], 'to know' [TNT], 'to know to be' [REB], not explicit [NJB].

QUESTION—Who is Silvanus?
It is the same person as the Silas spoken of in Acts and the Silvanus who was a companion of Paul [Alf, BNTC, ICC, IVP, NCBC, NIBC, NIC, NTC, Sel, TNTC, WBC].

QUESTION—What relationship is indicated by διά 'through'?
1. It refers to the actual writing of the letter [BNTC, EGT, ICC, IVP, NIC, NTC, Sel, TG; CEV, NIV, NLT, TEV, TNT]. Silas wrote the letter, but the thoughts behind it are those of Peter [NIC]. Silas drafted the letter acting as Peter's spokesman [BNTC]. Silas helped as a secretary by putting Peter's remarks into good Greek [NTC]. Silas assisted in the composition of the letter [IVP, Sel].
2. It refers to the sending of the letter, that is, Silvanus was the bearer of the letter [Alf, TNTC, WBC]. He could be trusted to expand on it in person [Alf].
3. Silas helped in the writing as well as the delivery of the letter, and was able to supplement, interpret, or expound on the letter in person as its bearer [EGT, ICC, NTC, Sel].

QUESTION—What is meant by ὀλίγων 'briefly'?
1. It was a conventional polite statement, since letters were supposed to be brief [BNTC, IVP, NCBC, NIBC, NIC].
2. It is brief in comparison to how much could have been said about the topics addressed [Alf, NTC, Sel]. He has said a great deal in a short space [TNTC].
3. It is a device used to keep things in perspective, which is that he has written a few lines about a suffering a little, the temporal being seen in the light of the eternal [WBC].

**encouraging[a] and testifying[b] this to-be (the) true grace of-God, in which stand.[c]**

TEXT—Instead of στῆτε 'stand' (aorist imperative), some manuscripts have ἑστήκατε 'you stand' (perfect indicative, translated as present indicative). GNT does not mention this alternative. Only KJV reads 'ye stand'.

LEXICON—a. pres. act. participle of παρακαλέω (LN 25.150) (BAGD 2. p. 617): 'to encourage' [BAGD, LN, NIC; CEV, NIV, NJB, NLT, NRSV, REB, TEV], 'to express encouragement' [NAB], 'to give encouragement' [TNT], 'to exhort' [BAGD, BNTC; KJV], 'to make an appeal' [WBC]. See this word at 2:11 and 5:1.

b. pres. act. participle of ἐπιμαρτυρέω (LN **33.262**) (BAGD p. 296): 'to testify' [BNTC; KJV, NIV, NRSV, REB], 'to express testimony' [NAB], 'to bring testimony' [WBC], 'to give testimony' [TEV], 'to witness' [LN], 'to bear witness' [BAGD; TNT], 'to declare' [NIC], 'to tell' [CEV], 'to attest' [NJB], 'to assure' [NLT].

c. aorist act. impera. of ἵστημι (LN 85.40) (BAGD II.1.d. p. 382): 'to stand' [WBC; KJV], 'to stand fast' [BNTC, NIC; NIV, NRSV, REB, TNT], 'to make stand' [LN], 'to stand firm' [BAGD; NJB, TEV], 'to hold one's ground' [BAGD], 'to keep on having faith' [CEV], 'to be steadfast' [NAB], not explicit [NLT].

QUESTION—What is the antecedent of 'this'?
It is the message of God's grace which the apostles preached and about which Peter has now written in this letter [Alf, NTC]. It is all that has been declared throughout the epistle [NCBC, TH]. It refers to the epistle itself and its message [WBC]. It is the grace of God which has been referred to in the letter, as well as the letter itself and its teaching [NIC]. It is what he has written about his experience of the grace of God [NIBC]. It refers to the glory which the readers will ultimately have, and of which they already have a foretaste [BNTC]. It is the grace they experienced in their conversion and Christian growth [Sel]. It is the entire way of life that the letter describes [TNTC]. It is the total experience described in the letter, which is that they are experiencing grace even in the midst of suffering [IVP].

**5:13** She[a] in Babylon, co-chosen,[b] greets you, also my son Mark (greets you).

TEXT—Some manuscripts include ἐκκλησία 'church' after Βαβυλῶνι 'Babylon'. It is omitted by GNT with an A rating, indicating that the text is certain. It is included or translated as implied information by WBC; KJV, NAB, NLT, NRSV, REB, TEV, TNT.

LEXICON—a. ἡ (LN 92.24): 'she' [BNTC, LN, NIC; NIV], 'the congregation' [WBC], 'the Lord's followers' [CEV], 'the church' [KJV, NAB, TNT], 'your sister' [NJB], 'your sister church' [NLT, NRSV, REB, TEV].

b. συνεκλεκτός (LN **30.94**) (BAGD p. 787): 'one who is also chosen' [LN], 'elected together with (you)' [KJV], 'chosen together with (you)' [BAGD; NAB, NIV, NRSV], 'chosen along with (you)' [NIC, WBC], 'elect like (you)' [BNTC], 'also chosen by God' [TEV], 'with (you) among the chosen' [NJB], 'God's chosen ones' [CEV], not explicit [NLT, REB].

QUESTION—Who is the 'she' referred to in this verse?
1. It is a Christian congregation [BNTC, EGT, IVP, NCBC, NIBC, NIC, NTC, Sel, TG, TH, TNTC, WBC; all versions except NIV].
2. It is Peter's wife [Alf, ICC].

QUESTION—What is Babylon?
1. It is Rome [BNTC, EGT, ICC, IVP, NCBC, NIBC, NIC, NTC, Sel, TG, TH, TNTC, WBC; NLT].
2. It is the Mesopotamian Babylon [Alf].

QUESTION—Who is Mark?
It is John Mark, writer of the gospel, and companion of Paul [BNTC, ICC, IVP, NCBC, NIBC, NIC, NTC, Sel, TH, TNTC, WBC].

QUESTION—What is meant by the term 'my son'?
It indicates close association or affection [ICC, NIBC, NIC, NTC, Sel]. It indicates that Mark was Peter's helper [TG, TNTC]. It indicates that Mark was Peter's disciple [NIC, Sel, WBC]. It means that Peter probably brought Mark to faith in Christ [IVP].

**5:14** Greet each-other with a-kiss[a] of love. Peace to-you all, the (ones) in[b] Christ.

TEXT—Some manuscripts include Ἰησοῦ. ἀμήν 'Jesus. Amen' after Χριστῷ 'Christ'. This reading is omitted by GNT with an A rating, indicating that the text is certain. Only KJV includes it.

LEXICON—a. φίλημα (LN 34.62) (BAGD p. 859): 'kiss' [BAGD, BNTC, LN, NIC, WBC; all versions except CEV, NAB, NLT], 'embrace' [NAB]. The term 'kiss of love' is also translated 'kiss of Christian love' [TEV, TNT], 'in Christian love' [NLT], 'warm greeting' [CEV].

b. ἐν (LN 89.119): 'in' [BNTC, LN, NIC, WBC; KJV, NAB, NIV, NJB, NLT, NRSV], 'one with, in union with' [LN], 'who belongs to' [CEV], 'who belong to' [REB, TEV, TNT].

www.ingramcontent.com/pod-product-compliance
Lightning Source LLC
Chambersburg PA
CBHW070331230426
43663CB00011B/2282